Sex, Abortion
and Unmarried Women

Sex, Abortion and Unmarried Women

Paul Sachdev

Contributions in Women's Studies, Number 133

Greenwood Press
Westport, Connecticut • London

Library of Congress Cataloging-in-Publication Data

Sachdev, Paul.
    Sex, abortion and unmarried women / Paul Sachdev.
      p.   cm. — (Contributions in women's studies, ISSN 0147-104X ;
  no. 133)
    Includes bibliographical references and index.
    ISBN 0-313-24071-X (alk. paper)
    1. Abortion — Canada — Psychological aspects. 2. Single women —
  Canada—Sexual behavior. 3. Birth control—Canada. I. Title. II. Series.
  HQ767.5.C2S2 1993
  306.7'08652 — dc20   92-33303

British Library Cataloguing in Publication Data is available.

Library of Congress Catalog Card Number: 92-33303
ISBN: 0-313-24071-X
ISSN: 0147-104X

First published in 1993

Greenwood Press, 88 Post Road West, Westport, CT 06881
An imprint of Greenwood Publishing Group, Inc.

Printed in the United States of America

The paper used in this book complies with the
Permanent Paper Standard issued by the National
Information Standards Organization (Z39.48-1984).

10 9 8 7 6 5 4 3 2 1

To all the pioneers, women and men, who have fought and continue to fight with dedication and conviction for the right of all women to uninterrupted reproductive freedom, so that every child that is born is a wanted child.

Contents

Tables and Figure

TABLES

FIGURE

Acknowledgments

This book is about young unmarried women who experienced one of the most difficult and, in most cases, lonely decisions of their lives. They freely and openly shared with me the most intimate details of their sexual, contraceptive, and abortion experience. Their only selfish interest was to convey to others how it feels to face an unwanted pregnancy and the abortion decision, in the hope that society's attitudes and abortion services would begin to change for the better for other women. I share that hope.

To all these women I feel indebted for giving generously of their trust and of themselves, even if it was at times painful to reveal an intimate part of their lives. Without their willingness to confide there would be no stories, hence no book. Bearing the yoke of the male perspective, I have attempted to understand and interpret the many emotions and feelings these women shared with me. I would feel at least partially successful in this mission if the women feel that I have relayed their stories with accuracy and as forcefully and cogently as they were expressed. I hope that the statistics and scientific structure of the report did not dilute the intensity of their affect but rather heightened the salience and credibility of their experience.

Without the extraordinary cooperation of the participating hospitals and the counseling agency I never would have had a sample. I am, indeed, grateful to the chief gynecologists of these hospitals, without whose generous support and confidence this study would not have been possible. I also wish to thank their staff, who were very cordial and pleasant. I express my deep appreciation, in particular, to Ms. Margaret Reid and Ms. Phyllis Curry whose assistance and support enabled me to endure many frustrations and difficulties during the data collection. I want to specifically thank Dr. Mirian Powell, one of Canada's pioneers in the fight for voluntary motherhood, for her invaluable help during the data collection phase and also for inspiring me on this issue.

My special thanks are owed to Dr. Stanley Henshaw, who not only was helpful in answering my inquiries over the years with prompt dispatch of material and information but also provided many helpful and thoughtful comments on chapter 1. However, I alone remain responsible for any shortcomings. He deserves my heartfelt appreciation.

To Professor Jeffrey Bulcock I am forever grateful for painstakingly reading the entire manuscript and providing the benefit of his many constructive comments and suggestions.

Many thanks to Bob Crocker for "being there" when I needed his advice and expert opinion and for rescuing me more than once when I felt immobilized.

I owe a special debt of gratitude to Dr. Alfred Kadushin, my professor and mentor at the University of Wisconsin-Madison, who provided inspiration and intellectual stimulation. To him, I remain eternally grateful.

I am grateful to Dr. Bill Rowe, Director of the School of Social Work at Memorial University of Newfoundland for providing the much needed supportive environment that facilitated the writing of this book.

Thanks to Duncan McAndrew, my research assistant, who responded to my importuning with equanimity and humor, and who brought his computer craft, efficiency and endurance to the deciphering of my numerous revisions, turning them into an intelligible manuscript. I highly appreciate his assistance.

A special thanks should go to my editor, George Butler, who believed in the project from the beginning and who encouraged me throughout the writing. I am grateful to him for his patience and a friendly but persistent nudge at just the right times.

1

Abortion in Perspective

Abortion . . . this insolvable problem. I say insolvable because it has bothered mankind for at least 2500 years.

Aleck Bourne[1]

ABOUT THE STUDY

About 1.6 million abortions are performed each year in the United States, representing about 29 percent of all known pregnancies (legal abortions plus live births six months later).[2] More than 70 thousand pregnancies, or about 19 percent of all known pregnancies are terminated preterm annually in Canada. A large proportion--two thirds--of these abortions occur among young, single women. Most of these pregnancies are unintended and result from unprotected or inadequately protected sex acts. One wonders: Why do these women get pregnant when they do not wish to continue their pregnancy? Do they have knowledge of and access to contraceptive methods? How do they and the key persons in their environment (e.g., the sex partner, family members, girlfriends) feel about the pregnancy and the decision to terminate it? Why do these women choose abortion, and how do they feel before and after the termination? Does abortion affect these women's sexual and contraceptive practices, and their future relationship with the sex partner? How do they come to terms with the abortion experience? One also wonders how the service providers (physicians and nurses) respond to the unmarried women who need abortions.

---

[1] Quoted in B.F.R. Gardner 1972: 41.
[2] Henshaw and Van Vort 1992.

To seek answers to these questions, seventy Caucasian unmarried women aged 18-25 were personally interviewed six months to one year following their first abortion, which they sought in the first trimester on mental health grounds. The sample women who provided material for this book were drawn from three major hospitals and one counseling agency in a metropolitan city in Ontario, Canada. Through conversational depth interviews these women provided insight into the sequence of events and their intimate experiences starting with the occurrence of the pregnancy and following through the abortion and its consequences. They also discussed their social environment (peers, family, sex partners, service providers) and how it influenced their experience as they passed through each situation.

Research data on the problems of abortion are easily available; however, their interpretation is highly inconsistent for three major reasons. First, most previous studies are based on women with diverse characteristics, such as married, single and never-married, primiparous and multiparous, white and nonwhite, the teenagers and the more mature, who obtained abortion through suction and saline procedures. Researchers have often lumped together all or any combination of these characteristics and have treated these women as a homogeneous group. It seems possible that each of these characteristics influences differentially a woman's contraceptive and sexual profile, her reaction to unintended pregnancy, her decision to terminate, and her experience with the abortion. These diverse characteristics constitute a source of possible differences in the women at the baseline and thus can contribute to the women's reactions (see chapter 3 for detailed explanation). The women selected in this study were homogeneous in terms of marital status, race, gestation period, grounds for abortion, and previous pregnancy and abortion, which standardized their prior experience before they faced a problem pregnancy and abortion.

Second, a bulk of earlier studies interpreted the consequence of abortion in moral and clinical terms; little consideration was given to a woman's social networks and how they influenced her perception and her coping responses to a problem situation. The role of social environment, peers, family, and colleagues in shaping attitude and behavior has been extensively documented in the literature on social learning and interactionism.[3]   According to these authors, human beings attribute meaning to events and interpret the significance of their situations as a result of their reciprocal exchange with key members of their social groups making judgments. It follows from this view that whether a woman defines her unintended pregnancy as problematic or how she reacts to abortion is greatly affected by her interaction with the key persons in her social networks and their influence over her. Also, professionals in the human service field have shown that most people in need first turn for support and assistance to their social networks and that this informal support system has proven quite effective in offering much needed responses to problematic situations.[4]   A pregnancy that is not desired can be a crisis for an unmarried woman; she is most likely to approach her social support network for emotional reassurance and reinforcement of her decision, which will determine her coping responses to this crisis.[5]   Recent studies on unwed fathers and prospective fathers have shown that a sizable proportion of male partners feel isolated and left out from the decision making in which they would like to be involved. They have also found that male partners feel and care about the trauma the women experience and remain committed to them.[6]   A few studies have suggested that male partners play a significant role in influencing the contraceptive practice of young females.[7]   Viewed in this context, this study, unlike many previous studies, examines the pregnancy and abortion experience of unmarried women in the context of their social networks. It focuses on these women's interaction with key persons in their lives--girlfriends, parents, siblings, sex partner--and the role they played in shaping the women's responses to pregnancy and abortion.

Third, once a woman decides to have the pregnancy terminated, she must seek the assistance and cooperation of medical professionals to implement her decision. The manner in which the

---

[3]Bandura 1969; Blumer 1969; Volkhart 1951.

[4]Whittaker and Garbarino 1983.

[5]See, for instance, Belsey et al. 1977; Bracken et al. 1974; Bracken et al. 1978b; Moseley et al. 1981; Shusterman 1979; Talan & Kimball 1972.

[6]Christmon 1988; Robinson 1988a; Robinson 1988b; Rotter 1980; Shostak and McLouth 1984; Smith 1979.

[7]Cvetkovich & Grote 1982; Friedlander, Kaul & Stimel 1984; Herold & Goodwin 1980; Niemela et al. 1981.

woman is treated and her perception of the attitudes of the medical staff are likely to influence her emotional state, which can have a bearing on the way she reacts to abortion. An unmarried woman is particularly sensitive to behaviors of the service providers because of the moral view the society takes of the nonmarital pregnancy. Earlier investigations of abortion patients have devoted little or no attention to the hospital/clinic milieu, the scruples associated with the surgical procedure, and the way they affect a woman's reactions to abortion prior to and following the surgery. In view of this, it was important for this study to examine the unmarried women's experience with the medical services they received, the abortion procedure they went through, and the attitudes of the medical staff to which they were exposed.

Thus, in arriving at a final decision to terminate an unplanned pregnancy, an unmarried woman goes through a sequence of stages of decision making, beginning with her acknowledgment of pregnancy. She then must come to terms with the reactions of key people in her life (parents, male partner, friends, etc.), consider alternatives and their merits relative to her situation, and determine her own moral scruples. She must also negotiate with the hospital or clinic environment. Theoretically, a woman must resolve each stage before moving on to the next. The conflict a woman experiences at each stage is determined by the difficulty in decision at the preceding stage. Each woman attempts in the final analysis to minimize her cognitive dissonance and maximize her net gains.[8] According to this conflict resolution model of decision making a woman experiences emotional distress pre- and post-abortion when she is emotionally attached to the pregnancy, takes longer to arrive at the abortion decision, considers other alternatives, holds conservative attitudes about abortion, and has a stable and romantic relationship with her sex partner.

The principal consideration in conducting this study was to ensure that it proved useful and relevant for abortion clinic staff, pregnancy counselors, and the concerned public. The study design was made sufficiently flexible, therefore, to encompass a variety of issues that confront an unmarried woman faced with a problem pregnancy. A conversational in-depth interviewing method was used

---

[8]The conflict-resolution approach to decision making was proposed by Janis & Mann (1968) and was applied to abortion by Bracken et al. (1978).

to ensure that the emotions, attitudes, and underlying motives of these women were fully captured and comprehended. To preserve the depth and candor with which these women shared their feelings, the study findings are presented in jargon-free, conversational language, while using statistical tables only sparingly. Vignettes from the interviews are liberally used, since they tell the story of these women more forcefully than figures do. In sum, the research design, of necessity, includes aspects of both quantitative and qualitative-descriptive studies.

The book provides the reader with a rare insight into the issues and problems of abortion among seventy never-married women, who spoke freely and at length about contraceptive and abortion experiences that are highly intimate. To locate and secure the participation of these women was a monumental task, because of the highly sensitive nature of the issue. However, it was both rewarding and challenging to study the problem that affects women so directly and so profoundly. Becoming pregnant out-of-wedlock when the woman does not want and is not prepared for parenthood is emotionally distressing. But a woman's trauma is compounded when society restricts her choices or imposes penalties on her for exercising her options. The current debate on abortion centers on the question of whether a woman has the choice to decide to have an abortion as a solution for her problem pregnancy and whether she can exercise this choice without bureaucratic and legal barriers. The forces that oppose the woman's right to make reproductive choices argue on the basis of the competing rights of the fetus, requiring state interference. The debate between pro-choicers and pro-lifers is so intense that the issue has become an emotional battle that is being fought in the courthouses and legislatures and on the streets. The following section examines the abortion controversy.

THE ABORTION BATTLE: THE U.S. SCENE

For centuries, abortion or its euphemism such as menstrual regulation has existed as a solution for unwanted pregnancies. It, however, has rarely been treated like other surgical procedures and has generally been available under certain conditions that vary from highly restrictive to less restrictive, depending upon cultural, economic, and religious forces, sexual and marital values, contraceptive profile, and forms of government.[9]

Although abortion has been practiced for centuries, it has only recently become a highly emotional and divisive issue. A number of factors have contributed to the polarization of society into two opposing and irreconcilable camps, pro-choice and pro-life. These include the women's liberation movement asserting the right of women to have control over their reproduction, medical advances improving the chances for a fetus to survive outside the womb, the science of fetology showing graphic fetal development from conception, the phenomenal rise in the number of unwanted pregnancies among unmarried women, and back-alley abortions occurring in dangerous conditions when abortions were illegal. The pro-choice forces advocate the right of the woman to reproductive freedom, and the pro-life groups emphasize the obligation of the state to protect the fetus as developing life. In a pluralistic society, the problem of finding a satisfactory resolution is compounded by conflicts between medical indications and moral precepts.

Roe v. Wade Decision

In 1973, when the U.S. Supreme Court handed down a landmark decision in *Roe v. Wade*, it was thought that the ruling, which was based on the trimester approach, would be viewed as a workable compromise by both sides. The Court recognized a constitutional right of privacy that encompasses a woman's decision to terminate her pregnancy. The Court found that the fetus is not a person in common law or under the Constitution. The right to abortion is absolute during the first trimester, but abortion may be subject to regulation necessary to protect maternal health in the second trimester, when the risk of complications is higher. The state may ban abortion in the third trimester, when the fetus is viable and the state's interest becomes compelling in protecting potential life,

---

[9]Sachdev 1988. In the book *Life Itself: Abortion in the American Mind*, Rosenblatt (1991) traced the anomalous 4,000 abortion history and noted that most societies have simultaneously deplored the killing of fetuses and more or less permitted the practice of abortion.

except when abortion is necessary to save the woman's life or health. In one decision, the Supreme Court swept away all the laws in every state that prohibited abortion.

The Court decision, which struck a middle ground in its trimester approach, was supposed to put the abortion controversy to rest. Instead, it touched off a new wave of political debates and court challenges. Much of the debate is aimed at restricting women's right to make a personal choice to have an abortion. With this goal in mind, the anti-abortion forces have focused their energies on Congress, state legislatures, and various candidates for office.

Since *Roe v. Wade*, state legislatures have passed numerous restrictions, including requirements that second-trimester procedures must be performed in hospitals, specific counseling must be provided to all abortion patients, one or both parents of women under the age of 18 must be informed or give consent, husbands must give consent, and public funds and facilities may not be used to provide abortions. Most of these restrictions have been found to be unconstitutional.

Missouri Case: The Never-Ending Battle

The desire of the anti-abortion forces to have *Roe* overturned came close to being realized in July 1989, when the Supreme Court, refashioned by the Reagan conservative appointees, upheld most aspects of Missouri's restrictive abortion law. In a series of rulings, in *Webster v. Reproductive Health Services*, the Court upheld the Missouri law banning the use of state funds, employees, and hospitals to provide abortions. It also upheld the provision requiring doctors to carry out viability tests before performing abortions after twenty weeks, to determine whether the fetus could survive outside the womb, on the grounds that such testing furthers the state's interest in protecting potential human life. The Court, in a 5-4 decision, sidestepped a preamble to the law that says life begins at conception and did not rule on its constitutionality, arguing that it has not yet been applied by the state to restrict any rights or practices. Although the Court did not overturn *Roe v. Wade*, the Missouri case gave an invitation to the state legislatures to restrict and perhaps ultimately to outlaw abortions.

The court ruling made abortion a more contentious political issue than ever and set the stage for more ferocious battles in state legislatures. The anti-abortion forces saw in it another opportunity to redouble their efforts to restrict abortion in the country and to turn every state or federal election into a referendum on the issue. To pro-choice groups, this ruling signalled a further rollback of the abortion rights guaranteed by the *Roe v. Wade* decision. Justice Harry A. Blackmun, author of the *Roe* opinion, characterized the ruling as "very ominous." "A chill wind blows . . .," he said, because he saw in the ruling an explicit approval of those who wanted to do away with *Roe*. His portent was based on the signals given by willingness of the court majority to review additional abortion restrictions and ultimately to revoke its 1973 decision guaranteeing a woman's right to terminate her pregnancy without government interference. For example, Chief Justice Rehnquist and Justice White stated that the Constitution did not guarantee women the right to choose abortion. Chief Justice Rehnquist warned: "We do not see why the state's interest in protecting potential human life should come into existence only at the point of viability and that there should be a rigid line allowing state regulation after viability but prohibiting it before viability."[10]   Justice O'Connor articulated that the *Roe* framework is "on a collision course with itself" because of new technology that is moving the point of viability to an earlier stage of pregnancy. In her opinion, the right to abortion was a limited "fundamental right," and she added that she would allow state restrictions as long as they were not "unduly burdensome" on women.

States Vote to Limit Abortion

Since the *Webster* decision, nearly 600 bills restricting women's right to choose abortion have been considered by state legislators across the country. Only Louisiana, Utah, and Guam have so far been successful in enacting legislation that bans most abortions in their states. The Louisiana law would permit abortions only in the case of rape or incest, but only up to the thirteenth week of pregnancy.[11]   To qualify for an abortion, rape victims must be

---

[10]*Globe and Mail*, July 5, 1989: A6.

[11]Louisiana's stringent law was overturned on September 22, 1992 by the 57th U.S. Circuit Court of Appeals. Details of the ruling were not available at this writing (*Globe and Mail*, September 23, 1992). On November 30, 1992, the U.S. Supreme Court, by a 6-3 vote, refused to

examined by a doctor within five days and must report the crime within seven days. Doctors violating the law would face ten years in prison and $100,000 in fines. The Pennsylvania law, one of the strictest in the nation, requires women under eighteen to get parental or judicial consent for an abortion, and married women must inform their husbands. It also obliges women to receive a state scripted lecture on risks and alternatives to abortion and mandates a twenty-four hour waiting period after such a lecture and before an abortion is performed. Planned Parenthood of Southeastern Pennsylvania challenged the constitutionality of the law, but the U.S. appellate court upheld its key provisions, except the spousal notification requirement.[12] The court of appeal based its decision on Justice O'Connor's assertion that abortion was a "limited fundamental right" and that state law would not impose an "undue burden" on a woman's decision to have an abortion.

On June 29, 1992, the U.S. Supreme Court delivered the final verdict that upheld all restrictions of the Pennsylvania abortion law, except the spousal notification for married women. The justices ruled that these controls do not amount to an "undue burden" (i.e., substantial obstacles in the path of a woman's choice) on a woman's right to choose to have an abortion. The plurality stressed that states have a strong interest throughout pregnancy in preserving potential life and argued that the *Roe* trimester framework was too rigid in view of the advances in medical technology making viability of the fetus at an earlier stage possible. Despite the support for *Roe*, the sharply divided court has gravely imperiled women's right to abortion in the United States. The split ruling has certainly set the stage for new restrictions on the procedure in the states, especially where the

---

review a lower court decision that declared Guam's anti-abortion law unconstitutional. The court action was significant in that it reaffirmed women's basic right to abortion. It also suggested that the women in Louisiana and Utah can rest easy because the Supreme Court will probably not take their cases, thus leaving intact lower court rulings striking down their state laws.

[12]*New York Times*, October 22, 1991: A1. Nine states, besides Pennsylvania, have laws requiring that husbands be notified or give their consent before abortion, and twenty-five states have informed consent laws (*Wall Street Journal*, June 30, 1992: A4).

anti-abortion forces are vocal.[13]   At the same time, a majority support for *Roe* suggests that the new laws in Utah, Louisiana, and Guam, which ban abortion, will have to go.   But the ruling, which imposes serious hardships especially on teenagers and poor women, surely inflames rather than quells the political firestorm over abortion. As most clinics do not have full-time physicians, women will have to wait longer and travel long distances to get abortions and teenagers will face a serious dilemma.   In this sense, the state law will impose "undue burden" on the women, which is contrary to the Supreme Court's ruling.

As expected, anti-abortion forces were buoyed by the possibility that the highest court might use this as an opportunity to rule that restrictions on abortion such as those in Pennsylvania are constitutional, thus overturning *Roe v. Wade*.   The ominous probability has increased with the appointment of Clarence Thomas, another conservative, in October 1991 as a Supreme Court justice. He replaced Justice Marshall, a champion of women's right to reproductive freedom.   Although the Supreme Court ruling on the Pennsylvannia law did not overturn *Roe v. Wade*, the justices were one vote short of doing just that.   The appointment of another conservative justice to the court after the imminent resignation of Justice Blackmun, the only liberal justice on the Reagan-Bush court, could provide that critical vote.[14]   To keep the controversy going and to ignite passions among public and politicians alike, certain anti-abortion groups have been resorting to vile tactics, making the fetus the cornerstone of their campaign.   Their tactics include picketing and bombing the abortion clinics and the harassment of patients and doctors who perform abortions.   They also show a film depicting

---

[13]In April 1992 Kansas passed a law requiring mandatory counseling and parental notification for women under eighteen, restrictions on late abortions and a mandatory eight-hour delay for all women seeking abortions. A similar parental notification measure was passed in Wisconsin, requiring young women to obtain parental consent or judicial bypass. In August 1992, the state of Missisippi passed a law requiring a twenty-four hour waiting period for women seeking an abortion.

[14]The election of Governor Bill Clinton as the next President of the United States may forestall this possibility. Bill Clinton and his Vice President, Al Gore, ran on a pro-choice platform and they promised to lift most of the current government restrictions imposed by the Bush administration.

gruesome pictures of fetuses in "excruciating pain" as surgical instruments poke at them. The film "Silent Scream," narrated by a reformed abortionist, is being shown on some television stations and in churches across the country. Many medical experts, however, dismiss the film on the grounds that its claims lack scientific validity. The objective of the film is intended not to satisfy scientific truth but to create revulsion against abortion.

The public has not become more accepting of a ban on abortion. Polls and surveys since 1980 regularly show that a sizable majority of the American people--54 percent to 60 percent--still occupy an uneasy middle ground.[15] Sixty-four percent are still in favor of the court's 1973 *Roe* decision. Sixty-five to seventy percent would like the decision to have an abortion to be left to the woman and her doctor.[16] A large majority--62 percent--favor choice in the first trimester. Only 12 percent of adult women and men surveyed favor a ban on all abortions.[17]

However, the abortion foes have made some significant political gains, as reflected in the Helms/Hyde amendments. Over the past decade, all but thirteen states have ended almost all public funding for abortion. Only ten states pay for abortions in which rape and incest are involved.[18] Regulations written by the administration would end federal aid to family planning programs that do abortion counseling, and foreign aid money is unavailable to programs that

---

[15]*USA Today*, April 27, 1989: 13A.

[16]*The Plain Dealer*, April 18, 1989: 10; July 24, 1989: 8; *Time Magazine*, May 1, 1989: 20-21; *Gallup Poll News Service*, January 18, 1992; *Parade Magazine*, May 15, 1992.

[17]*Wall Street Journal*, July 5, 1989: A12; *Time Magazine*, November 6, 1989: 51. Since the abortion question is notoriously sensitive to wording, these survey results should be treated only as trends. The abortion opponents have been strengthened over the past two decades by the support of black leaders who equated abortion with genocide. Although they may favor abortion, for many black women the issue is not a high priority. Recently, many prominent black leaders have taken up pro-choice banners, declaring that the right to choose is equivalent to civil rights (*Time Magazine*, November 6, 1989: 51).

[18]In November 1989, President Bush vetoed a bill permitting Medicaid to pay for the abortions of the victims of rape or incest, and Congress failed to overturn him (*Time Magazine*, November 6, 1989: 57; *Time Magazine*, July 9, 1990: 27).

offer abortion counseling.[19] These regulations also stipulate an end
to federal support for research in fetal tissue transplants on the ground
that such research would lead to more abortions.[20] Such research
holds promise for finding new treatments for a host of conditions such
as Alzheimer's disease, Parkinson's disease, diabetes, leukemia,
schizophrenia,   and   several   inherited   metabolic   disorders.[21]
Ironically, a number of members of Congress opposed to abortion are

---

[19]The U.S. Congress enacted, in 1970, Title X of the Public Health
Service Act, which provided federal funding for preventative family
planning services. The act forbade use of funds to finance abortions, but
agencies were required to advise pregnant women of all their medical
options, including abortion. But the Reagan Administration revised the rules
in 1988, banning federal funds for providing counseling on abortion or
providing referral for abortion. In May 1991 the U.S. Supreme Court
upheld, by a 5-4 vote, in *Rust v. Sullivan* the ban on abortion counseling in
federally funded clinics. The rule which has not yet been implemented,
would bar clinics from discussing abortion with pregnant women or from
telling them where to get one. The Court said that the ban on abortion
counseling, called the "gag rule," does not violate free speech or alter
women's right to end their pregnancy. In reality, the court ruling affects
about 4 million low-income women served by 4,000 clinics that receive
federal money. The clinics, which provide services ranging from birth
control to breast examinations to AIDS testing, may have either to stop
mentioning abortion or to risk losing millions in federal funding (*Globe and
Mail*, May 24, 1991). The U.S. Senate and Congress once again declared
their overwhelming opposition to the "gag rule" and passed a bill on April
30, 1992 to overturn the Supreme Court decision in October 1991, but
President Bush vetoed it and Congress was unable to override the veto.
President-elect Bill Clinton is opposed to the "gag rule" and has vowed to
repeal it upon taking office.
[20]As a strange corollary to the ban, the Bush administration also
withdrew support for research in in-vitro fertilization on the grounds that the
accidental but inevitable destruction of some embryos is murder.
[21]*New Republic*, June 29, 1992:10; *Time Magazine*, August 5, 1991: 40.
At this writing, the U.S. Senate has passed a bill by a wide margin, 85-12,
lifting the administration ban. However, Congress doesn't appear to have
enough votes to override Mr. Bush's certain veto. But this could change
with the new Congress and the new President, Bill Clinton, in office on
January 20, 1993. The law, if carried, contains measures that will deal with
issues such as the woman's consent and the confidentiality of the recipient
of the tissue.

convinced that the use of fetal tissue will save or improve lives. But President Bush remains adamant in accepting the argument of anti-abortion activists that fetal tissue research will legitimize and even encourage abortions.

Privately funded abortions, of course, are still legally available to everybody, even in the state of Missouri, if you have the money. But for the young, the poor, and those in rural areas, abortion is not as easily accessible. Even if *Roe v. Wade* is overturned, abortion will probably remain legal and available in most states, some of which guarantee reproductive rights in their state constitutions. Fearing the ominous threat to women's right to reproductive choice, the Judiciary Committee of the House of Representatives approved, on June 30, 1992, the Freedom of Choice Act, which seeks to enshrine in the law *Roe*'s principles establishing a woman's constitutional right to have an abortion. The bill, if passed by Congress, will undo the Supreme Court's decision on the Pennsylvania law.

Controlling Teenagers

The long-running debate over abortion rights focused on teenagers in June 1990 when the highest court upheld the Minnesota and Ohio laws requiring that parents of minors be notified or the minors obtain court authorization for an abortion. Minors must wait for at least forty-eight hours in Minnesota and twenty-four hours in Ohio after notification before having an abortion. The Court reasoned that such requirements further the state's legitimate interest in encouraging parental involvement in minors' abortion decisions and their support for the child.[22] Forty-one states have passed such laws

---

[22]Documents (1990), *Family Planning Perspectives*, 22 (4): 177. Interviews with 174 minors at four Minnesota abortion clinics showed that 43 percent of them used the court bypass option. Reasons for not notifying parents included fear of disapproval, absent fathers, and feelings of having betrayed the family (Blum et al. 1990). Crosby and English (1991) assessed the impact of mandatory parental involvement laws and concluded that such laws failed to promote family consultation and have had adverse consequences for the pregnant adolescents. However, Worthington et al. (1991) disagree with this assertion. Using research studies, the authors argue that two-thirds to four-fifths of parents have been reported to be supportive when approached by their daughters, which contributed to the

requiring notice to one or both parents or the parents' consent to abortion for unemancipated minors (women under age eighteen). Alternatively, minors can go to court to get authorization for an abortion without parental involvement (except in Utah and Idaho) if they can demonstrate to the court that they are mature enough or that the abortion would be in their best interest.[23] A recourse to the courts to avoid parental involvement and to find a sympathetic judge is not easy, however. Besides, the bypass statutes lack guidelines for courts to discriminate mature from immature minors and to determine best interests (Pliner and Yates 1992). The public seems to favor giving parents a veto over their unmarried teenage daughters' abortions. According to a Time/Cable News Network survey, seven out of ten Americans (69 percent) support the requirement of parental consent for minors to have an abortion.[24] However, the only time the public has voted on parental involvement in a referendum, in Oregon in 1990, it rejected the restriction. These laws affect a large number of teenagers. More than 400,000 U.S. teenage girls under age eighteen become pregnant each year, and almost half (175,000) choose to have abortions, which account for 11 percent of all abortions in the United States. The chief effect of such laws, which include waiting periods of days to a week or more, is that the teenagers are forced either to have babies or to have late abortions when risks and expense increase. In the state of Massachusetts, the incidence of abortion dropped significantly, by 43 percent, among minors during the twenty months after the state put its parental consent law into effect in 1981, while births were more numerous than would have been expected in the absence of the law.[25] Clearly, the requirement of notifying their parents or justifying their personal decision to a black-robed stranger restricts abortion for teenagers and forces some to endure pregnancy and childbirth against their will. As

---

quality of the decision making. Rogers et al. (1991) also examined the impact of the Minnesota Parental Notification Law on abortion and birth. Comparison of the outcome before and after enactment of the law showed that more minors were having late than early abortions.

[23]Greenberger and Connor 1991. Seventeen states that have passed parental involvement laws have been enjoined by the courts or have not enforced for other reasons (Henshaw & Kost 1992).

[24]*Time Magazine*, July 9, 1990: 24.

[25]Cartoof & Klerman 1986.

abortion is safer than childbirth, it is unlikely that parental involvement requirements further either the state's interest in protecting health or the women's own best interest.[26]

Abortion Rights on the Ropes

The anti-abortion forces continue their assault on women's right to make reproductive choices. Determined to prevent public funding for abortions, even those following rape or incest, the anti-abortion lobbyists are pressuring state legislatures where such laws exist to permit such funding only if the rape or incest is promptly reported to the police. They contend that women lie about rape and hope that the reporting requirements will discourage women from seeking abortions on false claims. Energized further by priests, by television preachers, and indeed by the presidents of the United States, Mr. Reagan and Mr. Bush, Operation Rescue, an aggressive group, is pushing the abortion issue onto the front pages by resorting to violent tactics that include blocking abortion clinics in some cities, and harassment of doctors and patients. One result of these tactics has been that abortion has become less and less available. In 83 percent of the counties in America there is no clinic, hospital, or doctor who performs abortions. Some clinics survive by importing doctors from other cities and states. The shortage of doctors is intensified because few medical residents are trained to perform abortions. Only 28 percent of the medical schools in the U.S. now provide abortion training, and in these it is optional.[27] While all sides brace for a major Supreme Court showdown on abortion, the reality is that abortion rights already are being eroded. The tactics of the abortion opponents, while stirring passion, deflect the public attention from the prospect of returning to the days of coat-hanger, illegal back-alley abortions. The tactics of the anti-choice activists have succeeded in limiting access to abortion services. Minority

---

[26]Henshaw and Kost (1992) surveyed a nationally representative sample of more than 1500 unmarried minors having an abortion and found that 61 percent of them told their parents of the abortion in advance even without any law requiring parental notification or consent. The authors question whether obligatory parental knowledge is necessary and helpful.

[27]*NBC Nightly News*, November 10, 1991.

women and those from an economically deprived class are most likely to suffer, as was documented by Judith Belsky, who surveyed the condition of medically indigent women seeking abortion at a publicly funded hospital in New York City under the state's restrictive abortion laws.[28]

THE ABORTION BATTLE: THE CANADIAN SCENE

In Canada, as in the United States, abortion is an issue that has split the public and politicians for decades and is stirring intense emotions across the country. In fact, there are many fascinating parallels bctween the American and Canadian experiences. Prior to August 1969, abortions in Canada could be obtained on the ground of strict necessity, and the law was largely vague on specific indications. The liberalization of abortion laws in Britain in 1967 and the fierce abortion debate in the United States stimulated the Canadian public and professional interest in reforming the country's archaic abortion law.

Federal Abortion Law

In August 1969, the federal government responded to the calls for a new abortion law, with one that changed the rules under which a woman could have an abortion. It permitted abortion in an accredited hospital if a therapeutic abortion committee of three doctors agreed that the continuation of the pregnancy would be likely to endanger the woman's life or health. The new law represented no major changes in the existing abortion practice, except that it added the term "health," which was subject to interpretation by each abortion committee. Because the hospitals were not required to set up therapeutic committees and because many committees approved few if any abortions, the law rendered abortion services uneven across the country. In fact, more than 75 percent of all abortions in

---

[28]Belsky (1992) found that the medically indigent women had more restricted access to therapeutic abortions and received more impersonal care than the women who sought abortion at a hospital for private patients. Also, more than one-third of the poor women attempted to abort the pregnancy themselves.

Canada in 1987 were done in only 15.4 percent of the eligible hospitals. As a result many women had to travel hundreds of miles to other parts of Canada or the United States to get what was their legal right. The opponents of abortion, however, argued that the law worked only too well, as it had legalized the killing of the unborn, usually for social or economic convenience. A heated and passionate debate between pro-choice and right-to-life groups continued for almost two decades, with the opponents of abortion using all too familiar techniques that included targeting pro-choice candidates, harassing doctors, bombing abortion clinics, taking over hospital boards and committees, and displaying pictures and film of torn fetal tissue, all intended to intensify controversy and inflame passions. The abortion debate was further fueled by the Canadian Charter of Rights, enacted in 1982, which protects the rights of all people. Some Canadian courts extended the same rights to the unborn child under charter in tort, property, and equity cases.

Supreme Court Nullifies Law of the Land

At the heart of the debate was Dr. Henry Morgentaler, a passionate crusader for abortion on request, who performed many abortions in his Montreal clinic in defiance of the federal abortion law and thus forced its review by the Supreme Court of Canada in January 1988. A majority court struck down the federal law, ruling that the legislation threatened women's health by permitting arbitrary delays and unfair disparities in access to abortion across the country. It went on to say that the abortion committees often imposed serious delays, causing increased physical and psychological trauma to those women who met its criteria. The justices said the law limits the pregnant woman's access to abortion and violates her constitutionally protected right to "life, liberty and security of the person" within the meaning of the Charter. The justices admitted that the decision to terminate a pregnancy is basically a moral decision and that in a free and democratic society the conscience of the individual must be paramount over that of the state. The majority of the justices did, however, say that the protection of the fetus is a valid objective under Canadian criminal law. However, they decided that the abortion law did not reach the proper balance between that objective and the woman's basic rights.

Patchwork Abortion Policy

With the historic Supreme Court decision, abortion was no longer a criminal issue and was put on the same level as an appendectomy or any medical procedure. The pro-choice forces hailed the decision as the biggest step since women won the right to vote. To those who opposed abortion, this decision was a stunning blow. The decision was also a nightmare for members of parliament, who now had to write a new law that uniformly defined for all provinces exactly when and how an abortion should be available. Though stunned by the court ruling, the opponents of abortion did not resign themselves to it. Forces on both sides of the issue started to intensify their campaign to influence Parliament. The chief effect of the court ruling was a wide range of provincial policies and confusion in the country. At one extreme, the British Columbia government announced that it would refuse to pay for abortions unless the woman's life was endangered.[29] At the other end, Ontario extended funding to abortion clinics.[30] Although the court ruling removed many obstacles to an abortion, there was nothing to force an unwilling doctor or hospital to perform the procedure. Thus, the New Brunswick government continued its policy of refusing to provide abortion services. The Prince Edward Island government said that no hospitals on the island would perform abortions, but it would pay for out-of-province abortions only if a five-doctor panel approved the woman's reasons. Alberta announced that women seeking abortions must get a second opinion. In Regina, for example,

---

[29]In March 1988, the B.C. Supreme Court ruled the B.C. regulation out of order as it violated provincial health statutes and "common sense." Consequently, on March 20, 1992, the new provincial government ordered hospitals in the province to provide abortion services even if their boards wanted to ban them. The new government, under pressure from pro-choice groups, also agreed to pay for abortions performed in Vancouver's two free-standing clinics.

[30]Other provinces do not cover the full cost of abortions performed in abortion clinics but do pay for various portions such as doctors' fees or the cost of laboratory tests. Newfoundland is the only province that refuses to pay for abortions obtained outside a hospital (*Evening Telegram*, November 28, 1991). Manitoba Court of Queen's Bench ruled on June 12, 1992, that the government must pay doctors' fees for abortion performed at private clinics, a decision that the government might appeal.

just one doctor performs abortions; many Saskatchewan women have to travel to neighboring provinces if they need the procedure. Saskatchewan will approve financing of abortions only when the pregnancy is declared life-threatening or medically necessary by the doctor, and it was the first province to pass a law that permits hospital workers to refuse to participate in the provision of abortion services. The College of Physicians and Surgeons of Saskatchewan requires that a woman obtain a second medical opinion or approved counseling that must identify to the woman the stage of fetal development.[31] Despite the Supreme Court's 1988 ruling, the new New Democratic Party government remains opposed to free-standing abortion clinics, which deliver high-quality and low-cost care to women. Nova Scotia passed legislation to allow abortions to be performed only in provincially approved hospitals, a provision that violated the spirit of the Supreme Court's 1988 ruling.[32]   Nova Scotia's government is trying to drive the Morgentaler clinic in Halifax from the province. Alberta will not pay for abortions unless they are performed in a hospital after consultation with a second doctor. In Manitoba, abortions are permitted up to the fourteenth week of pregnancy; and in the provincial city Dauphin, new hospital boards have drastically restricted abortion services. Meanwhile, the Canadian Medical Association issued guidelines for its member physicians to recognize abortion up to the twentieth week of pregnancy as a decision for the woman and her doctor.

The patchwork of abortion policies in the country flew in the face of the federal government commitment to equal access to health services. A part of the problem was that Canadian politicians were as deeply divided on the issue as the Canadian people. According to a CBC poll in 1988, a slim majority--53 percent--were in favor of a limited restriction on abortion, while less than one half--41 percent-- were opposed under any circumstances. Six percent did not want any restriction imposed. Another survey conducted by Angus Reid and Associates in March 1988 confirmed these results. A slim majority of those polled favored some form of restriction on abortion based on

---

[31]*Globe and Mail*, May 6, 1992: A2.

[32]The provincial law was struck down in October 1990 by the Provincial Court of Appeal, ending a year-long legal battle, but the provincial government has appealed the ruling to the Supreme Court of Nova Scotia.

the duration of pregnancy. Twenty-two percent wanted abortion to be permitted only to save a woman's life, while 10 percent favored unrestricted abortion.[33]

The Legal Stalemate

In July 1988, the federal government introduced a compromise resolution in Parliament before drafting legislation. The resolution was based on the trimester approach, which would have allowed abortion early in pregnancy and imposed tougher restrictions in the later stages. After a vigorous and emotional debate, the government's resolution was soundly rejected on a free vote (147 vs. 76), which left the government no closer to producing legislation that could appease the anti-abortion forces while complying with the Supreme Court's ruling.

The rights of women to make their own reproductive choices came under attack in the summer of 1989, when in two separate judgments (Ontario and Quebec) the lower courts granted injunctions sought by ex-boyfriends that prevented their former girlfriends from having an abortion. These rulings recognized the rights of the fetus as having precedence over those of the mother. These decisions were also interpreted to mean that fathers do have a right in the decision making. However, in both cases the injunctions were lifted and the women were allowed to have an abortion, thus reaffirming the women's rights to privacy and liberty. The Supreme Court of Ontario overturned the injunction on technical grounds, while the Supreme Court of Canada, in an unanimous decision, set aside the injunction upheld by the Quebec Court of Appeal, declaring that there is no statute in Canada, in Quebec or elsewhere, that recognizes an unborn fetus as having rights, including the right to life. The Court by implication ruled that fathers of unborn babies have no rights. The ruling was a landmark in that it rejected the grounds that could expose other women to judicial harassment by men who want to use the lower courts to impose their will upon them. These cases, however, were not without precedents, as the Canadian judges have been requested in the past by jilted lovers and estranged husbands to grant injunctions blocking women from having an abortion. In 1984,

---

[33]*Globe and Mail*, March 7, 1988: 2.

a lawyer failed to prevent an abortion by a Toronto woman on behalf of her estranged husband. In 1986, the Alberta Court of Appeal rejected a bid by a Mormon couple to keep their 16-year-old daughter from getting an abortion. In 1987, a Montreal man lost a bid to prevent a woman he had contacted through a newspaper ad from having an abortion. She had reneged on an alleged deal to bear him a child to replace a son killed in a traffic accident. In 1988, an Edmonton man could not stop his former girlfriend from aborting her pregnancy.[34]

By bringing down the curtain on the Quebec case, known as the Chantal Daigle abortion case, the Supreme Court gave a clear signal to the federal Parliament as to what might be a constitutionally acceptable abortion law that is congruent with the trend of international jurisprudence. In recent years, for example, courts in countries such as the United States, Britain, Italy, France, Australia, Yugoslavia, and Israel refused to recognize a husband's or boyfriend's right to veto a woman's decision to have an abortion.[35]

The Fetus--Is It a Person?

At the center of the abortion controversy is the thorny question of whether a fetus is a person having legal rights. Although there are irreconcilable differences among people as to the personhood of the fetus, its legal status was recognized in 1987 in an unusual case involving an Ontario woman. The woman refused to obtain medical treatment during pregnancy and planned to give birth in an underground parking garage, thus putting the fetus at risk. The provincial judge ruled that a fetus is a child and granted the Belleville Children's Aid Society a protection order making the 38-week-old fetus a ward of the crown.[36] However, a year later in 1988, the B.C. Court of Appeal ruled that a fetus is not a person until it has completely left the mother's body. The Court thus overturned a conviction against two midwives charged with criminal negligence in the death of an infant during their attempt to conduct a home birth. The right of a fetus as a legal entity was again recognized in 1989

---

[34]Brown 1989: 7.
[35]Cook 1989.
[36]Lipovenko 1987.

during the trial of a Quebec woman, Chantal Daigle, in Quebec Superior Court and later reaffirmed by the Quebec Court of Appeal. The Quebec Court of Appeal ruled that the fetus is a living human entity distinct from the mother and has rights equal to that of the mother. Meanwhile, the Law Reform Commission of Canada in its working paper, "Crimes against the Fetus," recognized the competing interests of the life of the fetus and the security of a woman's body and concluded that, in general, life is "clearly more fundamental than bodily security" and added that, as the fetus "is not yet independent, but is only a potential person," giving life priority over security may not be relevant in such circumstances.[37]   The question as to the personhood of the fetus remained unresolved in the Canadian criminal law when in March 1989 the Supreme Court declined to rule on an appeal from a Manitoban anti-abortion crusader, Mr. Borowski, on the right to life of the unborn. In a unanimous decision the Court said that to decide the issue outside the context of an abortion law would intrude in a policy area reserved for Parliament. Two years later on March 21, 1991, the highest court was presented with the B.C. abortion case of the two midwives whose acquittal by the Court of Appeal was appealed.   The Court upheld the acquittal and reaffirmed that an unborn child is not a legal person with its own rights.[38]

Federal Government's Attempt at New Abortion Policy

Nearly two years after the Supreme Court struck down the country's old abortion law in January 1988, saying that it violated women's rights, the federal government tabled Bill C-43 in November 1989 in the House of Commons. The bill permitted abortion at any time during pregnancy if one doctor believed a woman's physical, mental, or psychological health was threatened. Abortions were not limited to hospitals, however. This bill was not as bad as the old one, but it still limited a woman's right to choose by making her dependent upon a doctor's approval. Because the bill put abortion back into the Criminal Code, the bill did not treat abortion like any

---

[37]Law Reform Commission 1989: 26.
[38]Fraser 1991.

other surgical procedure under the Canada Health Act.[39] Both the woman and the doctor could face imprisonment of up to two years for defying the law, discouraging many doctors from performing abortions. Worse still, women were being treated as criminal for having an abortion under this bill but not for obtaining other medical procedures. Wary of risks of criminal charges, doctors were refusing to perform abortions even before the law was enacted, which severely restricted the availability of and equal access to abortion.[40] Also the bill did nothing to change the situation in which a physically and mentally healthy woman could obtain abortion. After months of intense debate between anti-abortion and pro-choice MPs and civil strife in the media and on the street, the bill was narrowly passed on May 30, 1990, in the House of Commons, but was defeated by a tied vote, 43-43, in the Senate on February 1, 1991. Although abortion remains a legal medical procedure, its availability is unequal across the country and is severely restricted. Also, most doctors who stopped performing abortions because of Bill C-43 are not returning to abortion provision. In November 1991, the federal government rejected a recommendation from the all party Commons Committee on health and welfare that Ottawa use its power by withholding transfer payments to ensure that provinces make abortions accessible to all women.

Legal Vacuum

Canada has been without an abortion law for over four years. That means that abortion is not in the Criminal Code and women are able to make choices regarding their pregnancies without government interference, theoretically at least. Is the legislative vacuum encouraging young women to have abortions, as the anti-abortion people charge? The Statistics Canada figures on abortion for the period 1980-1990[41] show that the abortion rates reported a slight

---

[39]According to a survey, 66 percent of Canadian people were against putting abortion in the Criminal Code (*Pro-choice News*, Spring 1991).

[40]Balsara 1990; McLaren 1990; Priegert 1991.

[41]*Health Reports: Therapeutic Abortions*, 1989, Supplement no. 9, vol. 3 (1), Table 5; 1990, vol. 3 (4), Table 10.

upward trend since 1986 in a narrow range from 18.6 to 20.1[42] per 100 live births, which continued after the abortion law was struck down and remained until 1990, the latest year for which statistics were available (see Appendix A figure 1). Thus, the increase in the abortion rate in each successive year was too slight to represent any significant impact of the absence of the law on the women's attitude toward abortion. The factors that could account for the general upward trend in the numbers and rates of abortion were the increased number of women in reproductive years, increased sexual activity among young people starting at an earlier age, and the lack of effective contraception. Furthermore, inconsistency in the reporting of abortion cases possibly contributed to the increase. For instance, some clinics that had not reported abortions started to report for the first time after the law was struck down. Also, since the reporting of abortion information from clinics in the border states in the United States is on a voluntary basis, the figures from these clinics are at best estimates, which are likely to fluctuate depending upon the cooperation of these clinics. One significant impact of the legal void, however, was that far fewer Canadian women travelled to the United States after the law was removed than before the Supreme Court ruling. The percentage of women who sought abortions in the United States sharply dropped, by 30 percent, in 1988 compared to 1987; that decrease was followed by another big drop of 20 percent in 1989.

It appears that, despite the legal void, Canadian women were making responsible choices and were not frenziedly having abortions. More women sought earlier abortions, in the first trimester, 88 percent in 1990 compared to 83.1 percent in 1975. As in other medical procedures, physicians made sure that reasonable standards of care were met as fewer complications resulted from abortions in 1990, at 1.2 percent, compared to 3.2 percent in 1975.[43] Even

---

[42]The Statistics Canada figures for 1990 show 12,524 therapeutic abortions performed in clinics in Newfoundland, Nova Scotia, Ontario, Manitoba, and British Columbia, which the provinces reported for the first time. But these were excluded from figure 1 (Appendix A) to maintain consistency with previous years. Similarly, the 1,383 therapeutic abortions performed in Centres locaux de services communautaires in the province of Quebec, reported for the first time, were also excluded from this analysis.

[43]Concerns have been raised about the adverse effects of induced abortions on a women's subsequent reproductive function. Data from twenty-one countries show that women with one induced abortion by

without Section 251, which was struck down by the Supreme Court, there are enough safeguards in the Criminal Code of Canada to ensure that doctors follow responsible and reasonable medical practice. In view of the above, one wonders why there should be a separate legislation governing abortion and why this procedure should be criminalized and not treated as any other health matter for which women should be able to take the initiative and responsibility. Quebec has defied federal law since 1976, but no anarchy has resulted. The province consistently reported abortion rates until 1990 that were lower than the national average and lower than those of seven other provinces and the territories, including British Columbia, Ontario, and Manitoba.[44]   Any attempts at a new law will undoubtedly restrict abortions by creating additional and unnecessary barriers to women's obtaining early, safe terminations.

Abortion opponents, however, interpret the rise in the number of abortions as evidence that Canadian women are having abortions for personal convenience, not because of ill health. This allegation implies that women are irresponsible, clearly an unsubstantial charge. The increase in the numbers only shows that modern birth control methods are imperfect and that women need abortion because society fails to provide social and economic support for women who become pregnant against their wishes. The militancy of the anti-abortion groups has steadily intensified since the Supreme Court decision of January 1988. They adamantly oppose any law that fails to recognize the fetus as a person and treat abortion as murder. They have

---

vacuum aspiration are at no greater risk of failing to conceive at a later date or of ectopic pregnancy or of spontaneous abortion than women with no history of abortion (see Hogue 1986). Another study of 9,823 deliveries at the Boston Hospital for Women was even more optimistic in its assessment. It noted that women who have had one or more prior induced abortions do not appear to have "substantially increased risks" of adverse effects in subsequent pregnancies (see Linn et al. 1983: 136). The mortality rate from abortion has significantly dropped to 0.5 deaths per 100,000 abortions. The risk of dying from medical abortion is one twenty-fifth or less than that of carrying a pregnancy to term, and one one-hundredth the risk of major surgery. The mortality rate from tonsillectomies is twice as high (U.S. Centers for Disease Control 1990).

[44]Sachdev 1988: Table 5.3; Statistics Canada, *Health Reports: Therapeutic Abortions*, 1990, vol. 3 (4). The latest year for which statistics were available was 1990.

resorted to violent methods to intimidate women such as bombing of abortion clinics and harassment of doctors and the women who enter these clinics.[45]

The abortion battle rages on in the United States and Canada, and the parallel between the two countries becomes complete with the continual assault from anti-abortion forces on a woman's right to make reproductive choices without state interference, a right reaffirmed by the highest court of each country. No law, short of banning abortions altogether, is going to satisfy abortion opponents and resolve the abortion issue. If they cannot make abortions illegal, their strategy is to make them inaccessible. As long as their game is all or nothing, the divisive question will remain in front and center.

The year 1992 was significant for the abortion rights movement in the United States. In June, the Supreme Court reasserted in the Pennsylvania case that women have a constitutional right to abortion. In refusing for the first time in 20 years to review a major abortion case from Guam, the Court reinforced the view that *Roe v. Wade* is safe, at least for now. The election of Bill Clinton radically changed the national landscape, guaranteeing a Supreme Court friendlier to abortion rights. But the fight for abortion right forces is not over yet. In upholding the Pennsylvania law, the Court made it clear that although abortion cannot be outright banned, it can be regulated by certain restrictions. The big fight in 1993 would be over how far states can go in restricting abortion. Legislatures in as many as seven states (Alabama, Louisiana, Utah, Michigan, Ohio, South Dakota, and Indiana) would consider restrictions upheld by the Supreme Court in the Pennsylvania case.   These restrictions, undeniably, impose undue burden and endanger the lives of poor and young women. It is clear that the focus will shift from the Court to the U.S. Congress and particularly on the Freedom of Choice Act. That bill languished in the last Congress because President Bush would certainly have vetoed it. Anti-abortion forces are gearing up to make sure that Congress does not approve the bill and current state restrictions stay, and that many more states join in imposing even

---

[45]On May 18, 1992, anti-choice extremists bombed the Toronto Morgentaler clinic, a horrendous example of the way these groups are escalating their war on women's right to choose.

stricter obstacles. The battle over this bill is likely to be one of the most divisive fights in the next Congress. In the abortion war, only the battle field seems to change.

ABORTION PROFILE

Like the abortion battle, the demographic profile of women undergoing abortion in the United States and Canada is similar. A typical woman who seeks abortion in both countries is young (54 to 59 percent under twenty-five years), unmarried (75 to 82 percent), childless (55 to 58 percent), and white (65 to 74 percent) and terminates her pregnancy in the first trimester (79 to 90 percent).

Demography of Abortion: United States

Approximately 1.59 million abortions were performed in the United States in 1988, representing an abortion rate of 27.3 per 1,000 women (aged 15-44). Stated differently, there were almost 29 abortions for every 100 known pregnancies (live births plus abortions), the highest among the western industrialized countries (see Apeendix A table 1). Though the number of abortions has been relatively unchanged since 1980, when 1.55 million abortions were reported, the abortion rates both per 1,000 women and per 100 live births declined moderately since 1980, when the respective rates were 29 per 1,000 women and 30 abortions per 100 known pregnancies. The drop may have been caused by aging of the "baby boomers," reflected in a lower incidence of abortion among women 25 and older.[46] Unmarried women, including single, separated, divorced, and widowed women[47] continued to be the biggest contributors, with 82.6 percent of the total in 1988. This represents an increase of more than 16 percent since 1973 and 4 percent since 1980. Not only did unmarried women represent a huge majority among the abortion seekers, they were more likely to have an abortion than were married women (46 vs. 9 per 1,000 women or 56 vs. 9 per 100 known

---

[46]Henshaw, Koonin, and Smith 1991: 77.

[47]The U.S. statistics do not provide separate figures for single, never-married women as do the Canadian statistics.

pregnancies). Lower abortion rates among married women may be attributed in part to their higher use of the most effective contraceptive method, sterilization. Unmarried women are less likely to plan their contraception, because of the unpredictable nature of their sexual activity. In terms of age-specific abortion rates, women 20-24 posted the highest abortion rate, 54.2 per 1,000 women, in 1988, followed by teenage women (under 20), who reported an abortion rate of 45.5. This trend has been consistent since 1973. However, abortion continued to be more common among older teenage women 18-19 than in any other age category. For instance, there were about 63 abortions per 1,000 women in this age group in 1988, and approximately this proportion has held since 1979 (see Appendix A table 2).[48]   The reasons for high abortion rates among teenage women may be attributed to early initiation of sexual debut, increased sexual activity, less effective contraceptive use or nonuse, higher failure rates, and delayed childbearing.[49]

In 1988, the majority of women (51.2 percent) had no previous live births, and this percentage has shown little fluctuation since 1974. The proportion of women who reported at least one previous induced abortion increased from 15.2 percent in 1974 to 43 percent in 1988. The upward trend in repeat abortions is not a reflection of these women's acceptance of abortion as a primary method of regulating fertility. A survey of Canadian women who had had repeat abortions shows that nearly one-half of them reported using contraception at the time of conception.[50]   Tietze (1983), having surveyed the contraceptive prevalence among aborters, concluded that it is the women on contraceptives who are more likely to have an abortion rather than those who do not use birth control.

Increasingly, women are seeking earlier abortions, mostly in the first trimester, when they are considered safest. In 1988, one-half (50.3 percent) of all abortions were performed before nine weeks of gestation, and almost nine out of ten pregnancies were terminated under thirteen weeks, up from 85 percent in 1973. Less than 1 percent (0.7 percent) of all abortions occurred later than twenty weeks. It is frequently the youngest women who seek late abortions,

---

[48]Also see Jones et al. 1988; Tietze et al. 1988.

[49]Forrest and Singh 1990; Jones and Forrest 1989; Trussell and Westoff 1980.

[50]Committee on the Operation of the Abortion Law 1977: 352.

because of their ignorance of the signs of pregnancy, their denial of its occurrence, the laws and regulations requiring parental consent for minors, lack of money, and fear of disclosure.

There are some striking black-white differences in the abortion rates. Blacks have consistently posted higher rates during 1973-1988, a difference due to higher pregnancy rates resulting from failure or nonuse of contraceptives.[51]   In 1988, among white women the abortion rate was 21 per 1,000 women aged 15-44, compared to the abortion rate of 57 among blacks and other minorities, which was 2.7 times higher.   Expressed differently, there were 25 abortions for every 100 known pregnancies (live births plus abortions) among whites in 1988, compared to 39 for blacks and other minorities, which is 1.6 times higher than that for whites.   While the abortion rate among whites steadily dropped since 1980, when it was 24.3 (per 1,000 women) and 27.4 (per 100 known pregnancies), the rate among blacks remained steady around the 1988 level since 1976. Similarly, black and minority teenagers had a higher rate of abortion in 1988 than did white teenagers (80 vs. 37 per 1,000), and this disparity held true for all age categories. However, white and minority teenagers are equally likely to choose abortion, once pregnant. For instance, the percentage of termination of known pregnancies was the same, 41 in 1988, in both groups.

White and minority women also differed by marital status, and this difference prevailed in all categories.   Black and minority married women were more likely to obtain abortions in 1987 than were white married women (27.6 vs. 6.9 per 1,000). A similar disparity held between white and minority unmarried women. There were 38 abortions per 1,000 white unmarried women in 1987 compared to 71 for minority unmarried women.

Demography of Abortion: Canada

The abortion trends in Canada are similar to those in the United States; however, its comparable rates are low compared to the United States and other western countries (see Appendix A table 1). A total of 94,108 abortions performed in Canada in 1990 represented

---

[51]Henshaw and Van Vort 1989, 1992; Henshaw and O'Reilly 1983; Henshaw et al. 1991.

an abortion rate of 14.8 per 1,000 women (aged 15-44) or 23.2 abortions for every 100 live births. Both the abortion rate and the abortion ratio showed an increase of 20.3 percent and 24.7 percent respectively from 1978, when abortions performed in clinics were first reported in Quebec (see Appendix A table 3).[52] Never-married women continue to make up the largest percentage, sixty-five, in the total abortions in 1990 (or 77 percent if separated, divorced, and widowed are added), which represents an increase since 1974 of 12 percent, but little change since 1980 (see Appendix A table 4).

Although the proportion of abortions to teenage women under twenty has steadily declined between 1974 and 1990, from 31.5 percent to 20.4 percent, teenagers are still the major contributors to the overall yearly number, compared to all age categories except women aged 20-24, who consistently held on to 31 percent of the total during this period (see Apppendix A table 4). As in the United States, teenagers in Canada also recorded the highest abortion rates in 1990 (15.9 per 1,000), only after the women 20-24 years (21.9 per 1,000) (see Appendix A table 3). While abortion rates among teenagers have steadily declined since 1978 by more than 6 percent, women 20-24 years have shown an increase in rates by more than 27 percent during the same period. Abortions continue to be more common among older teenage women 18-19 (around 19 to 22 per 1,000) than in any age category since 1977 (see Appendix A table 3).

Women with no previous live births continued to make up the majority (52.7 percent) in 1990, although their percentage has been slipping since 1980, the peak year, when it was 62.4 percent (see Appendix A table 4). Increasingly more women are seeking repeat abortions. In 1990, 30 percent of the women who obtained abortions have had at least one pregnancy terminated previously, compared to 9 percent in 1974. Generally, it is the older woman (20-29 and 30-39 years) who is more likely to seek repeat abortions. Women are seeking repeat abortions not because there is a growing acceptance of abortion as a preferred method of birth control but because these women experienced a genuine contraceptive or personal failure.

---

[52]The figures for 1990 reflect for the first time abortions performed on Canadian women in clinics in the provinces of Newfoundland, Nova Scotia, Ontario, Manitoba, and British Columbia, which resulted in a total of 12,524. These abortions largely account for the big jump in the abortion rates over the previous years.

Most abortions (88 percent in 1990) are being performed under thirteen weeks of pregnancy. Of the first trimester abortions in 1990, one-third were performed on pregnancies of less than nine weeks. Only 0.3 percent of all abortions were performed on late pregnancies lasting more than twenty weeks (see Appendix A table 4). Married women and older women (20 years and above) are more likely than single and younger women (under 20) to seek first trimester abortions, but this difference has been narrowing over time.

From the foregoing, it is clear that the overall abortion rate in both countries has been declining or has held steady (in the case of Canada) since 1980. However, certain groups such as older teenage women 18-19, women 20-24, and black and minority adolescents defy this trend. The increase in abortion rates among these subgroups is attributed to greater sexual frequency and less effective contraceptive use or nonuse. The limited access to abortion and contraceptive services by women of minority status is largely attributable to economic and psychological barriers.

Increasingly, despite intensification of anti-abortion movements, public opinion has held steadfast with two-thirds of the U.S. adult population supporting the current legal status of abortion. Forty to forty-three percent endorse it for any reason, and nine-tenths approve its legal availability according to the circumstances involved.[53] Interestingly, even anti-abortion activists are willing to tolerate termination of pregnancy in cases of rape and incest. Elizabeth Fox-Genovese notes that while anti-abortion forces are doggedly committed to oppostion to abortion, they seem to be more flexible in practice than in principle.[54] Evidence of this is provided by a recent survey of 533 physicians in Kansas. Almost eight out of ten respondents said that abortion should be legal, but only one-half (56 percent) described themselves as pro-choice. Similarly, less than one-tenth were in favor of a total ban, even though one-third said they

---

[53]Tietze et al. 1988; *The Plain Dealer*, January 22, 1989: 14A; *Time Magazine*, May 1, 1989: 20, November 6, 1989: 51; *USA Today*, July 7, 1989: 5A. A more recent survey by *Parade* magazine also confirmed previous survey results, with a slightly higher percentage of adult Americans (71 percent) approving of legal abortion. See *Globe and Mail*, May 15, 1992. Interestingly, according to a *Life* magazine survey, more men than women (54 percent vs. 46 percent) favor abortion rights. See, *Evening Telegram*, May 7, 1992.

[54]*New Republic*, May 18, 1992: 43.

were pro-life.[55]   Likewise, Canadians are approving of legalized abortion, although their support is not as strong as that of their American counterparts.   Close to nine-tenths (86 percent) of Canadians approve of legalized abortion generally, three-fifths support it on selective grounds, and over a quarter (27 percent) are in favor of it under any circumstances.   Canadians have held their attitudes consistently over time since 1975 (see Appendix A table 5).[56]

SUMMARY

The trends in abortion consistently show that, in both the U.S. and Canada, young unmarried women are the biggest contributors to the total abortions.   Most of these pregnancies are unintended and result from unprotected or inadequately protected sex acts.   Becoming pregnant out-of-wedlock and terminating a pregnancy pre-term can be in itself emotionally distressing for some women, but a woman's trauma is compounded when she is subjected to the forces that oppose her right to make reproductive choices free from state interference. Pro-choice and anti-abortion forces are polarized in the United States and Canada and have created a fierce battle over abortion.

In 1973, the U.S. Supreme Court handed down a landmark decision in *Roe v. Wade* sweeping away all the laws in every state that prohibited abortion.   The Court decision, which struck a middle ground in its trimester approach, was supposed to have put the abortion debate to rest.   Instead, it touched off a new wave of political controversies and court challenges.   The court rulings have especially come down hard on teenage access to abortions, enforcing various restrictions.   A similar battle has been going on in Canada, splitting the Canadian public and politicians for decades.   The Canadian federal law was struck down in January 1988 as unconstitutional, and there is no law yet governing abortion

---

[55]Westfall et al., 1991.

[56]*Evening Telegram*, January 15, 1990; *Globe and Mail*, March 7, 1988. A more recent poll, conducted by Environics Research Group Ltd., found that 79 percent of Canadians surveyed agreed that "an abortion is a medical decision that should rest with the woman in consultation with her physician." This figure represents a dramatic increase in support from a similar poll in 1988 in which 71 percent agreed that abortion is a private matter (*Globe and Mail*, July 22, 1992).

procedures except a patchwork of provincial policies. However, the rates of abortion have not significantly risen, despite the absence of law. The abortion battle rages on in both countries and any likelihood of truce is not in sight. However, women who are faced with problem pregnancies continue to seek terminations, abortion debate or not. A typical woman who seeks abortion is young, unmarried, childless, white, and terminates her pregnancy in the first trimester.

2

The Abortion Experience

The only people who know what an abortion is like are the women who have gone through it.

22-year-old university student

PSYCHOLOGICAL REACTIONS

How does abortion affect women psychologically, and how do they subsequently adjust? These questions are as controversial and polemic as the moral acceptance of abortion. Despite the massive data on the psychological effects of abortion, studies in this area are contradictory and inconclusive. The conclusions range from the suggestion that psychological complications are almost inevitable after abortion to a finding of their virtual absence. Depending upon the seriousness of the disturbance, these studies can be organized into three sections: (1) serious psychological reactions, (2) insignificant or negligible psychological reactions, and (3) minimal psychological reactions.

Serious Psychological Reactions

Representing one end of the extreme position are the studies, mostly clinical, that claim that abortion almost always results in psychological disturbances such as guilt, depression, and self-reproach.[1] These authors warn that these reactions are serious,

---

[1]See Anderson 1966; Aren 1958; Calderone 1958; Dunbar 1967; Deutsch 1945; Ebaugh & Heuser 1947; Hefferman & Lynch 1953; Malmfors 1966; Taussig 1936; Wilson 1952.

traumatic, and in some cases lasting. Bolter (1962) contends that these disturbances could interfere with the woman's role as child-bearer and child-rearer. Several of these studies were done on samples of European and Soviet women, and the authors found a majority of them (50 to 55 percent) reporting a considerable degree of guilt feelings and distress, lasting two to three years after they had an abortion.

Insignificant Psychological Reactions

The other extreme is represented by those investigators who dismiss any evidence of trauma resulting from abortion. They maintain that, with rare exceptions, the women's emotional health was the same or improved over their preabortion condition. These women felt content because abortion rid them of the emotional distress caused by an unwanted pregnancy and the consequences that would have followed the birth of a child.[2] Some investigators report maturing experiences being predominant among their sample.[3] Post-abortion psychiatric illness and guilt are rare and a myth, declared Kummer (1963) after surveying the experiences of thirty-two psychiatrists in Los Angeles.

Minimal Psychological Reactions

Other investigators occupy a middle position, suggesting that women who have undergone abortion experience psychological disturbances afterward, but that these reactions are mild and disappear with time.[4] They maintain that abortion itself is rarely the cause of

---

[2]See Brody et al. 1971; Ewing & Rouse 1973; Gebhard et al. 1958; Laidlaw 1966; Lask, 1975; Levene & Rigney 1970; Niswander & Patterson 1967; Peck & Marcus 1966; Schwartz 1968; Todd 1972; Tredgold 1964; Werman & Raft, 1973; Weston 1973; Whittington 1960.

[3]See Monsour & Stewart 1973; Marder 1970; Patt et al. 1969; Smith 1973; Wallerstein et al. 1972.

[4]Anderson 1966; Bacon 1969; Brekke 1966; Ekblad 1955; Ford et al. 1971; Greenglass 1976; Handy 1982; Illsley & Hall 1976; Ingham & Simms 1972; Kretzchmar & Norris 1967; Lee 1969; Lidz 1967; Lipper et al. 1973; Major et al. 1985; McCoy 1968; Meyerowitz et al. 1971; Mueller & Major 1989; Osofsky & Osofsky 1972; Patt et al. 1969; Payne et al. 1976; Perez-Reyes & Falk 1973; Simon et al. 1967; White 1966.

psychiatric conditions.   Rather, these symptoms are simply a continuation of the woman's psychiatric complaints existing before the abortion, or else precipitated by other life stresses occurring around the same time as the abortion.   Very often the woman may have latent or hidden mental problems or a poor mental state which make her susceptible to any stressful life events, such as pregnancy and childbirth. In other words, psychologically healthier women respond to the abortion without significant problems.   Anderson from England, referring to Ekblad's study of 479 Swedish women and based on his own study of twenty-four women, reaffirmed the risk of unfavourable reactions amongst women with a history of psychological problems and cautioned that a careful recommendation of abortion should be made.[5] Ford et al. (1971) reached a similar conclusion from their study of twenty-two women that "it is the seriously ill woman who does less well emotionally after abortion than the more 'normal' ones" (p. 117). One of the earliest studies by Hamilton (1966) in 1941 concluded that "there is a trend, with time, to find relief and satisfaction in abortion" (p. 379).   Subsequent studies affirmed that most of the women experience recovery from their symptoms of anxiety and depression in a relatively short time, up to six months after the abortion.[6]

Unscrambling the Professional Judgements

As is evident from the above reviews, the professional opinions on the psychological effects of abortion are confusing at best and they do not offer secure conclusions. Much of the literature, especially earlier studies that emphasize serious complications of abortion, is so poor it can be dismissed on the basis of gross methodological flaws such as biased samples (e.g., volunteers or only women with complications), unreliable measurements, lack of clarity about evaluation of certain diagnostic categories (e.g., Ekblad, "non-psychiatric patients;" Malmfors, "eugenic;" Siegfried, "serious psychiatric impairment").   Samples selected for the studies were generally drawn from women in therapy and therefore had weak personalities susceptible to stressful situations. Furthermore, during

---

[5]Anderson 1966: 82.
[6]Greenglass 1976; Lee 1969.

the period most of these studies were conducted, abortion was not legal and therefore was treated as a taboo subject. The medical profession considered the procedure beyond the range of "normal experience" and this conviction outweighed the importance of the data.[7] These studies are aptly described by Brody et al. (1971) as "maximum amount of theorization on a minimum amount of data" (p. 347). Callahan (1970) attempted to find consistency in the findings of earlier studies and lamented the lack of "reliable judgement" on the psychological effects of abortion (p. 30). At best, no general statements can be made about the women's psychological reactions due to the diverse sample of women who obtained abortion for diverse reasons (medical, mental health, or socio-economic) via different surgical procedures (suction or saline), under diverse conditions (legal or illegal). All of these factors can affect women differently and produce psychological reactions of different degrees and natures.[8] These are discussed in detail in the next section.

Illegal vs. Therapeutic Abortion

Abortions were illegal in several states in the United States prior to 1973 and were available only in case of a pregnancy posing a threat to a woman's life or mental health. In Canada, prior to August 1969 abortion was lawful when in "good faith," it was considered necessary to preserve a woman's life. After August 1969 the Criminal Code was amended to permit a therapeutic abortion if the continuation of the pregnancy would endanger the woman's "life or health." This law remained in effect until January 1988 when Canada's abortion law was declared unconstitutional. Under this law, in order to justify their requests for abortion, many women had to feign psychiatric symptoms, express suicidal ideas and present themselves as emotionally disordered. Research evidence shows that women who seek illegal abortions experience greater emotional problems than those seeking legal abortions.[9] Since laws represent society's moral codes for social behavior, a woman seeking an illegal abortion can experience guilt and anxiety emanating from dual sources of morality--one arising from breaking the law and thus

---

[7]Adler 1979; Lazarus 1985.

[8]See Wilmoth et al. 1992.

[9]Adler et al. 1990; Callahan 1970; Glenc 1974.

violating the society's moral code, and the second originating from personal morals. In contrast, a woman seeking a legal abortion faces the question mainly at a personal moral level.

Mental Health vs. Medical Reasons

The women who desire a pregnancy and intend to keep it but are compelled to terminate it because of the risk of a child's deformity or danger to their own health are more likely to react unfavorably after an abortion than those who seek termination voluntarily.[10] An outright rejection of the pregnancy in the first place makes it easier for these women to cope with the abortion experience.[11] Lazarus (1985), for instance, found in his study that the women who reported dissatisfaction with their abortion were the ones who terminated their pregnancy for medical reasons. Simon et al. (1967) also noted in their study of forty-six women that "transient and mild depression were more characteristic of the rubella group, while the psychiatric group reported the lowest incident of depression" (p. 60).

Likewise, the circumstances under which the pregnancy occurs determine the kind of post-abortion reactions a woman will experience. A woman who becomes pregnant from incest or rape is more likely to reject the pregnancy because of its association with the man toward whom she may feel hatred and repugnance. To such a woman seeking termination means seeking to erase unpleasant associations. Very few moral qualms are likely to arise, and the woman rarely regrets the termination of such a pregnancy. Also, society is more favorable toward abortion granted on these grounds than toward that permitted on social or economic reasons, as is evident from all opinion polls.[12]

---

[10]Adler 1975; Ashton 1980b; Donnai et al. 1981; Freidman et al. 1974; Leiter 1972; Meyerowitz et al. 1971; Niswander & Patterson 1967; Payne et al. 1976; Peck & Marcus 1966; Simon et al. 1967.

[11]Senay 1970; Wallerstein et al. 1972.

[12]Sachdev 1988; Ebaugh & Haney 1985.

Abortion Procedure--Suction Curettage or Saline Induction

Of the two major surgical procedures used to terminate pregnancy, suction and curettage (S&C), or dilation and evacuation (D&E), are the most commonly used up to fourteen or sometimes sixteen weeks of pregnancy. They are by far the safest method and much simpler than saline induction. These methods take about 15 to 20 minutes and can be performed on out-patients. Between sixteen and twenty-four weeks (in the United States; in Canada, up to twenty weeks) of pregnancy, saline induction or "salting out" is the method of choice.   In the first trimester, except for slight physiological changes accompanied by occasional discomfort like "morning sickness," a pregnant woman remains most of the time unaware of its reality. It is not until the major bodily changes (e.g., weight gain, tenderness and enlargement of breasts, frequent urination, changes in complexion) occur that the woman begins to identify with the pregnancy and views the fetus as a potential "child." In a very advanced pregnancy, the experience of "quickening" further places credence in the event and reinforces her identification with the fetus in human terms. As can be expected, women undergoing termination of late pregnancy are likely to experience more intense psychological reactions than those having early termination.[13]

Furthermore, saline induction that induces labor-like contractions and causes expulsion of the fetus, adds to the woman's psychological stress.   Saline injection also must be done after "quickening" and the woman must be conscious of the fetal movement. Since the fetus in an advanced pregnancy also resembles a baby, there is always the possibility of the woman accidently seeing the dead fetus, adding to her emotional trauma.   Several reports indicate that some women happen to hear the cry or see the fetus delivered alive, the episodes that cause intense guilt reactions. Psychological trauma may thus result from (a) the procedure itself and (b) from the removal of an active fetus that, as Braken and Swiger (1972) suggest, has already "received some psychological investment" (p. 302). Thus, resolution of the painful experience, if any, is apparently much easier among D&E patients, who receive a very brief exposure to the event, than among saline patients.

---

[13]See, Adler & Dolcini 1986; Bracken et al. 1974; Cates 1980; Lazarus 1985.

Ideological Basis

Trained in Freudian psychology, the earlier investigators had a particular view of women and abortion, which influenced their conclusions.[14] The psychoanalytical perspective held that, despite the risk of pregnancy, single women who do not use contraceptives experience intrapsychic conflicts or have neurotic needs that are expressed in what Lehfeldt (1970) calls, "wilful exposure to unwanted pregnancy." Thus, considered within this framework, no pregnancy to a single woman is unwanted at the unconscious level, despite her claim to the contrary (Luker, 1975). Clearly then, when these women seek abortion, the most obvious judgment made about them is that they not only are emotionally disturbed but also run the risk of compounding their pathology by rejecting the pregnancy that, in many cases, would gratify their neurotic needs. Two earlier studies that appear frequently in the literature clearly reflect this bias against women who seek therapeutic abortion. Simon et al. (1967) described them as "highly selected in terms of their psychopathology" (p. 64), and Ford et al. (1972) concluded that "these women tend to be narcissistic" (p. 551).

Several references in the psychiatric literature describe pregnancy as an expression of a women's "femininity, her creativeness . . . her mothering capacities and her family," and regard desire for motherhood as intrinsic to every woman.[15] Strong suggestions, therefore, are made that giving birth is preferable to abortion. To Simone de Beauvoir (1953), pregnancy is a woman's "natural calling," and she regards a woman's organic structure as her "destiny" and the primary role for the perpetuation of the species. Elaborating on Simone de Beauvoir's theme, Galdston (1958) reasons that women have a natural desire for motherhood because of their uterus, which determines their personality and biology. In Lee Rainwater's view, pregnancy signifies to a woman "a kind of categorical maturity as an adult human being" (1967). Bolter (1962), another psychiatrist, agrees with Simone de Beauvoir's view of women's primary role when he states, "despite protests to the contrary, we know that woman's main role here on earth is to conceive, deliver, and raise children" (pp. 314-15).

---

[14]Adler 1979; Zimmerman, 1977: 24.
[15]Fleck 1970: 44.

The ideological basis of much of the psychiatric literature can be traced to the influence of Freud, who maintained that desire for motherhood is a normal compensation for the small girl's wish for a penis and symbolizes her normal personality development.[16] Freud gave a dire warning that a woman who rejects the wish for motherhood is psychologically maladjusted. Psychiatrists who followed Freud echoed his theme and regarded the mother's bond with her child as natural and instantaneous from the moment of learning of the pregnancy. To them abortion interferes with the woman's biology and her primary role as child bearer, causing serious psychological consequences.[17]

Current Orientation

Luckily, investigators have gradually shifted over the years from Freud's deterministic perspective, which narrowly focused on patient pathology. Today, research recognizes the situational factors governing unwanted pregnancies and especially a woman's relationship with key people and their attitudes as salient elements in accounting for her emotional reactions to abortion. The new orientation does not share the values that women's reproductive and family roles are natural and given but regards motherhood as a culturally determined behavior.[18] This view is influenced, among other things, by an acceptance of recreational sex as the legitimate goal of sexual activity, and by feminist writings.

Furthermore, more recent studies are precise, systematic, and methodologically superior and provide evidence of consistency in their findings: Psychological reactions such as guilt, anxiety, and depression may occur after abortion in the first trimester, but they are seldom of a serious nature. These reactions disappear with time, depending upon the coping ability of the woman. Other reviewers who surveyed the literature on the psychological effects of the first

---

[16]Zimmerman 1977.

[17]Bolter 1962; Calderone 1958; Ford et al. 1972; Galdston 1958; Lidz 1967; Rheingold 1964; Romm 1967; Senay 1970.

[18]Cappen 1964; Simon et al. 1967; Steele & Pollock 1968; Walter 1970.

trimester abortion have reached similar conclusions.[19]   After an extensive consultation with experts in the field, former Surgeon General C. Everett Koop reported in May 1989 to the 101st Congress of the United States regarding his review of research on psychological effects of abortion.   He testified that the effect of abortion on the physical health of women is not significant and that the psychological problems of abortion are "minuscule from a public health perspective."[20]   Assurance also comes from well-known American authors Adler et al. (1990) who reviewed methodologically sound studies of U.S. women who obtained legal, nonrestrictive abortions. The authors concluded that the incidence of severe negative reactions after abortion has been uniformly low, depending upon the ambivalence about the decision, the degree of unwantedness of the pregnancy, and the support the woman receives from her key people.

CORRELATES OF ABORTION EFFECTS

As stated earlier, this study takes the view that adverse psychological reactions following an abortion are not inevitable but are largely influenced by immediate psychosocial factors in the woman's life and how she defines and experiences them.   These factors include her emotional conflicts or dilemmas, her experience with the service providers, her attitude toward the pregnancy, and the support of her male partner.[21]

---

[19]Adler 1975, 1979; Adler et al. 1990; Armsworth 1991; Bhatia et al. 1990; Blumenthal 1991; Callahan 1970; Dagg 1990; Illsley & Hall 1976; Levene & Rigney 1970; Lemkau 1988; Lodl et al. 1985; Olson 1980; Osofsky and Osofsky 1972; Romans-Clarkson 1989; Shusterman 1976; Smith 1973; Wilmoth 1988; Zimmerman 1977.

[20]Committee on Government Operations 1989: 219.

[21]The literature on abortion provides a robust support for the idea that these variables are the best predictors of emotional distress post-abortion. See Adler et al. 1990; Llewalyn & Pytches 1988; Lodl et al. 1985.

The Abortion Dilemma

Faced with an unwanted pregnancy, some unmarried women are irrevocably committed to its termination, while others may be ambivalent and may consider alternatives before deciding on abortion. Ambivalence may result from a woman's commitment to the pregnancy and attitude toward abortion.

A woman becoming pregnant in a love relationship is more likely to feel emotionally involved in her pregnancy than one whose pregnancy results from rape or incest or a casual encounter. Norms concerning motherhood held by those around the woman toward pregnancy also influence how she reacts to it. If the woman and the people around her value the maternal role as child-bearer and child-rearer, deliberate termination of the pregnancy implies rejection of this role, which is likely to evoke guilt reactions pre- and post-abortion.[22] A woman may experience little emotional dilemma from terminating a nonmarital pregnancy that is disapproved of by her key people, and she may feel relief after the abortion because it provided an escape from embarrassment or social stigma.

Attitude toward abortion represents a significant source of personal dilemma when seeking termination of a pregnancy and thus may cause psychological reactions of guilt and depression afterward.[23] Some women may regard legal abortion as a minor surgical interlude used as a natural and legitimate extension of contraception, while others may treat it more seriously because of the moral and religious significance they attach to it. However, abortion attitudes are largely shaped by exposure to one's religious position on the issue and to the media. Obviously, the church can influence the values and attitudes of those who are religiously devout. Several studies show that women who are religious and involved in church-related activities hold more conservative attitude toward abortion than those who are not affiliated with any religious groups or affiliated with liberal denominations.[24]

---

[22]Bolter 1962; Cobliner et al. 1973; Fleck 1970; Romm 1967.

[23]Eisen & Zellman 1984.

[24]Adler 1975; Cobliner et al. 1973; Combs & Welch 1982; Ebaugh & Haney 1985; Gabrielson et al. 1971; Maxwell 1970; Miller & Moore 1990.

The news media and printed material with a deliberate use of inflammatory language and gruesome pictures of aborted fetuses can only ignite passions and prevent prudent reflection on whether to abort or continue a pregnancy. | Clearly, as long as abortion cannot be performed as any other operation, women are at risk of feeling emotional distress about their decision to have an abortion. Bearing in mind that different women react to their pregnancy differently, depending upon their psychosocial contexts and their conditioning, the pre-abortion dilemma will be felt variously by each woman. Recognizing individual differences, Ruth I. Pierce (1970) expressed this theme very succinctly: "Some girls will want an abortion, and that is all there is to it. To others, the thought alone may be highly offensive" (p. xiv). A number of investigators observed that a woman's reactions following abortion, such as guilt and depression, are related to the degree to which she continues to experience pre-abortion dilemma.[25] International studies on abortion show that in countries such as China, India, Korea, Japan, and Cuba, where there is a high acceptance of abortion and little of the religious and moral controversy about abortion found in the West, women experience little or no anxiety and psychological trauma before and after the procedure.[26] It seems that reaction to abortion is bound by culture and social values.

Hospital Experience

A woman's emotional state before and after the abortion is likely to be influenced by the ease in which she is able to negotiate with the medical system (i.e., physicians and hospital staff) and implement her abortion decision. A woman who encounters a physician who is sympathetic and sensitive, a nursing staff that is cooperative and friendly, and a hospital that presents few bureaucratic barriers will perceive the medical service as caring and supportive. In contrast, service providers who are moralistic and critical of unmarried women seeking abortion are likely to exacerbate the woman's existing psychological disturbances or evoke new anxiety.

---

[25]Bracken & Kasl 1975; Eisen & Zellman 1984; Ekblad 1955; Greenglass 1976; Lemkau 1991; Osofsky & Osofsky 1972; Smith 1973.
[26]Lemkau 1988; Sachdev 1988.

Laidlaw (1966) observed that "a cold and frightening commercial atmosphere" of medical services was responsible for the trauma among his patients (p. 544). Similarly, Mardar (1970) found that "hostility and resentment toward the patient by the staff and nursing personnel" contributed to the emotional disturbances among his 147 abortion patients (p. 1235). Another report by Clark et al. (1968) concluded that criticisms spoken or implied by gynecologists or nurses might have intensified guilt and depression among the women they studied. Walter (1970) noted that mild guilt in his patients was due to the clinic atmosphere and the attitude of the staff toward the patients. Studies have shown that physicians' attitudes towards abortion have a great bearing on the extent to which equal and easy access to abortion services is available.[27] The physicians' attitudes are shaped not only by religious beliefs or by the professional climate of opinion but also very significantly by the "perceived attributes of women seeking abortion and by the ways in which these women present themselves."[28] Physicians are also found to be highly sensitive to the moral characters they attribute to their patients. That is, the "bad, promiscuous girls" are least likely to be recommended for pregnancy termination, and "the nice girls who had made mistakes" are most successful in having their abortion requests approved.[29]

Abortion Impact: Sexual Relationship

How does abortion affect the woman's relationship with the man involved in the pregnancy and her attitude toward sex? This is an important question in that a woman's abortion experience, her decision-making, and her reactions take place in the context of her relationships with key people in her life. Obviously, one of the key persons whose support and relationship is thought crucial is her male partner. Research evidence shows that the nature of relationship with the sexual partner and the extent of his support are highly significant in determining the woman's psychological adjustment following

---

[27]COAL 1977; Miller 1979; Nathanson & Becker 1980.
[28]Nathanson 1985: 215.
[29]Joffee 1979; MacIntyre 1977; Nathanson 1985.

abortion.[30] Important as this relationship is, the majority of women report deterioration in their relationship and feelings of dislike toward the man involved subsequent to the abortion.[31] White (1966) says that women after abortion may turn vindictively on their lovers or husbands, especially if they had been pressured into the abortion against their wishes (p. 553). Women also find their male partners selfish and insensitive to their feelings, uncaring of their need, and mostly selfish about their own sexual gratification. Shostak and McLouth (1984), however, found in their study of 1,000 men whose female partners have had an abortion that the men who broke off were sensitive and caring. They experienced tremendous emotional stress brought about by guilt and remorse. They also felt angry because the female partners did not encourage any discussion on the subject, thereby depriving them of the opportunity to express their feelings. They abandoned the relationship to be relieved from the mental tension and to close off the painful experience that was likely to be stirred up by the female partner. Another source of tension according to these authors is the woman's indifference to sex and denial of sex, which most men find hard to accommodate. A few investigators observed lack of sexual desire among the women having an abortion.[32] However, most women resume sexual activity after a short duration.[33]

Abortion Impact: Immediate Emotional Reactions

Some women experience feelings of relief and satisfaction as immediate reactions to termination. They feel relief from the stress of unwanted pregnancy, from the threat of penalties--social, emotional, financial--they might have faced were they forced to continue their pregnancy.[34] The proportion of women reporting euphoric moods immediately following their abortion range from a

---

[30]Greenglass 1976; Hook 1975; Moseley et al. 1981; Zimmerman 1977.

[31]Ford et al. 1971; Freundt 1973; Greenglass 1976; Lee 1969; Lipper et al. 1973; Monsour & Stewart 1973; Perez-Reyes & Falk 1973; Smith 1972, 1973; Shostak and McLouth 1984.

[32]Ford et al. 1972; Hamilton 1966; Smith 1972.

[33]Ashton 1980b; Gebhard et al. 1958; Wallerstein 1972.

[34]Adler 1975; Pierce 1970; Peck 1968; Zimmerman 1977.

low of one-third to a high of more than two-thirds of the sample studied.[35]   Some investigators describe these feelings as "a deliverance from conflicts" or "being rescued from drowning."[36] However, other investigators claim that the women's overriding response immediately following abortion is one of indifference and that these women would not like to talk about their abortion.[37] Senay (1979) remarks of these women that they rarely talk about the abortion spontaneously. These investigators further noted that the women go through a phase during which they resolve or repress the abortion experience; the amount of time each woman takes to complete this phase depends upon her ability to deal with life crises.

SUMMARY

The data bearing on the psychological aspect of abortion are immense, but the earlier studies, that is, prior to the late 1960s, are largely polemic and contradictory. These studies reflect the view that serious psychological complications of abortion are almost inevitable. Much of the literature during this period is grossly flawed, and the samples involved women who obtained abortions that were illegal or under restrictive abortion laws that permitted termination only to save the mother's life or to preserve her mental health. In addition, the ideology of the investigators was mostly anchored in a psychoanalytical orientation, which emphasized preference for completing pregnancy without exception.

More recent studies are relatively systematic and methodologically sound, and the sample women obtained legal abortion mostly on socioeconomic grounds.   These studies consistently report that many women suffer psychological reactions of guilt or depression following abortion, but these responses are mild and dissipate with time.   Serious and prolonged psychological consequences are rare, even rarer than those following unwanted

---

[35]Hamilton 1966; Jansson 1965; Lazarus 1985; Lemkau 1991; McCoy 1968; Niswander & Patterson 1967; Osofsky & Osofsky 1972; Simon et al. 1967; Wilmoth 1988; Zimmerman 1977.

[36]Jansson 1965; Rheingold 1964.

[37]Patt et al. 1969; Shostak & McLouth 1984.

pregnancy and childbirth.[38]   The studies note, however, that psychological reactions are influenced by the woman's pre-abortion dilemma, her commitment to the pregnancy, her prior history of mental state, her attitude towards abortion, the support of her key people, the attitude of the service providers, and her coping ability. Research evidence shows that abortion adversely impacts on many women's relationships with their male partners and causes loss of sexual desire, though temporarily. Some investigators report that for most women the immediate reaction following termination is one of euphoria, while others contend that the women withdraw into their own world in order to resolve the abortion experience.

---

[38]Greenglass 1976; Hamilton 1984; Kolbert 1989; Orentlicher 1989. Watters (1980) reviewed the literature on the subject and concluded that the rate of postpartum depression is six times that of post-abortion and that women who are forced to bear pregnancy and motherhood are at greater risk of adverse psychological reactions.

3

The Sample Women and How They Were Studied

We can safely assert that the knowledge that men can acquire of women . . . is wretchedly imperfect and superficial and will always be so until women themselves have told all that they have to tell.

John Stuart Mill[1]

STUDY FACTORS

The seventy women who participated in this study all lived in a large metropolitan city in Ontario, Canada. They were selected from the records of three major hospitals and a referral agency according to the criteria that they were 18 to 25 years old, white, unmarried, and pregnant for the first time and that their pregnancy had been terminated in the first trimester through the suction or dilation and evacuation (D & E) procedure. All these women obtained a therapeutic abortion on mental health grounds six months to one year prior to the follow-up interviews. The selection of women with homogeneous characteristics was intended to obtain a common baseline prior to their abortion. That is, an attempt was made to eliminate factors that could contribute to differences in the response patterns of these women and alter their reaction to the pregnancy and abortion, as they passed through the various phases of their experience.

The following section explains why the study was limited to only those women with homogenous characteristics such as age, marital status, race, and previous pregnancy and abortion. It was discussed in chapter 2 how a woman's psychological state is

---

[1]Quoted in Germaine Greer, *The Female Eunuch*. Frogmore, Herts, UK: Granada Publishing Ltd., 1971, p.13.

influenced by certain situations. These include the reasons for seeking abortion (psychiatric vs. social), the type of surgical procedure (suction vs. saline), and the conditions (illegal vs. legal) under which abortion is provided. These factors can be sources of possible variations in the women's experience with abortion. Their discussion will not be repeated here.

Age Group (18-25)

This age group was selected for two reasons. First, in most North American jurisdictions women under 18 are required to obtain parental consent for a surgical procedure. A mandatory involvement of the parents in the decision making brings in a whole new set of factors which make these women different from those who are free to choose their own course of action. Just how parents' reactions to abortion can influence the emotional reactions of women who underwent abortion is demonstrated by one study by Perez-Reyes and Falk (1973). The investigators observed among their adolescent patients that those who regretted termination were the ones who had been criticized by their mothers, sisters, or relatives. Studies also show that adolescents as a group, compared to adult women, are more likely to have psychological distress following the abortion, to feel forced by circumstances to have the abortion, and to be dissatisfied with the choice of abortion. These problems may be due in part to the developmental limitations and the cognitive characteristics that are natural to all adolescents.[2] Second, as discussed in the abortion profile in chapter 1, abortion is most common (both in terms of proportion and rates) among older teenagers 18-19 and women 20-25, compared with all other age categories.

Almost one-half of all abortions are consistently performed on women in the age group 18-25 in Canada and in the United States. For women over 25, the abortion rate begins to drop (see Appendix A tables 2 and 4). Interestingly, several European countries show steady trends in the age group 18-25 for having the most abortions.[3]

---

[2]Campbell et al. 1988; Franz & Reardon 1992.
[3]Sachdev 1988.

Furthermore, older women are likely to be married, more educated, and contraceptively more vigilant, making them markedly different from the younger cohort.[4]

White Women

White women of Anglo-Saxon origin are markedly different from their nonwhite counterparts (black, Jamaican, Puerto Rican) in the norms and behaviors governing premarital sex, pregnancy, abortion, and contraceptive use.[5] Blacks appear to be more tolerant of sexual activity and birth out-of-wedlock and to rate marriage as less important, while white unmarried women have a greater tendency to seek marriage or abortion as a way out of an unwanted pregnancy.[6] Black females not only initiate sexual activity earlier, they engage in sex more often and have more partners than do white females.[7] They are also less likely to abort because out-of-wedlock childbearing entails less loss of opportunities for black women than for white women.[8]

Also, white females view unplanned pregnancy as a more negative consequence, and they are more consistent in the use of contraceptives than blacks.[9] As would be expected, black women have proportionally more unplanned pregnancies and abortions. Among white females under twenty about one-half of all births occur outside of marriage, while black teenagers experience some 90

---

[4]Bowerman et al. 1966; Bracken et al. 1972; Cho et al. 1970; Grauer 1972; Kantner & Zelnik 1973; Kazanjian 1973; Osofsky & Osofsky 1972.

[5]Abrahamse et al. 1988; Cutright & Smith 1988; Hogan & Kitagawa 1985; St. John & Grasmick 1985; Trent & Griner 1991.

[6]Cooksey 1990; Furstenberg et al. 1987; Kantner & Zelnik 1973; Miller & Moore 1990; Moore & Peterson 1989; Moore & Stief 1991; Moore et al. 1986; Pope 1969; Trent & Griner 1991; White 1990; Zelnik & Kantner 1974.

[7]Moore and Peterson 1989.

[8]Hogan & Kitawaga 1985.

[9]Bowerman et al. 1966; Bracken et al. 1972; Kadushin 1972; Kane et al. 1971; Moore & Peterson 1989; Swenson et al. 1989.

percent of births outside marriage.[10]   There are also black-white
differences in their attitudes toward abortion, with blacks less
favorable towards it than whites.[11]   Although white unmarried
women comprise the largest proportion of those who seek
termination, abortion rates are higher for nonwhites than whites.[12]

In Canada, two large nonwhite minority groups, Puerto Ricans
and Jamaicans, show greater acceptance toward nonmarital pregnancy
and view it as a proof of a woman's fertility and a man's virility
before marriage. Furthermore, they do not face community stigma
by keeping babies out-of-wedlock.   Unmarried women, on the
contrary, receive assistance from their parents and close relatives in
caring for their newborns. A cursory examination of the hospital
records revealed that a majority of the Jamaican unmarried abortion
patients have had previous deliveries and their children were placed
with their parents back home. Italians, who constitute one of the
largest ethnic communities in Canada, are officially classified as
whites. However, they do not share the norms and values held by
Anglo-Saxon whites. They hold very restrictive standards regarding
dating, premarital sex, and pregnancy. Thus, the cultural and value
differences between whites and nonwhites (i.e., Italian, Puerto Rican,
and Jamaican) are too significant to be included in one study. Each
of these racial groups can yield a decision pattern completely different
from the other.

First Pregnancy

The first pregnancy is more likely to evoke greater childbirth
fears than subsequent ones.[13] A woman with a previous pregnancy
had already experienced the decision-making process and the
consequence of the alternatives. Faced with a subsequent pregnancy,
she is much less likely to register the same degree of conflict as at the

---

[10]Kalmuss 1986; Moore 1988; National Center for Health Statistics,
1989; Pratt & Horn 1985.

[11]Combs & Welch 1982.

[12]Henshaw et al. 1985; Henshaw 1992; Prager 1985. For instance, in
1987 the abortion rate among black unmarried women was twice as high as
among whites (Henshaw et al. 1991). Also, see Appendix A table 1.

[13]Payne et al. 1976.

first pregnancy. Similarly, a woman with prior abortion experience would be less apprehensive regarding the surgical procedure. At the same time, an abortion repeater might suffer more intense psychological consequences afterward because of the attitudes of the people around her, who might view a second abortion less favorably than the first, especially if it was done for psychological and economic reasons.[14]   Further, women with previous abortion experience or pregnancy are reported to have a greater motivation for contraception.[15]

Unmarried Women

A married woman's reactions to an unwanted pregnancy and her decision-making process are shaped by a set of factors and a support system that are completely different from those of an unmarried woman. In our pronatalist culture, there is greater pressure on married women to carry a pregnancy to term than on unmarried women.[16] Furthermore, as a married woman does not experience the same social and emotional pressures of an unwanted or wanted pregnancy as does an unmarried woman, her motivations to seek termination can be entirely different.[17] Pregnancy and childbirth among unmarried women are more disruptive, more socially and economically costly, than among married women.[18] Besides, married women usually have the benefit of a more stable relationship and the emotional support of the spouse and family. Empirical evidence suggests that emotional support and assurance

---

[14]Freeman et al. (1980, 1981) noted that repeat aborters experience significantly less decline in the emotional distress symptoms within two to three weeks following the abortion than do first aborters.

[15]Inghe 1972; Monsour & Stewart 1973; Martin 1972; Smith 1973; Steinhoff et al. 1979; Zozaya et al. 1972.

[16]Bracken 1978; Diamond et al. 1973; Francke 1978. Torres and Forrest (1988) surveyed 1900 women who had an abortion in 1987 at nonhospital facilities in the untied States and found that unmarried women were 17 percent more likely than currently married women to choose abortion to conceal from others their sexual activity and their pregnancy.

[17]Callahan 1970; Francke 1978; Sloane 1969; Young et al. 1973.

[18]Payne et al. 1976; Trent & Griner 1991.

from key people, especially the male partner or parents, greatly influence a woman's pre-abortion emotional state and psychological adjustment afterwards.[19]   A study by Niswander et al. (1972) compared abortion groups with maternity groups and found that unmarried women experienced greater stress of pregnancy than did married ones. Other investigators also found that married women who seek abortion are psychologically healthier, better adjusted, and less impulsive than their unmarried counterparts.[20]   Because unmarried and married women interact with entirely different psychosocial worlds, their reactions and adjustment to abortion can also be different. Several studies have noted that married women experience fewer emotional and psychological disturbances afterward and fewer strains on their relationships with their husbands.[21]   In a Canadian study, Greenglass (1976) found that while only 4 percent of the married women in her sample of 188 women dissolved their marriages after the abortion, a little less than 50 percent of the single women broke up with their sexual partners afterwards. Other studies also report a higher incidence of deterioration of pair relationships following pregnancy and abortion among young unmarried women.[22]

Married women also markedly differ from unmarried women in terms of access to and use of reliable contraception. As married women do not face the same psychological and social barriers and their sex relation takes place on a more regular and predictable basis, they are far more apt to practice contraception successfully.[23]

---

[19]Adler 1975; Belsey et al. 1977; Bracken et al. 1974; Major & Cozzarelli 1992; Moseley et al. 1981; Payne et al. 1976; Greenglass 1981.

[20]Brody et al. 1971; Hook 1963; Sloane 1969.

[21]Beric et al. 1974; Brody et al. 1971; Bracken et al. 1974; Ekblad 1955; Adler 1975; Gebhard et al. 1958; Hook 1963; Jansson 1965; Kretzchmar & Norris 1967; Niswander et al. 1972; Payne et al. 1976; Smith 1973; Trent & Griner 1991; White 1966; Whittington 1960.

[22]Addleson 1973; Hamilton 1966; Lee 1969; Monsour & Stewart 1973; Martin 1972; Smith 1972.

[23]Bracken et al. 1972; Francke 1978; Grauer 1972; Greenglass 1976; Hall 1971; Ingham & Simms 1972; Osofsky & Osofsky 1972; Pratt et al. 1984; Trent & Griner 1991.

Various studies have shown that effective contraception is highly related to a woman's ability to regulate sexual activity and the stability of her sexual relationship.[24]

Time Interval for Follow-up

The women in the study were interviewed between six months to one year after their abortion. This decision was made to ensure that these women were able to recuperate completely from the effects of the surgery and resume their normal routine, including sexual activity. Further, recognizing that immediate reactions to abortion such as euphoria or indifference, as reported in previous studies, last for varying lengths of time, it seemed likely that during this interval most women, if not all, would pass through this phase and would begin to experience a cooling-off period, enabling them to have a more sober perspective on their abortion experience. At the same time, the upper limit of one year was chosen on the consideration that these women's recall of the events would not diminish or that repression of painful material would not occur, which was possible if the time interval were protracted. A longer interval would have provided a valuable perspective on the delayed effects of abortion, but it also had the risk of losing women who might not have been located.

It was found that there was no noticeable difference in the recall of the decision making and the abortion experience between the women interviewed in the six-month or one-year follow-up, as was evident from sharpness of the contents and outpouring of emotions. It may be noted that previous studies of women within a period ranging from a few weeks to a few years after their abortion offered no explanation for the choice of the time interval, nor did they comment on the recall of the women interviewed a long time after the abortion. The exception, however, was Zimmerman's study, *Passage through Abortion*, in which women were interviewed six to ten weeks after their abortion. Here, the author was guided by a similar rationale as in the present study. Another author, Arthur Peck (1968), suggested that short-term or immediate psychological

---

[24]Furstenberg 1976; Luker 1975; Pick 1980; Rainwater 1960; Wallston et al. 1976; Greenglass 1981.

reactions to abortion occur within six months of the abortion. Freeman et al. (1981) investigated emotional distress scores (on depression, anxiety, hostility, obsessive/compulsive) of women, mostly unmarried, at three weeks and again one year after their abortions. The authors found that their scores declined significantly by three weeks but increased one year after the abortion, particularly for the first aborters. In view of these findings the interval of six months to one year used in this study should have avoided the fluctuation in the study women's emotional reactions to abortion, at the time of interviews.

OBTAINING THE SAMPLE

A list containing the names of 114 women who met the study criteria was drawn up from the records of three hospitals and one referral and counseling agency. Of these, fourteen women were introduced to me by staff members (either a social worker, a head nurse, or a doctor) on the day of their return appointments for post-abortion checkups in the clinics. The decision to draw the study sample from more than one hospital and the referral agency was based on the consideration that any one hospital could be atypical and thus yield a biased sample. The inclusion of three major hospitals in different locations increased the possibility of securing a sample that reflected the socioeconomic and religious diversity of the metropolitan population. However, the procedures followed in processing a woman's application were similar in all the three hospitals. Further, as stated in chapter 1, Ontario posts the highest abortion rates in Canada after the Yukon and British Columbia, and a large majority of these abortions are performed at these three hospitals. This approach provided an added advantage, namely, that of obtaining a sampling frame that was presumably fairly representative of the kind of women who underwent abortion in Ontario.[25]

---

[25]Lyons et al. (1988) conducted a rigorous examination of sixty-one quantitative research articles on the psychosocial effects of abortion over the past two decades and found only one study (Lazarus 1985) that used a random sample of abortion patients. These patients visited one clinic in Philadelphia from June 1976 to September 1977. Also, see Wilmoth et al. (1992) for a comprehensive critique of the sampling procedures used in the fifteen empirical studies that are frequently cited in the literature. The

Of the 114 women, seventy (61.4 percent) were located and interviewed. Twenty-four women (21.1 percent) could not be traced because they had moved. Incorrect or unknown addresses were responsible for not being able to identify six women. Three women (2.6 percent) were living in faraway towns in Ontario, making it prohibitive both in time and money to travel. These women came to the city because they wanted to keep their abortion a secret in their hometowns or because they could not get an early appointment in the local hospitals. Only eleven women (9.6 percent) refused to participate in the study, either because they feared the interview would stir up painful memories or because their boyfriends forbade them to discuss their abortion. Two women had married since the abortion, and their husbands would not let them discuss their past. Interestingly, all of the fourteen women I was introduced to in the clinics returned for an interview, suggesting that a personal, face-to-face appeal is often effective in eliciting participation of respondents in studies of this nature.[26]

Given the sensitive nature of the subject, the rate of contact with eligible women was very high compared to earlier follow-up studies involving nonvolunteer or noncaptive abortion patients.[27] The moral aspects involved in the abortion issue and the society's disavowing attitudes toward unmarried women having an abortion compounds the difficulties in identifying these women, who, more often than not, would like to keep their abortion a secret. It was, therefore, not surprising that one-fifth of the eligible women used a pseudonym or gave a false address. Other investigators have also

---

authors observed that generally these investigators obtained their sample from a clinic or hospital where abortions were performed and approached all women who came there during a certain time period. The findings from such samples limit their generalization.

[26]Kinsey et al. (1953) demonstrated the effectiveness of the personal approach to respondents in their historic study of sexual behavior of the American people.

[27]See Adler 1975; Athanasiou et al. 1973; Cohen & Roth 1984; Ingham & Simms 1972; Lipper et al. 1973; Major et al. 1985; Martin 1972; Peck & Marcus 1966; Smith 1972; Smith 1973; Zimmerman 1977. These authors reported a rate of identification of unmarried women few weeks to one year following their abortion ranging from as low as 18.3 percent to a high of 60 percent of the eligible respondents. Women who refused participation accounted for 13 percent to 40 percent.

observed that unmarried women undergoing abortions do not wish to risk exposure and are therefore less cooperative in follow-up studies than married women.[28] Also, a high mobility among these women was expected. Being single with fewer attachments and relatively better job opportunities, at least prior to 1988 in the metropolitan city, made frequent moves easier. Although nearly two-fifths of the eligible women were not available to the study, the women interviewed were not different from those not obtained. Comparison of these groups on age, education and occupation characteristics suggests that the women selected for the study were fairly representative of those not interviewed (see Appendix A table 6). Another indication that the sample was not skewed was the variability in responses obtained and diverse backgrounds of the women interviewed.

LOCATING RESPONDENTS

Any research involving the follow-up of human subjects who are not captive faces the task of locating and identifying its sample. But the task of location in this study was more onerous and arduous because of the extra burden of safeguarding the anonymity of these women. The fact that the study was seeking access to personal and intimate information concerning abortion made it even more challenging to overcome the resistance or perhaps denial of identity that was highly likely when approaching these women. Frequently, abortion as a personal experience for an unmarried woman is seldom revealed, especially to a stranger. Another overriding concern was the preservation of the patient-doctor confidence. It is reasonable to say that a physician on the hospital staff conducting this study would be better able to inspire willingness to participate because of his/her power and control over female patients, who would also feel obligated to respond to an invitation to do the hospital a favor. Kadushin et al. (1990) and Richardson et al. (1965) also talk about the interviewer's academic status and his/her institutional affiliation as crucial factors

---

[28]Ewing & Rouse 1973; Niswander & Patterson 1967; Wilmoth et al. 1992. Barnard (1990) reported that 50 percent of the eligible women in her study could not be traced because they had provided a false phone number to the abortion clinic.

in winning the respondents' confidence. The fact that I did not have the affiliation as hospital staff and the matching status of a physician made the task of locating these women and enlisting their participation monumentally hard and at times frustrating. The key principles that helped me search and complete the interview were perseverance, ingenuity, and presence of mind.

The exploratory contact invariably was made via a telephone call. Writing a letter to the eligible women was deemed inappropriate, as it might get into the wrong hands, inadvertently breaching confidentiality. Extreme caution was taken to disclose my identity and the purpose of the call only after confirming the identity of the woman called. To avoid suspicion, the women were invited to verify my identity and credibility of the research project with the clinic staff. This approach proved highly effective in inspiring their confidence and encouraging them to participate, as was later confirmed by several women. One woman remarked, "Your reference to Mrs. [social worker] was a big help in making up my mind. I thought you knew what you were doing." Interestingly, only three women checked my identity.

Each woman was contacted preferably at work, because of the consideration that it would sound more professional than a social call made at home during the evening and would spare the woman embarrassment and perhaps inquiry from an inquisitive member of the household.

Once the woman was located and identified, it was ensured before discussing the research study whether she was free to talk or would prefer a call at another number and another time. Each woman was assured of strict confidentiality of the information provided and of her identity. An offer of cash payment for the interview accompanied the request to participate in the study. Reaction to the request was either wholly negative, a refusal, or positive, an unequivocal willingness. The typical positive response was, "Okay, I'll talk to you. When do you want me to come?" None of the women accepted payment for the interview. Even an attempt to make the payment less ostentatious by describing it as an out-of-pocket expense or transportation money failed to make them accept money as inducement. The reason that propelled most women (81 percent) to participate in the study was the desire to share their experiences, so that other women facing the dilemma of an unwanted pregnancy could be helped. One woman, a 22-year-old student, remarked:

> The only people who know what it's like are the girls who
> have gone through it and nobody can possibly understand
> it, unless these girls have spoken to someone like you
> about their experience.

Another woman requested:

> I do hope that you will convey through this survey and say
> out loud how the women who have an abortion really feel
> about it. Otherwise, I would not have spent this time.

Three women were animated by a desire to promote the cause of
abortion. "I'm glad to have the opportunity to give my opinion, so
that it can encourage freedom of access to abortion for those women
who need it." Two women saw the opportunity of giving vent to
their grievances against the hospital and the way they were treated by
the staff. Curiosity about the study questions inspired a few women
to participate.
Eight women (11.4 percent) sought through the interviews an
expression of their feelings so that they could "get it out in the open."
In most instances, these women had few people to whom they could
confide their intimate feelings unreservedly. One woman said, "I
wanted to talk about my abortion and how I felt which I don't do very
often at home. I have no one to turn to." Another woman, aged 24,
working as a model, had this to say:

> Having an abortion or being pregnant is such a sensitive and
> personal thing that it is upsetting to discuss with people who
> are not sensitive to the feelings. It's such a deeply felt
> emotional thing that you cannot extract yourself out of it.
> Here in the interview I could talk freely and I find it has
> now taken the tension out of me. I wanted to purge myself
> of the abortion that I ever had one.

Being a "Boyfriend," a "Cook" and a "Salesman"

Although it was anticipated that locating these women and
communicating, especially with those living at home, was not going
to be an easy task, a few sensitive situations surfaced unpredictably
during the locating phase. The most characteristic of these occurred

when the person answering the phone was the woman's mother. To spare the woman any possibly embarrassing inquiry, it was considered expedient to hang up whenever it was suspected from the voice that it could be the woman's mother. However, there were occasions when it was not possible to distinguish the mother from her daughter. I was then faced with an inquisitive mother who would insist on a full name and purpose of the call. I would simply give my first name and state that I was her daughter's former schoolmate. If the mother insisted on further details, I would disengage myself by saying that I did not want to ruin the surprise for my "friend," but I would call back. After I had run into a woman's mother frequently, a female staff member was asked to talk to the mother. Posing as the woman's girlfriend, the staff member did not arouse the mother's suspicion and was able to obtain the needed information regarding the woman's whereabouts or her contact number. This strategy succeeded in approaching several of these women, who were later told about the artifice and reasons for such an approach. They appreciated and interpreted these efforts as real proof of concern for keeping their abortion confidential.

A couple of unnerving incidents took place during the home interviews with the women who were living alone or with a girlfriend. The time for the home interview was so arranged as to ensure an uninterrupted period of four hours, but chance had a few surprises. In one instance, the woman's father dropped by unexpectedly. Astounded by his sudden presence at first, the woman soon managed to compose herself and introduced me as her classmate in a cooking class. I was then faced with a barrage of questions from her father: Why did I want to learn cooking? What did I do for a living? Why was I carrying a tape recorder? My unwavering and yet coherent answers seemed to convince the woman's father. After he left, the woman congratulated me for "doing a fine job."

In another case, a woman's roommate came home early from her office. As she entered, the tape recorder, briefcase, and papers piqued her curiosity and she decided to stop before proceeding into her room. The woman introduced me as a salesman for a cosmetics company conducting a survey of favorite cosmetics. Her roommate then started to ask: Why was I selling and what kind of questions did I ask? Why couldn't I interview her? Why did I use a tape recorder? Here I had to summon my knowledge of women's cosmetics.

INTERVIEW SCHEDULE

Description of the women's pregnancy and abortion experience was obtained by face-to-face, in-depth interviews using a semistructured and thoroughly pretested interview schedule. It combined open-ended and fixed alternative questions to permit both a spontaneous response and specific uniform information. The open-ended questions were also intended to allow free and full responses to the questions dealing with feelings, perceptions, motivations, and attitudes. To lead the woman to answer more fully and with greater specificity, the schedule contained nondirective probe questions. The questions were worded in a manner that more nearly approached that of social conversation rather than a question-and-answer process.

In constructing the interview schedule, all available questionnaires on abortion, fertility control, unwed mothers, and contraceptives were examined and the relevant questions were adapted and supplemented where needed. The schedule was pretested using a convenience sample of seven women having undergone abortion. They were asked to provide critical analysis of all aspects of the schedule, including their understanding of the various questions and any omissions. These efforts and the number of appropriate items and subitems totalling 160 were considered reasonable to yield an adequate representative sampling of contents.

To obtain responses to questions involving thoughts, values, or behaviors that may be embarrassing or self-incriminating, the schedule used a component that Richardson et al. (1965) call "informed expectation or a premise" and was successfully employed by Kinsey et al. in their classic study of sexual behavior of American males and females. This technique was intended to assure the women that I was knowledgeable about the subject matter and that any type of behavior or thought was not atypical or abnormal; therefore I would not be surprised or embarrassed by their admission of unsanctioned experiences. An example of "informed expectation or a premise" is this question in the interview schedule: "Women who undergo abortion experience different emotional reactions afterwards. What emotional feelings did you go through soon after your abortion?" Another question reads: "Some women have sex relations but don't do anything about keeping themselves from getting pregnant. They may worry about it, but don't use any birth control methods, or use them irregularly. I'll read a few statements about the reasons that you sometimes hear unmarried women give. Please tell me the ones that describe your situation." Informed expectations or premises, as Kinsey et al. contend, place the burden on the individual who is inclined to deny her experience. There was no indication from the great variation in responses obtained that such a technique generated false admissions of acts or feelings.

Built into the schedule were certain internal checks intended to ascertain the reliability of the information obtained. These included a few extra but roughly equivalent or closely related questions, a technique recommended by several research scientists.[29] Also used was the procedure called "confrontation," that is, a question that presented the women with an apparent inconsistency within a response or between a response and the source of information and asked for its resolution. In addition, several self-report inventories known as attitude scales were used as a projective device. These scales, which assessed the verbalized concept of the women's attitudes towards premarital sex, pregnancy, motherhood, contraception, and abortion, provided a further measure of consistency of responses. Tests of validity have confirmed the usefulness of self-reports to measure attitudes. Nunnally (1970) sums up his confidence in these words, "At the present time, most measures of attitude are based on self-report, and from what evidence there is concerning the validity of different approaches to the measurement of attitudes, it is an easy conclusion that self-reports offers the most valid approach currently available" (p. 421). Of the two widely used self-report measures, Thurston's Equal Appearing Interval Scales and Likert Scales, the interview schedule employed the latter for its proved superiority, ease, and reliability over Thurston's Scales.[30]

Construction of Likert Scales for Abortion Attitudes

To prepare Likert Scales, all the available questionnaires, monographs, and articles dealing with studies of abortion, contraception, and pregnancy were scanned and the relevant items were teased out. Items concerning attitudes toward abortion were drawn from four U.S. national surveys by Rossi (1967), Kanter and

---

[29]Green 1970; Nunnally 1970; Oppenheim 1966; Selltiz et al. 1976.
[30]Green 1970; Nunnally 1970; Selltiz et al. 1976.

Allingham (1968), the National Fertility Survey by Westoff et el. (1969), and the National Opinion Research Center's (NORC) General Social Survey by Davis (1978).[31]   The abortion attitudes scales developed in two studies, one by Gabrielson et al. and the other by Maxwell, were also examined.[32] Westoff et al. (1969) confirmed the interreliability of the various items of these various surveys.

This pool of items was edited and a list of statements containing the most common items was prepared. These statements were expressive of attitudes covering as far as possible all gradations from one end of the scale to the other. To ensure variance with respect to the attitudes, the statements included an equal proportion of items that were moderately positive and moderately negative. Further, care was taken that the items pertained to only a single issue or theme for that particular scale.   To optimize representative sampling of the items it was considered reasonable that the summative scales include an adequate number of items from twenty-six to thirty in one pool (see Appendix C). These items represented the largest number compared to the summative scales used in previous studies, which contained a maximum of seven to twelve items.   It is recognized that even the best sampling of items cannot eliminate the sampling error because of the limited number of items in any test.

In every instance, a woman was presented with a list of these statements and was instructed to select one of the six alternatives from a numerical scale corresponding to her agreement or disagreement with each statement. Usually, Likert Scales employ five scale steps from "strongly disagree" to "strongly agree," but the use of more response categories is believed to improve reliability of individual rating scales as it permits greater amount of discrimination in reporting an individual's stand on the issue. However, six to seven response categories are considered an ideal number.[33] Recognizing that some women may have a truly neutral stand on certain attitudinal issues and therefore would be more comfortable in making ratings of

---

[31]Gillaspie et al. (1988) used the Mokken method of scale analysis, a stochastic extension of Guttman scaling, and concluded that the six items used in the survey across the three periods (1975, 1980, 1985) were unidimensional; they therefore created a single scale to measure the change in abortion attitudes.

[32]Gabrielson et al. 1971; Maxwell 1970.

[33]Garner 1970; Guilford 1954; Nunnally 1970.

their attitude, the six-step Likert Scale contained "neither agree nor disagree" as a neutral or middle step. However, the "neutral" step did not generate a preponderance of a response style, as these women used this category only sparingly.

Construction of Depressive and Guilt Reaction Scale

One of the areas the study investigated was the extent to which these women experienced depressive or guilt reactions following abortion. A measure that can validly assess depressive and guilt feelings related only to the decision about the termination of a pregnancy must deal with two formidable problems. First, it must be able to filter out abortion-related moods from situational and circumstantial moods resulting from such events as the women's reaction to pregnancy, her relationship with her sex partner, parental reactions, fear of surgery, and stress involved in the search for a physician or hospital willing to perform an abortion. The boundaries between depressive and guilt reactions related to abortion and those associated with other events are diffuse and often indistinguishable. Second, the measure must be able to express depressive or guilt reactions in empirical observations of physiological, emotional, and behavioral responses that are synonymous with mood and the feelings disorder experienced by a woman.

In the construction of a *symptom-complex inventory*, the following steps were taken. First, several textbooks of psychiatry and monographs on depression and guilt were studied to identify symptoms that involve affective, cognitive, somatic, and behavioral components attributable to these reactions. A pool of these symptoms was thus created. Second, a final pool of symptoms was constructed from the items about which different writers had reached consensus. Third, since depression or guilt are often ubiquitous occurrences in a given patient, it was imperative to distinguish between the two constructs. But it was noted that some symptoms overlap, making the distinction between guilt and depression less discrete. For example, loss of sleep and appetite, emotional outbursts, distressed feelings, decreased work capacity, various bodily complaints like diarrhea or constipation, headache, weight gain or loss, impaired concentration, decreased sexual desire, and preoccupation with abortion thoughts can be found among both the guilty and the depressive patients. However, it became evident that despite the inevitable overlap a certain symptom cluster was attributed to either the depressive or the guilt state by general consensus of the literature. Fourth, the characteristic signs and symptoms of depressive and guilt reactions were graded in three steps of severity--severe, moderate, and mild reactions. The basis used for designating symptoms in three gradations is similar to the one employed by Beck (1967) in his study on depression (pp. 16-36).

The title indicating the degree of severity of each step was omitted from both the interview schedule and the Cards (see Cards 6 and 7 in Appendix B) that were given to the woman, who read the symptoms herself. It was believed that the terms "severe or moderate depressive and guilt reactions" most often carry unpleasant connotations implying serious mental pathology, which might deter a woman from describing her true feelings. It may be noted that the words, "depressive reactions" were replaced in the interview schedule by milder and nonthreatening terminology such as "blue moods" or "down in the dumps" or "tense feelings," the terms which "normal" people use to designate any lowering of their moods or anxious feelings.

Fifth, all the statements were rewritten in ordinary usage to replace the psychiatric nomenclature. For instance, depression or state of dejection was replaced by "blue moods;" suicidal ideation by "you couldn"t bear to live another day;" self-depreciation by "you felt you were no good and blamed yourself;" fatigue and exhaustion by "worn out;" sense of emptiness by "usual activities seem flat to you;" feelings of distress by "you felt you were going to pieces or going insane." The idea behind these conversions was that the women should be able to relate their feelings to these statements more readily. The corresponding everyday terminology was secured by reading the statements descriptive of depression and guilt to several university coeds and asking them to provide equivalent everyday terminology used and understood by young people.

In each instance, the woman was asked to read the symptom statements in all of the three gradations and underline the ones that best described the symptoms of depressive or guilt reactions she experienced anytime after her abortion. Her response was categorized as either severe, moderate, or mild, depending upon the number of symptoms checked in each cluster. Two important criteria were taken into account while characterizing any of her feelings or moods as depressive or guilt reactions. One, these feelings or moods were not transient sadness or fleeting moods but were complaints of inordinately dejected, hopeless, or tensed-up feelings. Two, these moods and feelings were occasioned by the termination of the pregnancy. In other words, a woman might have experienced these moods at the time because of other unhappy life situations or because of a usual unhappy disposition. The interview focused on the reactions, depressive or guilt, that were felt by the woman as a direct consequence of the abortion surgery and that had no ethical or moral overtones.

In each case an attempt was made to explain the intent of the question to make sure that the women understood it. But anytime during the interview, if it became evident that the symptoms described by the woman were the consequence of other life events or situations such as a frustrated love relationship, or the anxiety of going through the unwieldy process of obtaining an abortion and did not relate to the fact of losing her pregnancy, she was not considered as having negative reactions to the abortion. Excerpts from interviews may help elucidate this point:

One woman reported that she had been extremely depressed since the abortion and checked many of the symptoms reflecting depressive moods. But further examination of the reasons made it apparent that her depression was not related to the fact that she had had her pregnancy terminated. This is what she said:

> I'm extremely depressed and emotionally upset. I am sad and on the verge of tears right now because of having the abortion. I don't feel unhappy for ending a life. I don't condemn myself. I know I can start another life if I want to; I can go sleep with my boyfriend right now and get pregnant again. I'm sad that the whole thing had to have happened and that George[34] had to go through with this.
>
> I still feel depressed and cry a lot not for having an abortion, but having to have one, that has association with needles; I don't like needles, and intravenous injection frightens me. I'm depressed because of the aftermaths of abortion such as occasional spotting, not having sex for six weeks, and not doing my work efficiently, my being incapacitated physically though temporarily and because next

---

[34]The names used here are fictitious to conceal the identities of the women and their partners.

time I have to take tons of precautions. To have an abortion doesn't bother me at all; it's just the idea of what I have to go through because of this.

Another woman reported her guilt reactions in the aftermath of abortion. But it appeared that these responses were unrelated to the abortion and actually emanated from her inability to prevent premarital pregnancy, which to her represented a loss of self-esteem and a great personal failure:

I feel guilty and regret a lot, not because I had to terminate the pregnancy, but because of the embarrassment. I'm embarrassed that I got pregnant and I should have been taking precautions and I wasn't. That makes me look kind of stupid. Pregnancy and abortion are a kind of black marks against me. I would be number one on the gossip list. I didn't really think much about the fetus.

INTERVIEWING

Fifty-eight women (82.8 percent) chose to be interviewed in the clinic setting, either in the staff lounge of a hospital or in a doctor's office. Since most of the women were employed the only time convenient for the interview was in the evening. This time of day also facilitated the availability of office space in all three hospitals. It also permitted privacy and freedom from daytime interruption.

The staff lounge was comfortably furnished and well lit. Although the doctor's office was pleasant and cosy, certain changes were made in the setting before the interview, so as to lend it an informal and homy atmosphere reducing the effect of unpleasant associations. A supply of coffee and cigarettes was available and the women were invited to help themselves. A cup of coffee also proved handy when it was felt the woman was fatigued and a brief recess would help in relaxation or when she became emotionally upset and a diversion was appropriate to allow her to regain her composure.

Wearing a lab coat with a name tag when greeting the woman proved effective in instantaneously establishing professional credibility, the authenticity of the study, and my identification with the hospital. A woman remarked after the interview, "I wasn't sure if you were an imposter until I saw you in the hospital coat. This convinced me that you were truly connected with the hospital." Another woman said, "After you called me, I was very mad at the hospital that anybody could pull a patient's records there. I thought I'll meet this man anyway, but will not give him an interview. But when I saw you in the coat with the hospital name printed on it, I was convinced that you were not anybody."

In introducing the study, it was stressed there were no right or wrong answers to the questions asked. Also, the woman was assured of my experience with interviewing people, both males and females, on sensitive subjects such as contraception and sexual behavior. The interviewer's knowledge of and experience with the subject area are believed to be important components in establishing rapport and enhancing the respondent's confidence in the interviewer's ability to accept without surprise or moral judgment any of the thoughts or sexual behavior in which the respondant might have been involved.[35] Kadushin (1990) views the interviewer's knowledge of the subject matter as an effective tool in increasing the degree of veridicality in the information content. "If she [the respondent] perceives the interviewer as knowledgeable and realizes that any fanciful, deceptive responses are likely to receive scepticism, the interviewee is more likely to be honest and straightforward with the interviewer" (p. 89). To further ensure that the woman was able to discuss her experience with ease, I maintained a calm, comfortable, and forthright posture toward the issues of sex and contraception. This attitude was conveyed, for example, through a deliberate use of words such as "sexual intercourse," "orgasm," and "rubber," to emphasize that sexual behavior is a natural human activity that need not be viewed as dishonorable.

The experience with sex, pregnancy, and abortion involves feelings that can evoke reactions of fear, guilt, anxiety, irritation, hurt, and frustration. If a woman became emotionally upset, while reconstructing the past events, I couldn't help being empathetic and supportive. This approach helped the woman unmask her true feelings and attitudes and was also therapeutic for her. When asked at the conclusion of the interview, "What do you think of the interview and of the questions asked?" several women indicated that a full and frank confession on their part served their own interest as

---

[35]Gorden 1980; Kinsey et al. 1953; Richardson et al. 1965.

well.   For many women (62.8 percent) the research interview provided a greater insight into their own thinking.   Some of the comments were: "It gave me an opportunity to think more deeply how I really felt about it; it really straightened out my mind." "When you kept asking me why I didn't use birth control methods, it made me stop and think exactly my reasons for doing what I was doing."

Some women (27.1 percent) felt the value of the interview was in the catharsis of talking about their problems and relieving their anxiety. They commented, "The interview helped me see what I was feeling and thinking just by talking to you, rather than bottling it up all inside." "I feel different now. I'm glad I got it out in the open. I had never discussed so clearly about my feelings and attitudes." "I never thought about my abortion until you phoned me. I think it helped me reduce my tension and worry."   A few women (10 percent) viewed the interview as an expression of the hospital's interest in them and their problems.

The women's reactions to the type of questions asked were highly positive. A few responses are sampled below:

The questions were personal, but not embarrassing.
*   *   *
I didn't feel embarrassed in discussing anything with a person who knows the subject.
*   *   *
A few questions were a little embarrassing and personal, but I didn't mind answering them for a study of this kind.
*   *   *
I have trust in you and feel I could talk freely to you about my experiences; it didn't bother me.

Gender's Effect

Assertations are made that the gender of the interviewer is significant in determining how a female subject will cooperate in sharing her information freely and openly, especially when the subject area involves intimate matters. The implication is that a female respondent would be more willing to unmask her feelings to a female interviewer. To ascertain whether the women were inhibited by my gender, each woman was asked at the termination of the interview whether she would have felt freer and more frank in discussion if she had been interviewed by a woman. There was no a hint of suggestion from their statements that my gender had created any emotional screen or ambivalence among the women. Interestingly, most women seemed to prefer male to female as their interviewer because, in their view, women become unprofessional in their inquisitorial undertakings. Typical of their comments were the following

> I feel far more at ease with men than women, because women are too closely attuned to each other. If you were a woman, you probably would be too sympathetic toward me instead of maintaining a professional and unbiased type of relationship. I'm sure you have your own particular views on abortion. But they didn't come out at all. I think a woman probably couldn't have kept them inside.
>
> *   *   *
>
> I can talk more freely to a man than to a woman, because I figure if I tell something to a man he is just going to take it for what it is and ask me questions. A woman sees right through another woman. I like talking to men better; they seem to be more logical.
>
> *   *   *
>
> I always find it easy and comfortable to talk to a man, because I find the women to be catty and not as friendly.

Some women showed no preference for a certain gender, because for them the most significant condition that catalyzed their cooperation and willingness to reveal intimate experiences was the nonthreatening, emotionally secure, and accepting climate of the interview. Some of the comments were: "I don't think I was shy or inhibited. It depends on the interviewer. You put me at ease and I didn't feel nervous at all." "The fact that you were male didn't make any difference to me. I had been as open to you as I would be with anybody. I was rather more open with you than I'm with my mother, because you accepted me the way I am." Only two women expressed preference for a female interviewer with whom they would have been freer and more comfortable in discussing sex.

A few studies on the effect of gender differences on the interview confirm the importance of a positive relationship, that is, a relaxed, comfortable, trustful, accepting, and emotionally empathetic one, between interviewer and interviewee, which encourages the interviewee to share painful and sensitive material.

Mattson (1970) concluded that a good rapport renders the sex and cultural differences non-operative. Malloy (1981) used the Tennessee Self Concept Scale on 48 female clients who were randomly assigned to male and female therapists. The author found that the sex of the therapist did not have a significant effect on the therapeutic outcome. Kadushin (1990), after a comprehensive review of research on cross-gender pairings of interviewer and interviewee, came to a similar conclusion: "It is difficult to delineate what effect gender contributes to the interaction . . . Despite difficulties, however, a good relationship can, and does, transcend sex differences" (pp. 333-34).

One might question the veracity of the statements of these women, as efforts to placate me.   However, this suspicion is dismissed by the evidence in the form of the extraordinarily rich sexual content obtained, which could only come from women who were relaxed and were willing to speak freely and at length about intimate matters.

RECORDING THE INTERVIEWS

To safeguard against misrepresentation, incomplete reporting, and distortion of the data, all the interviews were unobtrusively recorded verbatim by a portable tape recorder. The recorder was kept out of sight to avoid distraction, and only a small microphone was placed on the center table. The women were told that if during the interview they felt that the recorder was causing them embarrassment or inhibiting their responses, the recorder would be turned off.   Only one women made such a request.   Since the recording missed feeling tones, emotions, and moods, special notes of these emotional changes were taken as well as any manifestations of discomfort or hesitation were recorded. In addition to the accurate recording of the responses, the interview tapes were of great value in monitoring data collection, contingency cleaning, and assessing the reliability of the information received and coded. The interviews averaged about three hours in length and yielded a transcript of about 3,000 handwritten pages. The richness of the information obtained and its level of intimacy show that the tape recording had little or very transient effect on the women's responses. Most indicated either initial awareness of the recorder or did not notice it at all. That many women were able to display their intense emotions with sometimes painful frankness and that most of them wept during the recall of their experiences provides further evidence that the tape recorder did not interfere with spontaneity and forthrightness of their responses. The following excerpts from the interviews will capture the flavor of those outpourings, tales of personal dilemmas in sexual encounters, a mixture of sadness, ecstasy, and sometimes humor:

> I have a boyfriend, Ian, for four years, but we never had any sort of sexual intercourse. We had slept together, but gone only to the point of petting, etc., but never had intercourse, because he had some kind of problem, kind of impotency. If he didn't have sex, he wasn't missing anything. I did not tell him I wanted to have sex with him, but I felt frustrated. Last year I finally told him, "you better tell me or else I can't continue this relationship." I asked him if there was something wrong with him that I didn't know? He finally broke down and told me he was so afraid and anxiety ridden to have sex, because he was sure to be a failure.
>
> Having not experienced sex, I was kind of naive, a kind of utopia. I said to myself I'll go out with other guys just to see if I can have a relationship [sex] with somebody else.
>
> My boyfriend went away to India and I went out with another boy, Jim, only for two months before I became pregnant. The reason I went out with Jim was more or less for sex experience. You hear girls talking about it. I thought well, let's get together and find out what it is happening that way and learn something and that really was the main reason. But it was nothing that I anticipated at all. The first time I had intercourse with him was awful and terrible. I was trembling, it was distasteful. But after that I liked it.
>
> But I found out my relationship with him was not like it was with Ian. All he wanted to do with me was to have a bed partner. I'm not a bed partner. He liked to do it a lot. I used to get kind of fed up with it. He was oversexed. And I felt sooner or later it will hit, and it did. [Did he use anything?] He never used anything. One time I told him to pull out before he wanted to ejaculate. He

did that once. He was an animal as far as I'm concerned.
He really was. When he wanted it [sex] he wanted it, no
question about it.

*   *   *

[Did you use any preventative method?] We used a condom
every time I made love with Joe. [How did you get
pregnant?] I'm sure the condom broke during intercourse.
We were staying down in Nova Scotia at the time and were
not married. We were staying with some friends of ours and
their parents. We had not slept together for about two
weeks.

Pardon my frankness, but this was the way it was.
Our friend's parents were very religious, and it was like that
we couldn't even talk freely with each other. We had
separate rooms. His room was there and mine was the other
corner, and their parents were in the middle. I went into his
room one night about 10:30 and the father of our friends
said, "It is about time you went to your bed now." We felt
we had been really far apart and when we got together, boy,
it was wild, you know how when you haven't been together
with somebody for a long time and you're used to making
love to them.   Then you might go at it a little more
vigorously and that is why the rubber broke. I checked it
out by running some water in it. I knew for sure I that I
was pregnant.

CONFIRMING RESPONSE VALIDITY

Obtaining depth interview content alone would not provide
assurance that the women confided as honestly as possible, and this
assurance is even harder to guarantee when the interview content
involves attitudinal and affective questions. Ideally, one of the best
measures by which the credibility of the women's responses can be
determined is by comparing their accounts with a relevant source or
an independent external evidence of what "actually happened."
However, the difficulty with these measures is that the "relevant
evidence" itself can be unreliable and independent external evidence
is rarely available. A "true" answer simply does not exist. In fact,
it is hardly possible to obtain a "true" answer for the responses

pertaining to feelings and attitudes.   In view of these practical limitations such measures as internal and cross-checks on consistency, though imprecise, were used to gauge the credibility of the women's responses.

A cross-check was made with the medical records and questionnaires of the hospitals and the counseling agency for independent information that each woman provided at the time of her first visit.   Inconsistency between the responses obtained in the interview and the counseling agency records existed in only five cases. Two Catholic women informed that they falsely reported their religion to the hospital, fearing that abortion might be denied to them. One woman faked knowledge and the use of birth control methods to the social worker of the counseling agency in order to spare her any embarrassment.   Another woman related in detail how, in the interview with the hospital psychologist, she feigned her reactions to pregnancy and threatened to commit suicide if she was denied abortion:

> The lady psychologist asked me how about delivering the baby and giving it up [for adoption]. I knew right then she was trying to stop me from having an abortion. Until this point, I was quite determined that I didn't want this baby. I knew she was trying as hard as she could even to get me to call it a "baby." I was calling it "it," "the thing," "the little thing that grows," "the cancerous growth inside me." I kept up that attitude. But, in reality, I wanted to say, "I don't think I can face giving up my baby after nine months." I thought if I said that she was going to know that I had this stitch feeling toward my baby. I replied, as though I was indifferent, "I do not intend to have it. You get rid of it here, or I'll get rid of it some other way." Then she right away sent me to the doctor who gave me an appointment for an abortion before she even examined me.

Another woman confided that she got tips from her friend who had had an abortion on how to appear convincing and make her case compelling. Her friend had advised her to emphasize to the doctor that "I was on drugs and I don't want my kid deformed."

Such contradictions led me to conclude that I, rather than the hospital or the counseling agency, had been furnished reliable information about situations where accepted standards of behavior had been compromised. The remarkable fact about this conclusion was not so much that the correct information was withheld from the hospital or the agency but rather that these women were ready to supply it voluntarily to me.

Other indicators, intangible as they may be, were found useful in controlling the accuracy of the interview material. First, it is believed that the candor, depth, relevance, and richness of information obtained and the degree of the respondent's cooperation achieved are good measure of validity of attitudinal content.[36] As noted earlier, a large majority (81 percent) of the women participated in the study because of altruistic reasons, and none of them accepted payment as a compensation for their interviews or felt coerced into participation. Each woman answered all the questions freely, with sometimes painful frankness, and none of them used the option to forego her answer to any question.

Second, it was recognized that the nature of the subject matter was such as could cause uneasiness and defensiveness. Explicit efforts, therefore, were made to put the women at ease throughout the interview. By presenting them with a psychologically secure, emotionally supportive, nonjudgmental, and friendly atmosphere, it was possible to obtain full and frank disclosure of their personal and intimate experiences, as is evident from the abundant quotations. The general emotional climate and the interpersonal interaction of the interview experienced by these women were exemplified in their most frequent statements that expressed initial anxiety followed by gradually relaxed and comfortable feelings:

> At the beginning, I felt kind of scared. But then you gained my trust and it didn't bother me any more.
>
> *   *   *
>
> When I started the interview, I could feel my nerves started to go. Then I felt relaxed and it seemed that I had known you for ages.
>
> *   *   *
>
> First, I didn't know what kind of person you might be; I was nervous. But then I was very relaxed and honest and open.

---

[36]Cormier & Cormier 1985; Kadushin 1990; Gordon 1980.

Several women acknowledged that my attitude reflected sensitivity and nonjudgmental ascription of their behavior, as typified by this woman in her comment: "You didn't make me feel like sitting on a witness stand and trying me for my guilt."

Other investigators, notably Kinsey and his associates, have demonstrated in their interview studies that a secure atmosphere and good relationship contribute significantly toward ensuring credibility of the information obtained in sensitive areas of human functioning.[37] Kadushin (1990), citing abundant literature in counseling, confirms the validity of this claim: "It is easier to be an open person in such a benign emotional climate of mutuality . . . A positive relationship acts as an anodyne, an anaesthetic, to sharing of painful material on the part of the client; it heightens the salience and credibility of communication . . ." (p. 49). Deschin (1963) interviewed teenagers with venereal diseases and concluded that "given the emotional climate and interviewer-interviewee relationship most human beings--adults or adolescents--are likely to share significant, intimate personal data" (p. 16).

It is recognized that, despite the best efforts at controlling the source of bias, one cannot be certain that interviewing yielded completely accurate, valid, and "pure" data. There are factors that mitigate against securing valid content and that are beyond the control of the investigators. These include the unpredictability of actual behavior from reported attitudes, the motivations and feelings that are hidden from the conscious mind, memory loss, and the repression of painful and socially censored contents. The reality of these intractable problems proves the fallibility of social research measurements, which, in the words of Kahn and Cannell (1957), is "encountered in some degree no matter how refined the instrument or how precise the technician" (p. 169). In the final analysis, the best defense, permeable as it might be, that I as an experienced investigator can offer is the conviction that I "know" the women shared it all, as far as possible, "in the same way," Kinsey et al. put it, "a veteran horse trader knows when to close a bargain" (1953: 43). The problems of validity in social research are essentially attributable to the nature of human behavior, which is complex, variable, and at times inscrutable. Its precise assessment is beyond the tools of science currently available. In view of the inherent

---

[37]Kinsey et al. 1953; Pope and Scott 1967.

limitations of our technology one can at best simply describe one's work by the statement that "I believe that it is true" rather than "I have proved it scientifically.

SUMMARY

The seventy women who formed the sample for the study were selected from the records of three major hospitals and a referral agency in a large metropolitan city in Ontario. The women were between 18 and 25 years old, white, and unmarried, and were pregnant for the first time; their pregnancy was terminated in the first semester through the D & E procedure. The women obtained a therapeutic abortion on mental health grounds six months to one year prior to the interviews. The selection of the women with homogeneous characteristics was designed to obtain a common baseline prior to their abortion to eliminate demographic factors that could affect their response patterns. Research evidence shows that the factors such as age, race, marital status, prior experience with pregnancy and abortion, the type of surgical procedure, and grounds for termination can differentially influence women's experience with abortion. The selection of the sample from different location sources was intended to avoid any sampling bias and to achieve a fair representation of the women who undergo abortion in Ontario. The seventy women who were located and interviewed represented more than three-fifths of the eligible women. Less than 10 percent of them refused to participate in the study. The women interviewed were not different from those not obtained on age, education, occupation, and religious characteristics. Given the sensitive nature of the subject and the mobility of single women, the rate of location of the eligible women was very high compared to earlier follow-up studies. The reason that propelled most women to participate in the study was a desire to share their experiences for the benefit of other women facing a similar dilemma of unwanted pregnancy.

The information was collected through face-to-face depth interviews utilizing a semistructured and comprehensive interview schedule. Built in the schedule were components for ascertaining reliability of the information received and for eliciting responses to questions involving personal and intimate thoughts and experiences. In addition, the schedule included several self-report inventories, or attitudinal scales and a symptom-complex inventory to assess depressive or guilt reactions. The interviews focused on the women's psychological reactions felt as a consequence of the abortion surgery and not due to other life stresses.

Eighty-three percent of the interviews were conducted at the hospital or in a doctor's office and the rest in the women's homes. Each interview, averaging about three hours in length, was tape recorded. The richness of the information obtained, its level of intimacy, and the degree of their cooperation provided a measure of these women's truthfulness in sharing their experiences. Each woman answered all the questions freely, with sometimes painful frankness, and none used the option to forego her answer to any question. In addition, the findings of this study compare well with those of previous investigators. However, despite the best efforts at controlling the source of bias, one cannot be certain that the interviews yielded completely "pure" data because of the inherent fallibility of social research measurements.

4

The Women and Their Sexual and Contraceptive Dossiers

It's obvious, if you were going to sleep with someone and you weren't going to take precautions one thing is clear: either you got pregnant or you didn't.

21-year-old secretary

THE WOMEN

The seventy women were between the ages of 18 and 25, with an average age of 21.2. The women were concentrated in the younger age category, 18-21 (cutting point for the purposes of the study), comprising 57 percent of the sample. Nearly one-half were Protestants, less than one-third were Catholics, and 14.3 percent reported no affiliation. Jewish women represented 1.4 percent (See table 4.1).

The study women were classified according to their degree of religious commitment, which was measured by frequency of church attendance, degree of religious beliefs, and participation in church-related activities.[1] They seemed to be divided almost evenly between religiously devout and those not devout or religiously inactive. Fifty-four percent claimed to be either very religious or moderately religious, and 46 percent reported not being religious at all. The fact that many of these women were religious belies the impression that the women who seek abortions are not committed to religious norms.

---

[1] Frequently only one measure, church attendance, is used as a measure of religious commitment. (See, for example, Kinsey et al. 1953; Reiss 1967; Westoff et al. 1969.)

Table 4.1
Selected Demographic Characteristics of Seventy Women

Characteristics	Percentage
Age	
18-19	27.1
20-21	30.0
22-23	22.9
24-25	20.0
Religion	
Protestant	52.8
Roman Catholic	30.0
Jewish	1.4
Other	1.5
None	14.3
Religious commitment	
Very religious	13.0
Moderately religious	41.0
Not religious	46.0
Educational status	
Some high school	35.7
High school graduate	30.0
Some college	30.0
College graduate	4.3
Occupation	
Professional and technical	13.0
Secretarial and related work	45.0
Semi and unskilled work	16.0
Housewives	-
Students	16.0
Unemployed	10.0
Not stated	-
Father's occupation	
Professional, technical and related work	21.4
Administrative and managerial work	28.6
Clerical, sales and related work	20.0
Craftsmen and foremen	10.0
Unskilled or manual workers	20.0

Given their youthfulness, the women were not highly educated. Nearly two-thirds had not gone beyond high school. Only one-third had attended university or completed an undergraduate degree. Consistent with their low level of schooling, nearly one-half of all the women were employed as secretaries or clerical workers. Fewer than one-eighth held high-status occupations such as professional or semiprofessional. A little over one-sixth were attending a trade school or a college, while one-tenth were unemployed.

The occupation of the women's fathers was used as a measure of their general economic and social status. One-half of the fathers held high-status jobs--professional, technical, administrative, or managerial. Less than one-third of the fathers were currently or once employed as clerks, salesmen, or foremen and only one-fifth held low-status jobs such as unskilled or manual workers. Thus, it would appear that many of theses women belonged to middle-class families. Economically, too, the women's parents were placed in middle to high income brackets, with the median income being higher than that for Ontario.

The Sexual Dossiers

Sexual relations are more likely to be frequent if a woman is living independently where parental surveillance and policing are absent. Because in this context the fear of being noticed and facing embarrassment and occasional parental admonitions to "be careful" or "not get into any trouble" is absent, the pressure to conform to parental sex norms is greatly reduced. Although, parents often ignore signs of a daughter's sexual activity, independent living has an added advantage over living at home. The freedom of space makes it easier for the young woman to assert her freedom of choice by expressing her sexuality.

Since three-fourths of the women were employed and therefore economically independent, it was not surprising that a majority, 60 percent, were living either alone or with friends of their own sex or the opposite sex at conception. One-fourth were living with both parents, and less than 10 percent with one parent.

The process of initiation of pregnancy begins with sexual activity. These women were highly sexually active prior to becoming pregnant, as shown in table 4.2. Almost two-thirds have had sex

Table 4.2
Frequency of Intercourse among Seventy Women prior to Pregnancy

Frequency	N	Percentage
Almost every day	9	12.8
More than twice a week	14	20.0
Twice a week	13	18.6
Once a week	9	12.8
Once in two weeks	4	5.7
Less than twice a month	7	10.0
A couple of times (or once in a while)	4	5.7
Never since first time	10	14.3

with the man involved in the pregnancy at least once a week, with one-half of them having intercourse every day to twice a week. Low sexual activity, defined as once in two weeks to less than twice a month, was the characteristic of only one-sixth of all the women. Another one-fifth either engaged in sporadic sexual relations or experienced the only sex act with this man that resulted in pregnancy. It should be pointed out that the woman may have had intercourse with other men since her sexual debut, but these encounters are outside the concern of this study.   Not only were these women sexually active, they also initiated their sexual experience at an early age.   One-half (51.7 percent) of them lost their virginity by age 19.[2]

---

[2]These findings closely parallel those reported in the national surveys of sexual activity among teenage women by Zelnik and Kantner (1980) and Hofferth et al. (1987). A more recent study of U.S. high school students found that 48 percent of females have had sexual intercourse by the time they reach college age (Morbidity and Mortality Weekly Report 1992), which is approximately the same proportion of teenage women who reported having sexual experience in the surveys referred to above. Also, see Pratt

Evaluating Premarital Sexuality

The women reflect the emerging standards regarding sexual behavior that are less restrictive. They seem to reject the "new morality" of the 1960s and 1970s, "permissiveness with affection," in favor of the attitude that morals are a private affair and nothing is wrong as long as nobody "gets hurt." Fully three-fourths (75.7 percent) of them professed their disposition to engage in premarital sex "as long as the two people want it," as a 22-year-old waitress put it. For them, "having a good time" should be the primary criterion for acceptable sexual relations, as a 19-year-old college student said:

> There is no harm if a woman goes to bed with a guy (with proper precaution). It is just to enjoy sex and have a good time. She does not have to love the guy.

Implicit in the notion of "private morality" is the belief that sex before marriage is an adventure that should be not only acceptable but even desirable to ensure compatibility and optimal sexual pleasure. A 25-year-old sales supervisor had gone out with different men so that she could find out if the man she would marry compared well with his fellow men. She gave this reason:

> If you marry a virgin or if this is the only man you have had sex with, you will have nothing to compare with nor would you know any difference. You would just blunder along and lie there wondering if another man could give you better sex enjoyment. You might get fed up with him and look for somebody else.

---

and Hendershot (1984). In general, the various national surveys (e.g., National Surveys of Young Women--1971, 1976, and 1979; National Survey of Family Growth--1982 and 1988; Metropolitan Areas Surveys, 1971-1979) seem to indicate that while the proportion of teenage and young women having sexual intercourse continued to increase during the 1970s and 1980s, sexual activity of unmarried young adult women leveled off in the late 1980s at around 60 to 70 percent (Hofferth et al. 1987; MacDonald et al. 1990; Reinisch et al. 1992). These surveys also indicate that women are becoming sexually active at younger ages. That is, by age 15, approximately one-quarter of them have had sex and by age 19, four out of five females have had sexual intercourse (Miller and Moore 1990).

Only one-fifth of the women expressed their commitment to the standards that make sexual relations acceptable in the presence of affection. Two women supported adherence to traditional chastity norms, approving sexual relations only in marriage. They felt extremely guilty at having violated this norm, as this bank teller related:

> I always said to myself that I won't have sex before marriage, and I used to go to church more often. Since I started sleeping with Bob, my frequency of going to church went down, because I was committing a sin. I would never think of sin when I was having sex, but after the act I would feel terrible. So I thought there was no use of going to church and going to confession again and again because I was going to have sex again. I don't feel like having sex since my abortion because I strongly feel that sex is and should be for marriage.

The parents of these women largely manifest attitudes that evince a retreat from any pretence that "it is not happening" and an acknowledgement that their daughters were sexually active. Several women indicated their mothers were aware of their premarital sexual activity, accepting it as an inevitable consequence of the permissive climate in the neighborhood.[3] One 22-year-old woman shared the bedroom of her boyfriend at a wedding party while her parents were upstairs. The only warning came from her mother was, "be careful you don't get pregnant." She elaborates on her parent's attitudes towards sex:

---

[3] In a longitudinal study involving a probabilty sample of 916 parents and their children, Thorton and Camburn (1987) found that the attitudes and behaviors of adolescents are significantly influenced by maternal attitudes. Other studies have also shown that young women coming from families where very few rules and minimum parental discipline were applied are likely to be more permissive and at risk of pregnancy (Miller et al. 1986; Hogan & Kitawaga 1985). However, strong discipline and a high degree of parental control may be effective for the short term, but in the long run these strategies have potential for producing rebellious adolescents (Peterson et al. 1985).

> Parents accept the fact that this sort of thing is going on and there is nothing they can do to stop it. It is the age of the automobile and everybody is affluent, so there are plenty of opportunities.

Another woman aged 24, a teacher, describes her mother's attitude approving of her sister's premarital sexual activity:

> Some nights my younger sister, 23, does not come home and my mother will say, "I bet she's sleeping around." My mother knows what's going on and she does not get real mad at her.

These women's sexual attitudes are the manifestation of an emerging morality which Trippett (1969) describes as the "fun culture." Herbert Stroup, another American sociologist, considers the new morality an expression of the private ethic implying that the individual is the ultimate and autonomous measure of the moral life. These norms should not surprise Jetse Sprey, an American sociologist, who predicted more than two decades ago that "the societal game of sex" will increasingly generate its own set of rules (1969: 435).

Dating and Sexual Relations

The sexual activity of these women generally occurred in a fairly steady relationship. Three-fifths of them had had sexual relations with a man they had known for at least a year, with almost three-tenths having known each other for more than two years. One-quarter had gone together for less than six months before they became pregnant. Only three women became pregnant as a result of a "one-night stand." As a further measure of pair commitment, each woman was asked whether she had been seeing the man involved in the pregnancy no more than now and again or whether they had been going together regularly, fairly regularly, or never since the first time. Almost nine out of ten (87.1 percent) women had been seeing the man regularly or fairly regularly. A little over ten percent (12.9 percent) experienced a casual relationship. The majority of the women (87.2 percent) had been involved sexually before. The man involved in the pregnancy was typically two to three years older.

Thirteen of the men were either currently married or previously married. Although these women did not consider emotional closeness as an essential prerequisite to sexual interaction, the presence of love or the feeling of affection was characteristic of sexual interaction for more than two-thirds (68.6 percent) of the women. This presents an apparent value-behavior discrepancy. It shows that even those who believed in "free love" did not have the courage to embrace the lifestyle so easily. This concern aside, these findings are consistent with previous investigations that confirm that casual sex is not the dominant pattern among young Canadians.[4]

GETTING INTIMATE

Men and women participate in interpersonal sex for a variety of motives and purposes: procreation, release of physical tension, pleasure, passion, affection, popularity and acceptance, emotional security, self-esteem, marriage, career enhancement, and currying favors. Sex is also used to attain power and prove virility, especially by men.[5] The women in the study and their male companions were no exceptions.

"Nice girls do"

A few women had pledged allegiance to traditional standards of chastity because they were enjoined by their parents that "nice girls don't do it before marriage and stay out of trouble." But that was before they moved to the city, where they were overwhelmed by the new morality and discovered that "nice girls do." They felt as though they had been lied to and in a strange way sought revenge against their parents' injunction by refusing to refrain from sexual intimacy. To them sex was not necessarily an enjoyable experience, but they

---

[4]See, for instance, Barrett 1980; Bibby & Posterski 1986; Meikle et al. 1985; Herold 1984.

[5]Katchadourian 1989.

were glad to be liberated from virginity. One unemployed 18-year-old, a practicing Roman Catholic, had been delaying sex for six months. She finally decided to unlock the mystery of sensual ecstasy:

> I was very naive and did not really know about sex when I came to this city. My friends talked about sex and I decided to be modern and do it what the other girls were doing, and, believe me, lots of girls were doing it. But I still kept thinking at the back of my mind that it was wrong, because of what I was taught in school and by my parents' morals. I wanted to have sex because I was at a stage where I wanted to try anything once or twice. I think I was rebelling against my parents and against older people. I didn't even know the guy I made love to, but I said to him, "I'll have an experience tonight," something like that. And I did. I did not enjoy intercourse; it was awful and I did not have orgasm. That was the first guy I had sex with.

A 23-year-old woman, working as a shorthand typist, had been going with her boyfriend for six years but had resisted his sexual advances because she believed in "virginity and white gown stuff." Her views on traditional moral standards underwent a radical transformation following a trip to Europe. The liberalism of Europe and its permissive sexual standards made her realize the futility of her moral dilemma:

> I heard guys and girls talk about sex and say that a lot of girls were not virgins any more. I was afraid of men because the only thing they were interested in was sex. I enclosed myself and was scared to go on dates. I liked talking and meeting guys, but they had different ideas about me. However, that did not bother me, and I stuck to my belief in virginity. I figured this was my body and I wanted to do the way I liked and if anybody didn't like the way I was, hell with them. Then I went to Europe for about five months, and saw how easily the girls got laid. At first, it bothered me, but then I started to wonder, "How do you really know that you are compatible with a person? Are you missing something?" Having seeing things in Europe, my

ideas started to change and I came to a point of choosing between virginity or intercourse. So I decided to have sex experience and wanted to see if I could satisfy a man.

"Just a taste"

Some women had every intention of being virgin on their wedding night, but were driven to sexual intimacy by the desire to have "just a taste" of sexual experience or by plain curiosity. They did not expect that a one-time compromise would become sexual vagrancy, a way of life. They went through the moral conflict between sex as sin and sex as an opportunity for the ultimate expression of maturity and self-fulfilment and resolved the dilemma with a vow to do it only once for experience. However, once they cast off the traditional moral restraint and sexual timidity, they could no longer utter the final "no" to their aroused dates, as one 19-year-old bank teller said:

> I was raised with values that sex is only for marriage. But I thought I will have sex only one time because I cared about this guy. After I had sex I couldn't stop him. I realized that once you have intercourse with a guy, he is pretty sure that you'll have sex again with him, there was no way I could go back with the same guy and not have sex. He'll talk you into it.

Curiosity about sensuous joy enticed a 20-year-old chaste woman into premarital sex with her family's boarder. As several girls in her class had gotten rid of their virginity and talked about their sexual adventures, she wanted to see what it was like. However, her first experience shattered her delusion about the wonders of sex:

> I'm a very frigid, cold person as far as sex goes. This man used to live at our house as a boarder. He was a good looking guy. Every girl talked about sex, but I thought I was a good girl and would never do a thing like that. One day I said to myself that sex was supposed to be a part of life, a kind of utopia. So I decided to go out with this guy and to see what happened. I was naive about sex. My mother never told me anything about it. I used to wonder

"I'm human like her, why does she not tell me about sex and birth control." I had sex with this guy, but it was nothing what I had anticipated. It was awful and terrible. I was trembling. Every time he saw me he wanted to have sex. I hated it, but I still did it--about five or six times.

Drinking often preceded sexual debuts. Liquor lowered the women's inhibitions, released moral restraints, and made it easier to succumb to curiosity for "just this once, and not again until marriage." The drunken haze coupled with sexual desire heightened the vulnerability of young women. An 18-year-old receptionist describes her first sex act as follows:

I had always told myself that I would never have intercourse before marriage and I wasn't on the pill. On a Saturday night my girlfriend's parents had gone away for the weekend and my girlfriend and her boyfriend and my boyfriend and I went over to her house. We started to drink. I got drunk and my boyfriend did too and then everything just led from there. When I woke up the next morning I felt very bad and ashamed of myself about it. My girlfriend always teased me that "you can say no, but you can not plan it. It's something that just happens." It's true. I knew what was going on. I wanted it and so did he and so it just happened. Before, I always found myself stopping it, although he felt frustrated. That night I just didn't stop.

A 19-year-old nursing student had a similar story. She held on to her chastity for two years despite her boyfriend's persistence. It was "just once" that her defenses were too weak to push the stop button:

I'm the only girl of my parents and the big, white gown wedding is very important to them. I have been dating this guy for two years. Lots of times we had taken showers together and had slept together, but never had sex. I knew sex had been on his mind, but he consented to my wishes. A couple of times we tried to have sex, because I had birth control pills and I thought I'd be alright. But each time I had a terrible mental block and just went frigid. I just couldn't do it. I knew I was hurting what you call the male ego. I did not want to put George down anymore. I knew if he kept trying I'd just hurt his feelings. So I told him, "Don't even bother trying, let's wait for a while."

Other occasions we had drinks together, but I didn't want sex and he didn't bother. If he did insist, I would say no. But this time, I was too drunk to push him away. He kept talking to me and I kept answering. I guess if I had stopped answering he would have stopped. He was saying, "Do you like this?" and I said, "Yes." He was very gentle and I didn't feel he was forcing on me. I was half aware of what was going on, but I don't know why I didn't stop him.

"I was scared of being alone."

Although endowed with weak libido, a number of women engaged in sexual intimacy because they could not bear the burden of loneliness. Being emotionally starved, they were vulnerable to sexual exploitation. They allowed themselves to be "used" in the hope that they would be loved and admired. Sex was not the goal in itself, but a vehicle for obtaining affection and an aid in the struggle against loneliness and emptiness.[6] Some women went through the motions of sexual intercourse in anticipation of being held and cuddled. They wanted to believe that they were in love with the man. In point of fact, they resented him for his insensitivity toward their feelings and needs. These women were scared that the man might desert them. Fearing a threat to their security, they continued their compliance to the man's demands, which only served to reinforce sexual exploitation. One twenty-year-old bilingual secretary, from a small town in Quebec, discussed her reasons for sexual involvement with the man she had been dating for two years:

> I used to feel very lonely and unhappy especially after my father's death. I met this guy and I believed I loved him and he loved me. But inside I knew all he wanted was sex. As long as I gave him that, he could give me anything I wanted.

---

[6]A few studies have found that adolescents who do not experience emotional connectedness with their families are likely to feel socially and emotionally isolated. These adolescents are prone to premature sexual activity as a way of compensation for their emotional deprivation. See Barnett et al. 1991; Grotevant & Cooper 1986.

Let's face it, I'm one of the coldest. I don't feel it, hardly ever. And he could go to bed anytime he wanted to, anytime of day. He could hardly wait a week when I was on my periods. Even then he wanted sex. I couldn't have a minute of peace with him--never. As soon as he walked in the door. he'll ask me if my roommate was there. That really used to turn me off. Sometimes I wished he wouldn't ask for sex and just caress and hug me. Many times I asked him, "Why can't you do that for me and don't say anything about sex; just sit there and talk." He was very selfish and would always say, "Why can't you satisfy me; it doesn't take you long." As soon as he would come, which was very quick, he would finish and leave. He didn't care about my feelings. I told him many times, "Not tonight, I'm tired." He would say, "You are always tired; you always have reasons . . . ."

Sex was not enjoyable at all. To tell you the truth, I never experienced orgasm and my boyfriend was so selfish that he was concerned about his enjoyment and never bothered to know what happened to me and what I wanted. I wished he would kiss me, hold me before intercourse. I wished we would just lay there and cuddle and kiss each other. His idea of love was to get down to intercourse. I knew the bedroom was there just for sex, nothing else.

As soon as he found out I was pregnant, the first thing that came to his mind was, "What's it that we now have to worry about?" He was happy because as he said, "Well, we can make love as much as we want and we don't have to worry about precautions . . . ."

[Were you using any precautions?] No, I wasn't. I was scared of taking the pill or using anything because he would then ask for sex anytime.

[Was he concerned about you getting pregnant?] He didn't care a shit. All he cared about was sex. The more I gave him, the more he wanted and that's how I ended up being used sexually.

[What if you refused him sex?] If anytime I didn't give him sex, he would just say, "Listen, if I don't get you, I'll go out and get somebody else." And I was scared of that. [Scared, why?] I know I would miss him when he was not there. I didn't have anybody and I was scared of being alone. I've been brought up in a big family. I came to this city and I couldn't stand being alone and he was the only one I knew.

"Sex will bind us together."

A few women decided to abandon virginity because sexual intimacy seemed the only way to salvage a fractured relationship. They experienced tension in the pair relationship and were afraid that if they did not take concrete initiatives, the relationship might fall apart. Their concern for the relationship overcame their desire to remain chaste until marriage. Even the concern for the untoward consequence of an unwanted pregnancy was insignificant. Some women did not have a sexual desire but were driven to sexual relations out of consideration for the partner's sexual need. They hoped that the sexually content man would be able to express warmth and affectional attachment. An 18-year-old high school student explained why she did not use birth control methods to avoid unwanted pregnancy:

> I had been going out with this man I knew for three years and I wouldn't let him touch me. I was determined I would remain a virgin and that was instilled in me when I was a little girl. But after some time, we weren't getting along. I was worried and emotional at the time. My mind was so fogged at that time that I didn't think about getting pregnant. I knew I could get pregnant when I had sex with him without contraceptives, but I was blind to all other things. I was so glad to be with him.

A high school teacher became sexually involved for about four months with a man who was recently separated from his wife. She described the reasons for her sexual encounters with this man, which were in high frequency despite her low sex drive:

> I loved this man and I felt good when I was with him. But he started to drift back to his wife which bothered me. I did not want to lose him. He was oversexed, but for me sex was not a big thing that I had to have. I was perfectly content with just being held and kissed and did not have to

have sex for months. Most of the time I had sex with him because I wanted to satisfy his need. I didn't experience orgasm that often and he seemed to be worried about it. For me, the feeling of being with him, being that close made the sex relations enjoyable. I don't think it should be physical enjoyment; it is the emotional feeling between two people which brings them closer. There is a feeling of disappointment when you reach the height but do not get orgasm. But it didn't really matter to me, because I was doing it mostly to make him feel good.

"I wanted to have fun."

Some women were motivated by the desire to experience casual lovemaking, hitherto the prerogative of men. The force that propelled them into casual and impersonal sex was not sexual craving but rather their need to prove independence in sex decisions, free from worry about the consequences, or the inconvenience of contraception. "Sex is fun and the risk of pregnancy is worth the price" seemed to be their guiding attitude. The recurring comment made by these women was, "I just wanted to have sex at the time and didn't really care about anything," which meant that anything that's fun or worth something takes a few chances. This attitude is illustrated by the following excerpts:

[Were you concerned about pregnancy?] No, hardly at all. I was at a party and was drunk. I went with this guy to his hotel room. I wanted to have sex that night and didn't worry about anything. I thought I will have my fun and would worry about pregnancy later. *18-year-old bookkeeper*
*   *   *
I met this guy at a bar and had been going out with this man off and on for three months. I didn't really like him, so I used to put him off. I happened to have too many drinks that night and was sort of in a carefree mood. You know what I mean? [Were you worried that you might get pregnant without contraceptives?] I was not thinking of that at the time. I was out for a good time. *20-year-old billing clerk*

CONTRACEPTIVE USE BEFORE PREGNANCY

Why would a women get pregnant when she says she doesn't want to? Why would she not take the necessary precautions to prevent an unwanted pregnancy? Is it because she used the method incorrectly or because she failed to use a method? Did she believe that the risks of using contraceptive methods were too great and she would rather take a chance? Did she desire to have a child and then change her mind? Questions such as these are highly significant when considered in the context of national concern to prevent unplanned and unwanted pregnancies and thus reduce the demands for abortions.

First, what is contraception? The term contraception as used in this study includes any method employed either by the woman or her partner deliberately to prevent a pregnancy. In other words, if a woman used a device with the conviction that the method would prevent a pregnancy, although the method used was not recognized medically as a standard contraceptive, she was considered a "user." Examples of contraceptive methods that are not medically recognized are folk methods such as the superstitious ring, a hot bath, or standing up after intercourse.

A 24-year-old woman with a college education made sincere efforts to prevent her pregnancy through a hot bath, which "worked" for her for a long time:

My roommate was having an awful lot of sex and she told me that all you have to worry about is just to get it out in time and take a hot bath immediately after intercourse and there is no way you would get pregnant. So I used to jump in a bath tub right after intercourse and didn't have to worry about pregnancy.

A 22-year-old woman with some high school education used to stand up right after sex to prevent pregnancy and had a strong conviction that this method would work:

Somebody told me that if you get up right after you have intercourse it makes the sperm fall down. So I would get out of bed and run into the shower right after intercourse and I never worried about anything. I did it before all other times and it was okay.

A 19-year-old typist had to go off the pill in order to have a checkup. In the meantime she had sex relations, but she was not apprehensive about pregnancy because she had a superstitious ring to protect her:

> I did not think at the time I was off the pill that I'd get pregnant. I wore my girlfriend's superstitious ring which was supposed to protect me against having a child. I believed it, so I didn't let it enter my mind that I'll get pregnant.

The douche is another example in this category. If a woman douched following intercourse with the intention of preventing a pregnancy, she was considered a user. However, if the douche was used for hygienic reasons, she was designated a nonuser. The woman's intention to prevent a pregnancy was the relevant factor; whether she used a method improperly or ineffectually was not considered. This definition of contraception is in accord with that used in other studies such as the Indianapolis Study, the Growth of American Families Study, and the Fertility and Family Planning Study (FFP).[7] The FFP study, for instance, refers to users as "couples who tried to prevent pregnancy, regardless of which methods they used or how effective they were" (p. 138). The Indianapolis Study and the Growth of American Families Study refer to contraceptors as "motive users."

The contraceptive status of these women refers only to their use or lack of use of preventive methods during coitus with the man involved in the pregnancy. A woman might have a different contraceptive profile in her sex relations with other men, but those contraceptive behaviors were excluded from this discussion.

Contraceptive Use Pattern

The women were classified in four groups according to their contraceptive use patterns: (1) every-time users, (2) most-of-the-time users, (3) occasional users, and (4) never users or the do-nothing group.

---

[7]Whelpton et al. 1959, 1966; Whelpton and Kiser 1966.

Every-time users were highly motivated to prevent pregnancy. Afraid of pregnancy, they planned on contraception from the beginning of their sex relations and followed it through faithfully during every sex act. At times they were overly concerned about getting pregnant and used more than one method concurrently as an extra precaution. However, the pregnancy occurred because of method failure rather than human failure. A 24-year-old every-time user gave this account of her contraceptive behavior:

> The fear of pregnancy was so much in me that I didn't have feelings for sex and used to fight with him a lot over it. I always felt glad when it was over.
> [Did you use any methods?] Yes, I made him always pull out and never discharge inside me. He always wanted to keep it in and I always pushed him away or do something. I told him if he wouldn't pull out then no more sex. As far as I know he did pull out every time we had sex. I don't remember, but there must be one time when he didn't. I was also using a hot bath even if he withdrew, because I was still scared. I wanted to delete every possible chance for getting pregnant. And then I used to douche myself every once in a while.

A 21-year-old-ballet dancer was seized by pregnancy panic every month and made every attempt to prevent her pregnancy despite the inconvenience of the methods used:

> I would be worried about pregnancy from the middle of every month until I got my period again. We used a condom in spite of the fact that we hated it. It is a pain in the ass to whip out a rubber and put it on when you are feeling very passionate. We were so careful that we used rubber and withdrawal together, every time we had intercourse. I had thought I was not taking any chances with pregnancy. It must be an overflow of semen or ruptured sheath which caused this pregnancy.

Most-of-the-time users worried a great deal about pregnancy and made sure that their sex relations accompanied contraception. Unlike every-time users, they relaxed their efforts once or twice, believing that an occasional lapse in use might be forgiven. Their thinking was that if one was good most of the time, a few slips would be ignored. It was usually the single occasion that "deceived" them.

A 20-year-old legal secretary had had sex relations once a week. The couple had been using contraception regularly except one time when the pregnancy occurred:

> I worried quite a bit. We used either the rhythm or condom every time we had sex. [How did you get pregnant?] Well, (laugh) this is a long story. We went to the States to see my boyfriend's parents. I had too much to drink. He was drinking too. We were there for a couple of days and that's why he didn't think of buying any condoms down there. He usually had them on hand in my apartment or his. It was never a question of being stuck without them except for that time and to top it off I completely forgot all about my safe days. He was drunk too, otherwise, he usually asked me if I was safe. And it just happened all at once. It was funny how it happened because we had been so careful, yet it was just one time.

Another 22-year-old most-of-the-time user cohabited with her male partner for a year before she got pregnant. Coitus occurred almost every day. She had used contraceptives regularly, but got pregnant when she relaxed her efforts once or twice:

> I was not worried about pregnancy because I was using the pill. I had to go off the pill because of its side effects, but I used the foam instead every time I had sex. It was a few times when I didn't use it because I felt it was not going to hurt. But, obviously, it did hurt.

Occasional users practiced contraception, but only sporadically. They did not use any one method consistently and often hopped from one method to another. The female partner feared becoming pregnant, but was not preoccupied with it every time she had sex relations nor did she worry enough to lead her into effective contraception. When she did not use contraceptives, she trusted fate or simply liked to believe, "it won't happen to me." Occasional users were not committed to contraception as were every-time or most-of-the-time users but, unlike the do-nothing group, they made token efforts.

A 25-year-old teacher had gone with her male partner for over a year and had had sex relations more than twice a week. This is what she said about her contraceptive behavior:

> We talked about using safe [condom] but didn't follow through. We used sheath, but not very often. I did worry about pregnancy a lot, but didn't do anything to prevent pregnancy at the crucial time. I think it was very foolish. It was just a matter of disbelief that it won't happen.

A 22-year-old secretary with some college education had engaged in sex relations twice a week with a man she dated for over two years. This is what she did contraceptively:

> I used a diaphragm, but not very often. Sometimes I used rhythm, but most of the time I used nothing. [Any reason why you didn't use it more regularly] What can I say in my defense? You can chalk up that I wanted an experience or was trying to trap someone or putting myself in a masochistic trick. In reality as far as I'm concerned, all that it was neglect. I mean we are not all made perfect. How often I forget when I go out in the morning to get my street car tickets or whatever. Then you get into these things that you are not supposed to have it planned. It is supposed to be a big, romantic happening.
> [Did it worry you that you might get pregnant?] No, because I have a great deal of faith in my luck and I didn't really worry about it at that point.

Never users or the do-nothing group made no effort at all to avoid pregnancy. They were generally orientated to present interests, to here-and-now gratification, and were bothered by the inconvenience of contraception. They lacked self-control. They planned to use a method but never got around to it because they continued to rationalize their inaction, as if some external force had been frustrating their efforts. They seemed casual toward pregnancy and depended on the unrealistic belief that "it won't happen to me."

One 23-year-old shorthand secretary had had sex relations once a week with the partner she had been dating for six years. She never used any birth control methods, but she hoped and prayed:

[Did you worry about pregnancy?]   Yes, the thought did cross my mind once a while. [Did you use any preventions?] I didn't do anything.   I was scared to go to the doctor, because I don't like the hospital and anything associated with it.   The fact of seeing a doctor on top of the pill is really harrying. [Did you think of buying contraceptives off the shelf, for example, foam?]   No, because this stuff is not hundred percent foolproof. I used to think, why not go to the drug store that specializes in birth control methods and knows about it, instead of going to an ordinary drug store and buy it off the shelf without any directions on the package.
[Did your partner use anything?]   No, he gave me the impression that it was my problem and I should look after myself. Once or twice he pulled out, but I didn't like it. It gives you a sense of incompleteness, as if there was something missing.

An 18-year-old unemployed student had unprotected sex almost every day with her male partner of six months:

Fear of pregnancy was on my mind, but I wasn't really worried, because in my mind I had thought, "it won't happen to me." [Did you use anything to protect yourself?] No.   It seemed premeditated and it would cheapen the relationship if I would eat or use anything. Now I realize how stupid I was. [Did you ever discuss about birth control with your partner?] He told me to go on the pill and I kept putting it off, because I thought it would take the enjoyment out of sex.

Table 4.3 shows that a majority (55.7 percent) of the women either did not use any contraceptives or used them sporadically. Another one-tenth did not employ them with every sex act. Thus, two-thirds of the women were unprotected at the time of conception. One-third claimed to have used contraceptives with every sex act, but the pregnancy resulted because they used ineffective methods or used

Table 4.3
Contraceptive Use Status among Seventy Women prior to Pregnancy

Use Status	N	Percentage
Every time	24	34.3
Most of the time	7	10.0
Occasionally	18	25.7
Never	21	30.0

effective methods incorrectly. Although seven out of ten women had practiced a contraceptive method, their first intercourse was largely unprotected. Nearly two-thirds (65.3 percent) experienced their first intercourse without the benefit of contraceptive devices, giving evidence that adolescents begin their sexual encounters before they begin to use contraceptives. Consistent with the findings of this study, Mosher and Horn (1989) found in the U.S. nationally representative sample of 1,905 women aged 15-24 that three out of four women made their first visit to a family planning clinic or to a doctor on an average of 23 months after their first intercourse. Only 17 percent visited before they started to have intercourse. Similar to these findings, Zabin et al. (1979) found in their national survey that adolescents typically delay seeking and obtaining an effective birth control method often 12 months or longer following first intercourse. In the sample studied by Koenig and Zelnik (1982), only half of the sexually active teenage women living in metropolitan areas of the United States used any type of contraceptive method at first intercourse, most of which were nonprescriptive and less effective methods of contraception. These findings refute the argument that the availability of contraceptive methods encourages sexual activity. Mahoney (1983) argues that if the availability of contraceptive means motivated teenagers to initiate sexual experience, far fewer pregnancies would occur to unmarried teenage women each year.

The contraceptive practice of these women compares well with that of the unmarried patients of the metropolitan hospital from which most of the sample was drawn. The proportion of nonusers among the hospital women was 33.5 percent, and those who had used a preventative method at some time accounted for 66.5 percent. The only Canadian national study of abortion patients, undertaken in 1977 by the Committee on the Operation of Abortion Law (COAL), made similar observations. The survey found that 28.2 percent of the sexually active single women did not use any contraceptive methods. The surveys commissioned by the Planned Parenthood Federation of Canada in 1984 found a slightly higher percentage of nonusers among unmarried women, at 35 percent.[8] The findings of this study also parallel those of U.S. studies of sexually active unmarried women, confirming that much sexual experience among young people occurs without or with minimal use of contraception by either partner.[9]

---

[8]Gallup Poll 1984: 27; Canadian Gallup Poll Ltd. 1985: 6.

[9]The proportion of U.S. metropolitan white teenage women, 15-19, who had ever used a method in 1979 was 76 percent, and those who used a method with every sex act accounted for 35 percent. One-quarter (24 percent) never used a method of contraception (Zelnik and Kantner 1980: table 7). The U.S. study, however, reported that 51 percent of white teenagers attempted contraception at first intercourse (see table 8), which does not correspond to the findings of this study. More recently, the 1988 U.S. National Survey of Family Growth supports the findings of this study. Its analysis showed that one-third of all young women aged 15-19 had not used contraceptives the first time they had sex and that one-fifth of them never used any form of birth control (Forrest & Singh 1990). A U.S. survey of abortion patients in 1987 also supports the findings of this study. It found that one-quarter of never-married white teenagers never used a contraceptive method (Henshaw & Silverman 1988). Nearly the same proportion (27 percent) of never-users in the general population of teenagers in 1979 was reported by Koenig & Zelnik (1982).

A British national study of the contraceptive practices among teenage women also confirms the results of this study. The study involved 533 sexually active teenage women who were randomly selected from twenty-six areas of England and Wales during 1979. The authors reported that 30 percent of the women never used any form of contraceptive (Simms & Smith 1986).

Methods of Contraception

While infrequent use of a contraceptive device can expose a woman to the risk of pregnancy, the type of method used may further intensify the risks. As shown in table 4.3, a total of forty-nine women had used a contraceptive method at some time. The most effective methods, the pill and condom, were favored by 37 percent of the women, while one-half used the least effective methods-- withdrawal, douche, and rhythm (see table 4.4). The highly publicized side effects associated with the use of the pill were responsible for its low use. Interestingly, a majority (56.5 percent)

Table 4.4
Types of Methods Ever Used by Forty-Nine Women

Type of Method	Percentage*	Percentage**
Pill	12.0	22.4
Rhythm	14.1	26.5
Foam	7.6	14.3
Jelly or Cream	1.0	2.0
Diaphragm	1.0	2.0
Douche	4.4	8.1
Condom	25.0	47.0
Withdrawal	31.5	59.2
Folk Method (Hot bath, superstition, etc.)	3.4	6.1

*Percentages based on the total number of responses, i.e., ninety-two.
**Percentages based on the number of women, i.e., forty-nine, who ever used contraception. This is done so in order to conform to the practice followed by some authors whose findings will be compared.

relied on the methods of withdrawal and condom, for which the male partner was responsible.[10] In such situations, the possibility of a woman getting pregnant is linked to her ability to persuade the man to use protective devices. This process, described by Furstenberg (1976) as negotiation or bargaining, obviously did not work out for these women.

Knowledge of Contraceptives

Each woman was presented with a list of male and female methods of contraception and was asked if she knew how these methods worked and their sources. Based on the number of uses and sources correctly identified, the women were classified as having "good knowledge," "fair knowledge," or "poor knowledge." "Good knowledge" means more than two-thirds correct answers, "fair knowledge" more than one-third, and "poor knowledge" means less than one-third correct. Almost two-thirds (65.7 percent) of the women had good knowledge. Less than one-fifth (15.7 percent) had fair knowledge of contraceptive methods. Just less than one-fifth

---

[10]In the U.S. national study of unmarried metropolitan women referred to earlier, 48 percent of white ever-users initially used the least effective methods--withdrawal, douche, and rhythm--in 1979. The three most popular methods ever used were withdrawal, condom, and the pill, in that order (Zelnik & Kantner 1980: table 10). These findings are very similar to this study. Consistent with the findings of this study, Herold (1984) found in his study of 481 university and community college students in Ontario that one-quarter of them reported condom use and 27 percent practiced withdrawal. Only one-third of the students attempted any contraceptive use at first intercourse. The types of method used by the abortion patients in the Canadian national survey, referred to above, closely matched this study, with 18 percent using the pill, 26.2 percent using the condom, and 14.9 percent practicing rhythm at the time of conception (p. 352). However, the data from the U.S. National Survey of Unmarried Women, conducted in 1983 with a nationally representative sample of 20-29-year-old women showed higher use of the pill (55 percent) and lower use of condoms (11.4 percent) among sexually active women than the women in this study (Tanfer et al. 1992). The difference is more likely due to the younger age of the women in this study.

(18.6 percent) were assessed as having poor knowledge.[11] Curiously, most women tended to have the least knowledge about the rhythm method that many of them (14.1 percent) used and were most aware of condom and withdrawal, over which they had least control.

REASONS FOR NONUSE OR IRREGULAR USE OF CONTRACEPTION

Given these women's adequate knowledge of contraceptive methods and their source, why did so many, forty-six women, not practice contraception or practiced it irregularly? They were aware of the consequence of unprotected sex and indeed rejected the pregnancy, and yet they lacked commitment to contraception. Does there seem to be a contradiction? To find answers to these questions, each of the forty-six women was presented with twenty-five statements that described various reasons single women give for not using contraception or using it irregularly and was asked to check the ones that applied to her case. In addition, their motivations and underlying reasons became evident through probes and a series of questions on contraceptive experience. Their reasons are set forth in table 4.5.

"I thought I was too lucky for anything like that to happen."

Three-fourths of the women did not think that they could or would become pregnant either because they trusted the external force of luck that would always favor them or were convinced that the mere denial of occurrence of pregnancy will ward off the consequences of unprotected sex. They did perceive the risk of pregnancy and often

---

[11]Other investigators have reached a similar conclusion that most women--75 to 94 percent--claim familiarity with the modern methods of conception control, their uses and sources (see Sachdev 1985: 240-241). Clearly, absence or minimal use of contraception, which is constantly reported in studies of young people's contraceptive and sexual behavior, cannot be attributed, in most cases, to a lack of knowledge about or access to birth control methods. Rogel and Zuehlke (1982) reviewed studies involving antecedent factors that influence adolescent contraceptive behavior and concluded that "the problem is clearly more complicated than simply lack of information" (p. 197).

Table 4.5
Reasons Given by Forty-Six Irregular and Non-Users

Reasons	N[*]	Percentage[**]
Felt like pregnancy would never happen to me	35	76.1
Didn't get pregnant last time I had sex without contraception, so I thought I was not likely to get pregnant this time	20	43.5
Didn't want sex to seem planned	15	32.6
No boyfriend or no plans to have sex relation or too infrequent sex	12	26.1
Afraid to get hassled if I went to get birth control pills	9	19.6
Afraid pill would mess up my insides	9	19.6
Thought it was man's responsibility to use birth control	6	13.0
Most birth control methods are messy and take the enjoyment out of sex	10	21.7
I thought either I was sterile or my boyfriend was sterile or vasectomized	6	13.0
I kept putting it off	9	19.6
Thought abortion as a backup measure if pregnancy occurred	6	13.0
Deep down, I might have wanted to get pregnant	11	23.9
Didn't matter to me if I got pregnant, I wanted sex pleasure	12	26.1
Didn't know any preventative method	--	--

*The number of responses exceed the number of respondants because some of them gave more than one reason.
**Percentages are based on the number of respondents and not the responses.

became hysterical the day before the menstrual period was due, yet these women took the view that they had some magical immunity against pregnancy. In almost identical words, they expressed the conviction, "it won't happen to me." A 22-year-old waitress, an occasional user, typifies this view:

> I knew I could get pregnant when we were not using anything. It sort of entered my head now and then. Actually, he worried about it; he was the one who would always bring that up. He was using withdrawal and he told me that it was not reliable and asked me to get on the pill. But I just kept putting it off, because I thought I was too lucky for anything like that to happen.

> *"I didn't get pregnant last time, so I don't need contraceptives."*

The erratic or nonexistant contraceptive use of more than two out of every five women was reinforced when pregnancy did not occur during their first few sex relations, which took place either without contraceptives or with the least effective contraceptives. They became increasingly convinced that they would not become pregnant or the method was working:

> We didn't use anything. Well, before this man, I lived with a Greek fellow for three years and he wanted to have kids and I didn't. We never used any precautions in three years and it was strange that I didn't get pregnant then. I really didn't think that it was going to happen to me this time.
> *25-year-old sales supervisor*
>
> *   *   *
>
> I didn't worry about getting pregnant. I was on the rhythm and it worked so often before. [Do you know how to calculate your safe days?] I don't know. He is the one who knows how to count them and he used to keep track of my periods. *19-year-old cashier*

"It's supposed to be a spontaneous thing and a big romantic happening."

Another deterrent to the use of contraception is our cultural norms that make allowances for premarital sex if "love" or the feeling of love becomes a justifiable basis and sex relations stem from spontaneous and natural situations. Obviously, advance preparation and rational planning for contraception signify sexual intent not only to the women herself but also to her male partner. Despite sexual emancipation of women and a more permissive climate, it seems that the traditional norms of premarital chastity continue to hold sway along with the idea that sex is legitimized if it seems to take place as an uncontrollable act without conscious volition and in the spirit of romantic love. While these normative expectations protect the unmarried woman's self-image, they leave her at risk of pregnancy. Although worried about pregnancy, she may settle for the least effective methods of conception control, which do not imply planned and deliberate efforts. This perspective prevented almost one-third of the women from making consistent efforts at effective contraception. For example, an 18-year-old most-of-the-time user rejected contraceptive methods except withdrawal because all other methods involve rational planning and signify that she anticipated sexual relations:

We didn't use any birth control methods except taking out. I thought it would cheapen the relationship if we would eat or use anything. He told me to go on the pill and I kept putting it off, because it would seem as though I was expecting to be screwed.

A 22-year-old highly sexually active woman relied on a diaphragm to keep from getting pregnant. She used the method occasionally and gave this reason for not using it more frequently:

When I was using anything it was a diaphragm. However, I did not have it with me most of the time. [Why not?] You get into these things about how you are not supposed to have it planned; you should be swept away by romance. Well I mean, when intercourse does happen, I don't think there are many human beings who are ever going to stop, because they did not have contraceptives available.

"I was afraid of getting hassled."

In order to acquire prescriptive or nonprescriptive methods of conception control, a woman must come in contact with other people--pharmacist, doctor, or family planning clinic staff. Besides the inconvenience, she openly acknowledges her intention to engage in premarital sex, which may be embarrassing. In this sense, contraceptive preparation, as Rains (1971) put it, is a "reputational and self-definitional matter" (p. 23). As possessing a diaphragm or taking birth control pills is self-incriminating, some women would rather play naive about sex and contraception than risk a reputation that they are sexually available. This reasoning deterred almost one-fifth of the women from choosing effective contraceptive methods such as the pill. The following excerpts illustrate a dilemma of these women. They wanted to protect themselves against unwanted pregnancy, while preserving their image as a nonpromiscious woman:

> Before I got pregnant we used withdrawal. My roommate tried to talk me into taking the pills, but I didn't. I was just scared that people would find out that I was on them and would talk about me and think I was a tramp. They would think that since I was on the pill, I wanted to have sex all the time. *24-year-old college student*

Another 20-year-old woman working as a medical secretary intented to protect herself against pregnancy, but postponed taking effective action until she got pregnant. She explains the reason:

> I kept meaning to go on the pill and get a prescription, but never got around them. I made an appointment, but then I found out I was pregnant before I saw the doctor. [Why did you keep postponing?] I was afraid of going to see a doctor. I didn't know what he was going to say, and he might give me a rough time.

"I wasn't having intercourse that often."

Infrequent, inconsistent, and unpredictable opportunities for sex encounters were the reasons that one-quarter of the women did not use birth control methods or used them irregularly. When sex relations did not occur in a predictable manner, it seemed impractical and unjustifiable for these women to stay "prepared" in anticipation of the sex acts. This situation is well illustrated by a 25-year-old property manager who discontinued the pill when sex relations with her steady partner became infrequent and unpredictable. This is how she described her attitude toward the pill;

> I lived with my boyfriend for three months and we had sex almost everyday. I was on the pill. My parents didn't like my living with him and so I moved back home with my parents. As soon as I moved out I went off the pill. [Why?] My parents didn't like him and I had to see him sneakishly. So, we couldn't plan sex. Our meetings were all so unpredictable that I was there and it happened before I had any time to think anything or do anything about it. After each intercourse I used to think, "Well, it happened this time, and now I'm okay. But I'll keep away from this type of thing, so there was no sense of going on the pill."

A 22-year-old teacher relied on a douche. Although she recognized this method as highly unreliable, she did not switch to the pill because her sex relations were casual and inconsistent. She said:

> I used a douche all the time and I knew I was taking an awful lot of chances. I didn't want to take the pill because I knew I had to take it regularly whether I was having sex or not. But I wasn't going to get myself involved.

"I'll have an abortion if I become pregnant."

The availability of legal abortion weakened the resolve of a little more than one-tenth of the women to prevent pregnancy. They considered abortion as a backup measure if they became pregnant.[12] A typical response was given by this occasional user:

---

[12]That easy access to abortion does not encourage women to relax their efforts at contraception was also confirmed by Jone and Philliber (1983) who studied 119 sexually active women aged 21 and under who were never pregnant. The authors found that the consistent contraceptors were more certain that they would have an abortion should they become pregnant and that their parents would help them to have one than the women who were nonusers or irregular users of contraception.

A month before I got pregnant I said to myself if I ever got pregnant I would get an abortion.

Another woman, a nonuser, said:

I didn't want to get pregnant, but if I did, it didn't matter, I knew I had a good doctor in Canada and I understood from him that if by chance I happened to become pregnant, he could arrange a proper abortion.

"I planned on using contraceptives, but it didn't happen."

Almost one-fifth of the women planned on switching to the most effective and efficient method, the pill. They worried a lot about pregnancy, but postponed taking decisive action to realize their plan for some reason or another until it was too late. The following statements illustrate the phenomenon of procrastination:

Fear of pregnancy was always on my mind. I remember in the beginning I did not want to have intercourse because I was scared of getting pregnant. I had thought that as soon as my periods were over, I was going to go to a doctor and see if I could get the pills. But the periods never came.
          *   *   *
I did nothing . . . I was planning to go on birth control pills but after everything went wrong, I realized it was too late.
          *   *   *
I had gone out with this guy for one year. I was first using pills, then we broke up. Then I suspended their use thinking why bother using them . . . Then we went back together. But I didn't start using them. I didn't have a prescription and was putting it off thinking that I ought to go see a doctor, but somehow I didn't.

"When you're having intercourse, pregnancy is the last thing on your mind."

Twelve women (26.1 percent) presented themselves as pleasure orientated and believed in carefree, wholesome erotic experiences. Their desire for sex enjoyment superseded their concern for an unplanned pregnancy, because they believed that "anything that's fun or worth something involves some risk." This view of risking pregnancy is akin to risk taking behavior in other life areas. Their intolerance of birth control is understandable because the methods impose artificiality on something that is natural and interferes with sex pleasure. Their usual comment was, "It didn't matter to me if I got pregnant, I wanted sex pleasure." The following excerpts typify these women:

> We had sex almost every day in the horse field. It was in the spring and summer, so it was really nice out. It is fun, you get a body tan all over.
> [Did you use any contraceptives?] No, we didn't. Well, we started with condoms for a while, but I got sick of them. Then we tried the withdrawal method. But I hated that even more, because my excitement was just getting up and then he fell out. That really bothered me. He did not withdraw any more.
>
>   *   *   *
>
> I had a fear of getting pregnant, but I liked him so much I was willing to take chances. I wanted to have sex because I wanted to have the experience of it. Then I began to like sex very much, but I was not prepared for the consequences. [Were you worried about getting pregnant?] It didn't bother me. I said, "I won't worry about it until it happens."

"I thought I was sterile or my boyfriend was sterile."

More than one-tenth suspected sterility when they did not become pregnant despite their exposure to unprotected sex. Their fear that they would not get pregnant became reinforced as more time elapsed without conceiving. Although they did not want to become pregnant, they were becoming increasingly concerned about the possibility of being sterile. The longer they went without conceiving, the more likely they were indifferent toward contraception. These women experienced mixed feelings on discovering their pregnancy. They were relieved that it proved their fertility, but were also sad because pregnancy occurred at a time when they were ill-prepared for parenting. The following excerpts illustrate this point:

I always thought I couldn't get pregnant. I have a twin sister and she has two children. I had an ovary removed a few years ago and some people say that one of the twin sisters can't have children in some cases. I had been having sex relations for the past 2 to 3 years and I never took precautions. But I did not get pregnant. When I found out I was pregnant I was happy to know that I could get pregnant and someday when I'm married I will be able to have my family. But I didn't want the child in the situation I was in at the time. *22-year-old ballet dancer*

*   *   *

I was glad I could be pregnant. My boyfriend and I have been going out for three years and have been pushing it a little bit without any birth control method. At first, I was proud of the fact that I could have a baby because my oldest brother and his wife have been married for 8 years and have not been able to have a child. My sister has been married for 9 years and she has just got a baby. When I realized it is so hard to have children and it changed their lives so much when they got a child, I was glad that I was able to have one. I often wondered I might not be able to conceive because of my family history, which was an added reason why I did not use anything. *21-year-old sales manager*

"When you come right down to it, I really wanted to get pregnant."

Pregnancy was consciously desired by eleven women (23.9 percent) who admitted deliberately exposing themselves to unprotected sex with a desire to become pregnant.[13] The comments they made and the statements they checked acknowledged that these women wanted to conceive. Pregnancy was desired to serve a variety of

---

[13]The U.S. study of metropolitan unmarried teenage women, referred to earlier, reported that 18 percent of them had a conscious desire to become pregnant (Zelnik and Kantner 1980, table 6). An analysis of the 1988 data from the U.S. National Survey of Family Growth reveals that 18.3 percent of births to teenage women were intentional (Forrest & Singh 1990). The larger proportion in this study is due to the small sample of forty-six cases. All proportions in this section should be treated as trends.

purposes: to seek marriage commitment, fill a void in life, for self-retribution, for maturing experience, or for closeness with the boyfriend. Their motivation to experience pregnancy first existed on a fantasy level. It was only when they had a rude awakening to the harsh reality of parenting responsibility that they began the process of undoing their wish. Typical of the conscious wish to get pregnant are the following excerpts:

> I used to think it would be nice to have my own little baby and I really loved this man. But I didn't think marriage would be quite the same. But having a baby would be great. So when I went down to the states that weekend, it was very much at the back of my mind. When I found I was pregnant, I was very happy. [smiles and laughs]
> [Why abortion?] I was happy at first, when I got pregnant. I knew it would be a love baby. However, I hadn't really thought everything yet. Then my roommate started getting me sensible. How could I feed this poor little thing? How could I raise the baby all by myself? I couldn't run my own life, let alone a baby's. I began to realize there was no way I could support the baby. *22-year-old waitress*
>
> *   *   *
>
> I knew this man as a pen pal when he was in jail. I was sort of attached to him. The day he got out I met him and it just happened. We had sex and I never saw him again.
> [Did you or he use any birth control?] No. [Did you know you could get pregnant without protection?] I was happy when I found out I was pregnant. I was going through a stage where I was tired of being alone. Maybe I thought if I got pregnant I won't be alone. I have a lot of friends. But friends are just not enough, even though you go to places and do all sorts of things together. When you finally come home you are by yourself, you are really alone. When I knew I was pregnant I thought I won't be alone any more.
> [Why abortion?] Then I started to face reality that I couldn't afford it. I was not really mentally ready to have it. I was irresponsible; I pick up and run off for a couple of days for some place. I enjoy my freedom too much. I didn't want to be burdened down with a child. I knew I would just take all my frustrations on the child. *21-year-old unemployed*
>
> *   *   *

I used to have sex with this man twice a week. I was on the pill and then I stopped taking them. [Why?] I wanted to have a baby. I thought maybe this will bring us closer together. I was very mixed up. I had a very bad life and had seen lots of fights in my family. I wanted the baby so much because it was part of me and part of him whom I loved quite a bit. I was so happy after I knew I was pregnant. It is a feeling every woman gets. It gave me funny feelings inside that it was part of me that I could just bear something and give life. It is hard to explain.
[Why abortion?] I was having so much trouble with him; we were fighting constantly. I realized I wasn't just ready for a baby because I did not know how he would react to it or say because he was heavy on drugs. He could say that I did it on purpose and didn't want anything to do with it. We were not getting along. I couldn't see bringing the baby into the world without a father. *22-year-old film distributor*

FACTORS RELATED TO CONTRACEPTIVE USE

In addition to cultural, social, and technical barriers, other factors influence the extent to which a woman is likely to use contraceptive methods. In this study younger women appear to be less receptive to contraceptive methods (see Appendix A table 7). While 40 percent of the younger women aged 18-21 practiced contraception most of the time or every time they engaged in sex, one-half of the older women 22-25 years of age used contraception with the same regularity. Similarly, those who never used any form of contraception accounted for over one-third for the younger women, compared to nearly one-fifth of the women in the older group.[14]

---

[14]This finding is parallel to the trends observed in other studies (Bowerman et al. 1966; Bracken et al. 1972; Cho et al. 1970; Daily & Nicholas 1972; Grauer 1972; Kazanjian 1973; Monsour & Stewart 1973; Osofsky & Osofsky 1972; Tyler et al. 1970; Zimmerman 1977). Because the cutoff age between younger and older women varied from study to study, these studies differ from each other on the magnitude of relationship between age and contraceptive use. In the U.S. national sample of white unwed teenage women, Kantner and Zelnik (1973) concluded that "it

The more educated women were also more active contraceptors. However, this finding should be treated with caution because of the small number of women with college education. Also, the data on secondary school education were difficult to standardize, as some women were educated outside Ontario and a few outside of Canada. As shown in table 8 (see Appendix A), of the women with some or completed high school education, 41.2 percent practiced contraception every time or most of the time, while the same regularity in contraceptive use was reported by one-half of the women who had some college education or college graduation. Likewise, those who never or only occasionally used contraceptives comprised nearly 60 percent of the women in the school category, compared to one-half of the women in the college group. However, the relationship between education and contraceptive use did not reach statistical significance.[15] Similarly, religious commitment had no influence on contraceptive use. That is, active Catholic women were just as likely to be regular users as were the active Protestant women (see Appendix A table 9).[16] Far more women who professed no religion were active contraceptors than the women in either religious group.

---

appears that as age increases, those who, for one reason or another, did not use a method at younger ages tend to begin occasional use of contraception" (p. 21). Similar conclusions were reached in the Canadian study of the national survey, referred to earlier, that older women used such methods as condoms, withdrawal, and the diaphragm more often than young women or their partners (COAL 1977: 352).

[15]This finding is completely consistent with the results of the national Canadian patient survey, which did not find education having any effect on contraceptive use (COAL 1977:345). However, the two U.S. national studies found that a woman's level of education was positively related to her prior use of birth control methods (Kantner and Zelnik 1973: 24; Tanfer et al. 1992). The contradictory findings are attributed to the difficulty in standardizing educational level of the women in different studies.

[16]Several authors have observed that the influence of church on Catholics in shaping their attitude toward contraception has considerably weakened. See Cho et al. 1970; Whelpton et al. 1966. Ryder and Westoff (1971) concluded from the U.S. national surveys on contraceptive behavior among married women that "it is apparent . . . that from cohort to cohort at each age and for each cohort as age advances, the differences (between Catholics and Protestants) is seemingly attenuated" (p. 108).

Stability of the relationship seems to encourage the use of birth control devices. In this study, stability of relationship is gauged by the duration of time the sexual pair had dated each other. As shown in table 10 (see Appendix A), nearly one-half of the women who had known the sex partners for one year or more practiced contraception every time or most of the time they had sex, whereas the women who occasionally or never used birth control had dated the man less than six months.[17]

There are several reasons that durable romantic relationship fosters contraceptive use. First of all, with continued involvement, the communication between sexual partners progressively improves and becomes more open on sexual and contraceptive matters.[18] Second, deep involvement also fosters mutual planning and the male's readiness to assume responsibility in avoiding pregnancy by either using a contraceptive himself or encouraging his partner to use one.[19] Third, a stable relationship affords more opportunities for sexual liaisons, which tend to occur in a regular and predictable fashion. Under these conditions, the couple is likely to regard sex as less spontaneous and more under control, which makes methods of contraception such as the pill more acceptable. Fourth, in a casual relationship the man may not feel obligated to avoid pregnancy and therefore may ignore the woman's request to practice contraception. In a stable relationship a woman's bargaining position is improved; her male friend is less likely to ignore her request to assume contraceptive responsibility because he is emotionally involved and may feel more obligated toward the child, should pregnancy occur. Finally, in a continued relationship, the woman's mother is less likely to pretend ignorance about her daughter's sexual activity and is more

---

[17]A number of studies confirm the positive influence of continuing relationships on the frequency of contraception. See Anderson et al. 1978; Bachrach 1987; Friedlander et al. 1984; Furstenberg 1976; Kantner and Zelnik 1973; Luker 1975; Miller 1976; Reiss et al. 1975; Slonim-Nevo 1988; Sorenson 1973; Spees 1987; Tanfer 1987.

[18]A recent study by Catania et al. (1992) shows that heterosexual partners who had open communication and were in monogamous relationships were significantly more likely than others to use condoms with every sex act.

[19]Studies have shown that encouragement by the male partner is a strong contributor to effective contraceptive use in young women (Apkom et al. 1976; Cahn 1978; Herold and Goodwin 1980; Thompson 1978).

likely to recommend and encourage the use of contraceptive methods.[20]   Other factors such as perception of pregnancy risks, receptivity to contraceptive means, and acceptance of one's sexuality appear to promote contraceptive use.   However, these findings are presented with qualification because of limited information on these determinants.   The investigation of these patterns of contraception was not planned in this study. But they surfaced in the data in an interesting way and hence an ex post factum explanation is being offered.   As shown in table 4.6, a substantially higher proportion (61.3 percent) of women who perceived the risk of pregnancy reported using contraceptives every time or most of the time than of those (38.7 percent) who did not show such awareness.[21]   The women's perception of pregnancy risks was assessed by the following statements:

I felt like pregnancy would never happen to me.

I didn't get pregnant last time I had sex without contraceptives, so I was not too likely to get pregnant this time.

I thought either I was sterile or my boyfriend was sterile.

I guess I always left it to chance.

Similarly, women who rejected contraceptive devices as messy and inconvenient were more likely never to have used birth control or to have used it occasionally (32.6 percent compared to 67.2 percent who

---

[20]In a study of pregnant teenage women, Furstenberg (1976) found that women are more likely to use contraceptives if their mother discussed birth control or at least relayed expectations for their use.

[21]Reschovsky & Gerner (1991) examined contraceptive choices made by 673 sexually active teenage women and noted that perception of pregnancy risk was a predictor of contraceptive use.   Reis & Herz (1989) surveyed inner-city black adolescents concerning their attitudes toward birth control and sexual intercourse.   The authors found that these young people were egocentric and concerned with personal gratification with little thought about the consequences, which were largely responsible for nonuse or erratic use of contraceptives and a high incidence of unplanned pregnancies among this group.

Table 4.6
Personal Factors and Contraceptive Use

Personal Factors	Frequency of Contraception	
	Every/most of the time user	Occasional or never user
Perception of pregnancy risk	61.3	38.7

"I felt like pregnancy would never
     happen to me."
"I didn't get pregnant last time I had
     sex without contraceptives, so I was not
     too likely to get pregnant this time."
"I thought either I was sterile or
     my boyfriend was."

Receptivity to contraceptive means	67.4	32.6

"I didn't want sex to seem planned"
"I was afraid of getting hassled if
     I went to get birth control methods."
"My boyfriend would not let me use birth control."
"I was afraid the pill would mess up my insides."
"Most birth control methods are messy
     and take the enjoyment out of sex."
"I was too shy to use one myself or
     to ask him to use one."

Acceptance of one's sexuality	58.7	42.3

"It would be better if women would express their
     sexual desire with as much initiative,
     aggressiveness and enthusiasm as men."
"Masturbation seems no less natural for females than
     males."
"There is something not quite normal about oral sex."
"Girls should be prohibited from engaging in self-
     examination."
"A woman usually finds adequate satisfaction in sex
     relations even when she and her partner are not in
     love with one another."

accepted contraceptives).[22] Their receptivity was assessed by the following statements:

I didn't want sex to seem planned.

I was afraid of getting hassled if I went to get birth control methods.

My boyfriend wouldn't let me use birth control.

I was afraid the pill will mess me up inside.

Most birth control methods are messy and take the enjoyment out of sex.

I was too shy to use one myself or ask him to use one.

Finally, women who had a positive attitude toward their sexuality were much more likely to be regular contraceptors (58.5 percent compared to 42.5 percent who were equivocal about their sexuality).[23] The following statements indicated the women's attitudes toward their sexuality:

---

[22]Keith et al. (1991) compared cognitive processing between users and non-users of contraceptives among black adolescent females and found that non-users tended to report fewer benefits and more barriers to contraceptive use. Similarly, Orr et al. (1992) tested a health belief model of condom use among 390 sexually active adolescent females and concluded that reported condom use increased as cognitive maturity and positive condom attitude increased. Morrison (1989) also demonstrated the importance of attitudes toward contraception as a predictor of effective contraceptive use.

[23]Adler & Hendrick (1991) examined contraceptive behavior among 350 undergraduate male and female students using Rain's and Reiss et al.'s model of effective contraceptive behavior. The authors found that their study results supported the relationship between sexual self-acceptance and effective contraception. Similarly, Loewenstein & Furstenberg (1991) found in their study of contraceptive practice among 1,032 teenagers that the women's attitude toward sex, pregnancy, and birth control significantly predicted behavior. Also, see Berger et al. 1984; Cvetkovich et al. 1975; DeLamater & MacCorquodale 1978; Reis et al. 1975.

It would be better if women were free to express their sexual desire with as much initiative, aggressiveness and enthusiasm as men.

Masturbation seems no less natural for females than for males.

There is nothing wrong about oral sex.

Girls should be encouraged to engage in self-examination.

A woman can usually find adequate satisfaction in a sexual relationship even though she and her partner are not in love with each other.

The explanation of why acceptance of one's sexuality is conducive to the use of contraception can be understood in the context of the nature of the contraceptive means. As the act of contraception is intimately linked with sexuality and the use of most female-orientated methods require contact with their genitalia, women who accept their own sexuality are more likely to assume responsibility in contraception and are less inclined to rely on the male. It is the ambivalent woman who seeks to neutralize her family proscription by not thinking about contraceptives, which imply family planning and preparedness.[24] Nonuse may also serve as a defense against guilt feelings induced by violation of personal and family sex norms.[25]

From the foregoing discussion of the women's contraceptive profiles, it is evident that their pregnancies resulted from situations in which there were either genuine contraceptive failure or a failure to use a contraceptive method effectively. Indeed, motivation is an important factor in successful contraceptive activity. One should, however, not overlook the fact that society's structural arrangements and cultural expectations present realistic barriers to an otherwise

---

[24]See Brandt et al. 1978; Dembo and Lundell 1979; Fisher 1978; Furstenberg 1976; Miller 1976; Nadelson et al. 1980; Notman 1975; Rains 1971; Reis et al. 1975. Mosher (1979) found that women in his study with high sex guilt were less likely to use methods of contraception and to retain birth control information.

[25]Monsour & Stewart 1973; Rader et al. 1978.

highly motivated woman, preventing her from achieving fertility control. Coupled with these impediments are the currently available contraceptive devices, which are highly inconvenient or unsuited to young unmarried women. They are linked to sexual activity and require deliberate planning, which implies reputational implications. The claim that sex is something that "just happens" and pregnancy is a consequence that was neither anticipated nor desired will make sense when viewed in the context of our cultural norms regarding the sexual behavior of unmarried women, who are supposed to regard sex as a spontaneous, uncontrollable act.   This study refutes the psychodynamic explanation of out-of-wedlock pregnancies, which contends that a woman willfully exposes herself to pregnancy because of her "underlying motivation" to fulfil her emotional and psychological needs.   Only eleven women acknowledged that they consciously wanted to become pregnant. It is also worthy of note that, although abortions have been legally available in Canada, only a little over one-tenth of the women used abortion as a primary method of contraception, a finding that flies in the face of the claim made by anti-abortion groups that availability of abortions will encourage women to have one.

It seems that as long as the discovery of an "ideal" contraceptive eludes scientists, contraception remains a highly complex act in which chance or risk-taking behavior plays a significant and unavoidable role. How many times one takes chances when crossing the street or travelling by plane or by car. Most pregnancy will occur not because of some "special motivation," but because of risk-taking behavior that runs through many aspects of life. Bowerman et al. (1966) recognized the social and cultural forces that impinge upon young women's sexual behavior and concluded their study with these words: "Thus, en fin, it really isn't at all difficult to become an unwed mother" (p. 293).

SUMMARY

The seventy women ranged in ages from 15 to 25, with a concentration in the younger age category (18-21). About one-half were Protestants and less than one-third were Catholics. The women were almost evenly divided between the religiously devout and those not religiously active (measured by their religious commitment). Given their youthfulness, the women were not highly educated nor were they working in high status jobs. Two-thirds of them had not gone beyond high school and nearly one-half were employed as secretaries or clerical workers. Judging from their fathers' occupations, it would appear that a majority belonged to middle-class families. Three-fifths were living independently of their parents at the time of conception.

These women were highly sexually active prior to becoming pregnant. Almost two-thirds engaged in sexual intercourse with the man involved in the pregnancy at least once per week. One-half lost their virginity by age 19. Their sexual attitudes and behaviors reflected a largely "private morality." Only one-fifth of the women expressed commitment to sex relations in the context of affection. However, they did not give evidence of promiscuity as their sexual activity generally occurred in a fairly stable relationship. Their predominant motivations to engage in interpersonal sex were to seek acceptance and affection, satisfy curiosity, and attain emotional security. Very few had a prior commitment to pregnancy.

Four-fifths of them had fair to good knowledge of the modern methods of birth control. However, only one-third of all the women used contraception with every sex act. One-half of them relied on the least effective methods. Two-thirds of the women were unprotected at the time of conception. In the sociocultural and technological context of these women, it seems that effective use of contraceptives requires more than just information about the methods. Younger and less-educated women appeared to be less receptive to contraceptive use. Religious commitment had no influence on contraceptive behavior. That is, active Catholic women were just as likely to be regular users as were active Protestant women. The data show that stability of the pair relationship had a positive influence on the frequency of contraception. Other factors such as perception of pregnancy risks, receptivity to contraceptive means, and acceptance of one's own sexuality appeared to be positively related to contraceptive use. There is ample evidence that their pregnancies resulted from situations in which there was either a genuine contraceptive failure or a failure to use a contraceptive method effectively because of sociocultural factors. The study rejects the psychodynamic explanation of out-of-wedlock pregnancies that contends that a woman willfully exposes herself to pregnancy because of her "underlying motivation" to fulfil her psychological needs. The data also show that most women did not use abortion as a primary method of contraception. It seems that as long as the discovery of an "ideal" contraceptive eludes scientists, the act of contraception remains highly complex.

5

Facing the Pregnancy

"Before, nothing was serious, now it was a reality."

25-year-old teacher

Every time a young unmarried woman engages in unprotected or inadequately protected sex relations, she faces the risk of pregnancy. She copes with her lurking anxiety about the possibility of conception (unless she wishes to be pregnant) through denial and magical thinking, "It won't happen to me," and approaches her next menstrual period with hope and prayer. A few days of delayed period throws her into a panic, and she is relieved as though a lucky survivor when her period comes on. Sometimes as it may appear to her the magical force or luck may not favor her and the woman finds herself "caught." Indeed, a few women become a statistical casualty because the contraceptive method failed. The woman may extend her denial mechanism for some time and not recognize the existence of her pregnancy. But she must sooner or later come to grips with the realistic issue of making a decision about the pregnancy she does not want. Faced with the desperate situation she gropes for the alternative that is socially and psychologically less costly. All the women in this study, obviously, decided in favour of termination of their pregnancy.

THE DECISION

The decision to terminate pregnancy can be an agonizing experience for some women, while others manage it with little or no noticeable emotional upheaval. A woman's experience with her decision to abort depends largely upon such factors as her reactions to the pregnancy, the attractiveness of other alternatives, her attitudes toward abortion, apprehension about the surgical procedure, and the degree of emotional support she receives from the key people in her life such as her parents and her sex partner. All of these factors in concert influence her decision to seek abortion and its accompanying emotional reactions.

Recognizing Pregnancy

More than a majority (57 percent) of the women sought pregnancy confirmation either by a physician or a druggist within three weeks of suspicion. The remainder (43 percent) did not arrange for a pregnancy test until four to eight weeks after they recognized the pregnancy. Of these "late" women, two-thirds (67.2 percent) dismissed their earlier symptoms as a delayed period.[1] Afraid to admit pregnancy, they held out a vain hope that some magical force would make their pregnancy disappear. The following excerpts illustrate their denial of reality, which postponed pregnancy confirmation:

> I was four weeks overdue. I was very depressed and was crying almost everyday. I was upset that I had given life to something and it has started growing inside of me and I couldn't make some sort of magic wish to make it go away. I kept hoping that I'll miscarriage. I kept hoping if I sort of exercise too much, maybe something would happen and it will go away and I would not have to face the fact that I really was pregnant.

> *   *   *

---

[1] In a British national survey of women who sought "very late abortions" (at a gestational age of twenty weeks or more) during 1981 and 1982, Joseph (1985) found that 62 percent of these abortions were attributed to reasons that included denial of pregnancy, apprehension about the procedure, indecision, financial difficulties, and a change in the woman's personal relationship. In a national survey of 1,900 women, Torres and Forrest (1988) found that of the women who had late abortions (at 16 or more weeks' gestation) 71 percent attributed their delay to not having realized they were pregnant or to difficulty in arranging the abortion.

> I knew I got pregnant the minute he discharged in me, but I was so mixed up and hysterical that I kept putting the pregnancy test off for six weeks after I missed my period. I tried not to think about it. I thought, "Oh, my period is going to come, it'll come." I kept talking to myself, "Don't worry about it, it'll come." But it was not there the one day, it wasn't there the next day, it still had not come.

> Finally, I had to tell my friend that my periods are six weeks late. She decided for me to go to the drug store. I was too scared to go, because I was afraid to face the fact that the druggist will come to me and actually say to me, yes, you are.

Three women delayed seeking confirmation of their pregnancy because of the possible embarrassment of an internal examination. Two women could not get an early appointment, and another two delayed confirmation because they were not quite sure what exactly they should do with the pregnancy, as one woman stated:

> I waited for eight weeks before I went for the pregnancy test. I knew I was pregnant, but I just had to figure out what I was going to do about it. When I pretty well knew what I was going to do, I went to my doctor.

The above finding underscored the tendency of a substantial proportion of women who persisted in the denial of pregnancy despite their prompt recognition of symptoms.[2] The implications of this finding are worrisome in that delayed verification scarcely allows a woman time for a reasoned consideration of alternatives in dealing

---

[2]Consistent with this observation, a survey of the Hawthorne House girls reported by Rains in his study, "Becoming an Unwed Mother," revealed that over 50 percent of the girls did not have their pregnancy medically confirmed until three months after their initial suspicion (p. 180).

This finding is contradicted by Zimmerman's study, "Passage through Abortion," which found that 75 percent of the sample women had their pregnancy confirmed "as soon as they became aware" of the pregnancy symptoms (p. 97). The discrepancy in the findings could be due to Zimmerman's sample, which consisted of married and single women with previous pregnancies and living children.

with the pregnancy. As the pregnancy advances, she increasingly eliminates the possibility of a first trimester termination by a suction procedure, which is quite simple and safe.

APPROACHING THE PREGNANCY

Upon learning of pregnancy, the women reacted in one of three ways: negative, positive, or mixed.[3]

Negative Reactions

"I was shocked and hysterical, and I cried."

Thirty-eight women (54.3 percent) recalled feeling very upset, distressed, guilty, and embarrassed.[4] They were depressed, with occasional or regular crying episodes and suicidal ideas. They had irritable moods and were withdrawn. They were self-critical, nervous, and irrevocably committed to aborting the pregnancy under

---

[3]Because women's moods and feelings fluctuate through different stages of the pregnancy, it was appropriate to examine initial reactions of these women, that is, soon after the discovery of the pregnancy. The reactions were classified based on their answers to the question: "Now I'm interested in your immediate reactions to your pregnancy. Remembering back, can you tell me as fully as possible what were your feelings and thoughts about it as soon as you became certain that you were pregnant?" Their responses were compared to a check list of nineteen-item statements decribing initial feelings of unmaried women towards pregnancy. The concurrence betwen the two measures was 91.4 percent of the cases. The discrepancy in six cases was resolved using the women's most frequent feelings as well as their attitude expressed elsewhere in the interview. As should be clear, reactions do not occur in a single, discrete chorus, but they are tinged with different shades of feelings ranging from positive to negative emotions. Thus, for the convenience of discussion, women were classified in three distinct, but not strictly mutually exclusive categories based on their dominant feelings and emotions.

[4]Furstenberg (1976) in his Baltimore study of 306 teenage mothers found a slightly higher proportion (60 percent) describing their initial reaction in negative terms.

any circumstances.[5] At times they disavowed the pregnancy and wished it had disappeared by magical wish. Their attitude was, as one woman put it, "I had the feeling I was pregnant, but I didn't want to believe it." Illustrative of the negative reactions are the following excerpts:

> I was shocked when he [the druggist] said it was positive. I was upset at the thought of just what I was going to do. I was so depressed that I was almost tempted to commit suicide. I went for a long walk to a long bridge down to the city, and I was really tempted. I thought, maybe if I throw my purse first it will be easier. I don't know what came over me. I thought it was wrong and had to straighten it all out.
>
> I thought this [pregnancy] was going to change my whole life, my everything--my work. I had no intention of getting married. I thought I'm not going to be six months pregnant walking around my office. I definitely wanted an abortion. I tried to abort myself by taking hot baths, and cod liver oil. I exercised a lot hoping this will do the trick. I would have gone to a quack if I could not get an abortion here.
>
>   *   *   *
>
> My first reaction was, "Oh, hell." I started to cry and was extremely upset and very irritable. I yelled and complained and was nervous being pregnant. I felt very guilty and extremely depressed. I kept thinking I wasn't pregnant. I didn't like to talk to people. It was embarrassing because society puts guilt on you. I just kept thinking day to day, "Oh my God, my tummy is getting bigger and bigger."
>
> Abortion was my first and last and the only option. I was determined that I didn't want this child no matter what, even though I had to go all over the world to get one.

---

[5]Of interest, two-thirds (65.8 percent) of these women had engaged in sex relations when they were unprotected or inadequately protected and were aware of the risk.

Not all women in this category reflected negative emotions with intensity and vehemence. A few women (eight) were quite casual and sober in their reactions as though they anticipated risk involved in unprotected or inadequately protected sex. They appeared unequivocal that abortion was the only acceptable solution. Typical of this reaction is as follows:

> When the doctor told me I was pregnant, I felt depressed for the fact that something I really didn't want it to happen. But I kept it to myself and tried to put an "everything is okay" look on my face. It didn't really bother me or my job. I didn't have any other kind of reactions, like wanted to jump off the cliff type idea, because there is always a solution to your problem, if you are willing to accept the responsibility of what you got yourself into. I think you get yourself into and you get yourself out of it. So it is your problem. I knew that abortion was the easiest way out of not having something tie me down.

Positive Reaction

"Just being young and pregnant for the first time, it was really great."

Although all of these women eventually rejected their pregnancy, twenty-one women (30 percent) greeted its occurrence with positive feelings.[6] They were almost euphoric with pride in themselves for being a "complete woman," as one woman put it. They tended to identify with the pregnancy, usually referring to the fetus as "my baby" and themselves as "mother."[7] They usually did not appear depressed or guilty. If they did, it was mainly because they let their parents down ("what will my parents think of me") or

---

[6]A comprehensive British study involving a random sample of 533 teenage mothers in England and Wales found that 35 percent of the women reacted to pregnancy with positive feelings. The findings are very similar to this study (Simms & Smith 1986: 15).

[7]Nancy Kaltreider (1973) designates this behavior as "sense of baby" syndrome.

because the circumstances would not allow them to have the baby. These women considered other alternatives such as marriage, financial assistance, or support from the boyfriend, but none of them appeared acceptable. Of particular interest is the finding that a little less than one-half (42.8 percent) of these women made consistent efforts at contraception, suggesting that a woman who never desired pregnancy may come to regard it as wanted once it occurs. This, however, does not imply a discrepancy in their behavior, because the experience of being pregnant was a novel experience that was felt at a romantic level. Upon objective assessment of the choices available, feelings were replaced by the reality that continuation of the pregnancy was unrealistic. Typical of positive reactions are these excerpts:

> I felt happy as soon as I found out. I don't know, just being young and pregnant for the first time, it was really great. I was so happy because there was a child inside me and that was growing and I was his mother. It was a great experience. We did plan first to go through with the pregnancy, but we didn't think of the money angle and how we were going to raise the child. My parents wanted me to have an abortion. They started talking to us, "Where are you going to get the money to raise a child . . . ." I was just in a dream and then when I hit reality I realized I had to have an abortion.
>
> *   *   *
>
> When the doctor told me I was [pregnant], I wasn't shocked. I was just hoping I was pregnant, that's all. Then I also felt it was a good feeling, that I had something living in my body, and someone really belonged to me. I wanted to keep it because I really felt good that I was going to have a baby. I thought something miraculous was happening inside of me.
>
> I have a goddaughter who is almost a year old now and when I look at her I think, "Gee, if I can have one of my own like her." I think I was missing something in a way, by not having it.
>
> I was thinking about leaving the city and going somewhere for bringing up the child by myself. Then I thought my mother would be very ashamed of me; my dad would probably kill my boyfriend. I was happy but you

have got all these problems and you have to think what you are going to do. All of a sudden you have to grow up and you have to take care of another human being, etc.

Mixed reactions

"I was sort of happy, but I also hated the thought of a baby."

Eleven women (15.3 percent) seemed confused and ambivalent.[8] At times, they felt depressed and upset. At other times, these feelings were balanced by upswing moods. One minute the idea of continuing the pregnancy appeared feasible, the next minute they abandoned the idea as unrealistic. They seemed to alternate between the sense of the baby identity and detachment. In a sense, they teetered between the fantasy of motherhood and the reality of their circumstances. When they decided to terminate the pregnancy they could do so only by arguing that it was best for the child. The following excerpts exemplify mixed reactions:

When the drugstore told me it was positive, I was frightened not for myself, but for my parents. If I had been alone, I would have the baby and have kept it. I'm the only girl and the white wedding gown is very important to my parents. I loved my baby, but I loved my parents and I knew what they will say and feel. You see so many television programs where the wife walks in and says we are going to have a little one and from then on she is a very special person. Everybody treats her so well. And me, I felt like a scum on the earth, because I wasn't married.

    I was sort of happy, although I wouldn't want to admit it. I felt that I was capable of having life inside of me. It was just incredible, something that God had done

---

[8]This finding is in conformity with that reported by Furstenberg (1976) in his oft-quoted Baltimore study of 306 pregnant, unwed teenage women. The author found that one-fifth of the sample recalled having mixed feelings about getting pregnant (p. 53).

this. But I knew it couldn't last long. So I tried to make myself hate the feelings and manage to depress myself. I was at times very depressed and my sleep was broken.

One night when I did lay there I started thinking and I got all upset. I started thinking how I could get rid of the baby. I had these pills which I knew were strong for me. I took about a pack and a half that night and then I just rolled around the bed in pain. I thought, well, this would do it for sure; this would abort it, but it didn't. All it did was a lot of pain. Then I thought since it had deformed the baby, I had to get rid of it. I should not have done that.

But when I was away from home I could forget about my parents. Any day when I was walking along in the park by myself or with Gary we would have a good time. Gary wanted me to keep the baby. I was also thinking that it would be wonderful to have a baby. But then when I became realistic, I knew there was no way I could keep it and abortion seemed the only way.

*   *   *

I phoned the doctor the next day and he said the test was positive. I said, "Oh no, I just can't possibly be." Before that I had thought, "Well, if I'm pregnant, I'll have an abortion." A couple of hours I had thought, "How did I ever get myself into this and had to get an abortion?" Then I started having feelings, may be silly feelings, womanly feelings or something like, "This is the first time you have been pregnant and there really is a baby that I actually conceived." Then I sort of stopped myself out of these feelings because there was nothing I could do. There were times when I just hated the thought of a baby and then there were times when it seemed so great.

In summary, the majority of the women were initially shaken upon discovery of their pregnancy. Even the women who were having sex relations with minimum or no protection were shocked and distressed. It thus seems obvious that most women were not bent upon getting pregnant. This finding refutes the psychodynamic explanation of out-of-wedlock births that women who become pregnant before marriage are impelled by a deep-seated craving for motherhood or by some special motivation, unconscious or conscious, to seek love or self-worth. The biggest drawback with this viewpoint is that it does not explain the fact that numerous women who engage in unprotected or minimally protected sex do not become pregnant. Further, the psychological theory covers the entire group of women whose pregnancy results from genuine method failure or from the social climate encouraging this behavior. The assumption that this theory makes is analogous to presuming that if a person continues losing jobs he does so because he does not want to work, which is very simplistic reasoning.

ABORTION AMBIVALENCE

These women did not accept abortion with the cavalier attitude that some might contend. One-half (52.9 percent) considered other alternatives before choosing abortion. The other half (47.1 percent) of the women were certain from the moment their pregnancy was confirmed that they wanted to have an abortion, thus claiming no ambivalence.[9] It is reasonable to assume that consideration of other alternatives to abortion signifies a woman's emotional conflict or ambivalence in accepting abortion.[10] Their internal conflict was also gauged by their answers to the question, "Please think back and tell me if you came to the abortion decision after extreme ambivalence, great ambivalence, somewhat ambivalence or not at all." These responses were corroborated with the women's attitudes towards abortion and pregnancy. It should be made clear that their dilemma refers to moral, ethical, and sociopsychological considerations and is

---

[9]Consistent with this finding, Burnell & Norfleet (1987) found in their sample of 178 women who had received therapeutic abortions that nearly half found abortion preferable to other alternatives for future unplanned pregnancies.

[10]Kerenyi et al. (1973) in their study on "Reasons for Delayed Abortion: Results of Four Hundred Interviews" used serious consideration by their respondents of alternatives to abortion as a measure of ambivalence.

Cynthia Martin (1972) in her unpublished thesis on the "Psychological Problems of Abortion for the Unwed Teenage Girl" also used "active" or "bare" consideration by the women of other alternatives as an indicator of their ambivalence. Friedlander et al. (1984) used the conflict resolution model and suggested that consideration of other alternatives before deciding on abortion is an indication that the abortion decision was confusing and conflict-ridden.

not related to their fears regarding the abortion surgery. Based on these measures, 40 percent of them reported great to extreme ambivalence, while three-fifths experienced somewhat or no conflict in their decision (see table 5.1).[11]

Table 5.1
Degree of Ambivalence towards Abortion as Reported by Seventy Women

Degree of Ambivalence	N	Percentage
Extreme	14	20.0
Great	14	20.0
Somewhat	8	11.4
None at all	34	48.6

Their ambivalence was also reflected in the time they took in making a final decision to have an abortion after confirmation of the pregnancy. The more ambivalent woman is likely to take a longer duration in making the abortion decision. Table 5.2 shows that nine out of ten women who experienced great to extreme ambivalence took a long interval (more than one week). Similarly, more than four-fifths who reported slight or no pre-abortion ambivalence took a short interval for such a decision (one week or less following pregnancy confirmation).

---

[11]Other investigators have also reported moderate to considerable difficulties in accepting the decision to have an abortion. The proportion of women experiencing the dilemma varies from a low of 48 percent to a high of 70 percent, depending upon the method used by these studies in defining this experience. See Kerenyi et al. 1973; Lemkau 1988; Martin 1972; Osofsky & Osofsky 1972; Ullman 1972; Wallerstein et al. 1972; Young et al. 1973. A review of British studies also concluded that "few women found the decision to terminate easy." (Handy 1982: 29)

Younger women (18-21 years old) were more likely to be ambivalent about seeking abortion than their older counterparts (22-25 years old). While one-half of the younger women felt great to extreme ambivalence, only one-quarter (26.7 percent) of their older counterparts reported the same intensity of conflict. Likewise, among the older group seven out of ten felt somewhat or no conflict and the comparable percentage among younger women was one-half (see Appendix A table 11).[12] The reason that younger women are more

Table 5.2

Degree of Ambivalence towards Abortion and Time Interval between Pregnancy Confirmation and Abortion Decision

Interval between Confirmation and Abortion Decision	Degree of Ambivalence**	
	Great to Extreme	Somewhat to None
One week or less#		
% = 100	18.4	81.6
n = 49	(9)	(40)
Two to five weeks*		
% = 100	90.5	9.5
n = 21	(19)	(2)
N = 70		

*# Combined for test, $X^2 = 36.64$, df=1   P < .001
** Some cells had zero frequencies so categories were dichotomized

---

[12]This finding is congruent with the observation made by Alma T. Young et al. (1973) in their study of 382 abortion patients. The authors found that "most of the girls who were aged 21 or younger were placed in the distressed group" (p. 63). Other investigtors also confirm that delay in seeking abortion is the characteristic of younger women (Adler 1975; Ashton 1980a; Lemkau 1991; Olson 1980; Osofsky & Osofsky 1972).

susceptible to ambivalence may be a lack of emotional maturity, reality testing (i.e., sense of realism), ego development, and operational thinking, which are in a very general sense considered to come with age.[13] These endowments enable a person to cope with life's events more realistically and less emotionally.

The women's reactions to pregnancy also had bearing on the extent to which they felt ambivalence. Because of emotional commitment and identification with the pregnancy, the women who reacted positively experienced a more intense dilemma in seeking abortion than those who reacted to pregnancy in negative terms. The data show that nine out of ten women who reported positive feelings felt great or extreme conflict, whereas less than one-tenth (7.9 percent) of the women with negative reactions felt great ambivalence. The women with mixed reactions were almost evenly divided between those who experienced great ambivalence and those who felt slight or no ambivalence (see Appendix A table 12).

The woman's choice of the first alternative and her pre-abortion conflicts or ambivalence are highly related. The women who elected abortion as their first choice were less likely to be ambivalent, than those who first considered maintaining the pregnancy (91 percent vs. 11 percent) (see Appendix A table 13).[14] However, the sex partner's support did not ease these women's ambivalence regarding abortion (see Appendix A table 14).[15]

---

[13]Cobliner et al. (1973) consider that the degree of conflict is largely dependent upon the extent to which values stemming from moral principles, beliefs, commandments, and rules of the church are assimilated by the aborting woman. The greater the assimilation of these values, the more mature the individual and the less the conflicts.

[14]These findings are in accord with Bracken et al.'s (1978) complexity model of decision making, which suggests that the abortion decision is more difficult when a women engages in a more delayed consideration of the abortion alternatives and desires pregnancy.

[15]The relationship between partner's support and woman's ambivalence was not statistically significant, although the data tended to show that the women who had supporting sex partners compared to those with no support experienced less conflict about the abortion decision. This finding reflects the inconclusive observations of earlier studies. Bracken et al. (1978), for instance, noted that partner's support eases the abortion decison, whereas Friedlander et al. (1984) found that strong involvement with one's sexual partner tends to influence decision in favor of continuing the pregnancy. In

To give the reader a flavor of the emotional conflict these women experienced, a few excerpts follow:

Women with "extreme" ambivalence appeared mostly to have felt intense emotional conflict, which lasted right up to the time of surgery. They felt coerced by certain key people in their lives or were compelled by circumstances to have the pregnancy terminated or did not receive support that they needed in order to keep it.

> At first, I thought I was going to go through with it. When I went home my father told me, "Would you like to see your mother around or would you like to have your baby?" I was thinking, "Is it right for me to give up the baby? Is it right for me to keep it? Whether I'm doing the right thing? Is it easier to face the death of my child at 3 months or is it harder to give it up when it is mine at nine months?" So it was an argument inside me, which was the better thing to do for me and the baby and for those people whom I love and who love me?
>
> I couldn't get it out of my mind ever. I kept thinking there has got to be a place I can go; there has got to be a way of packing 9 months quick and getting back home, and not have anyone to find out. Then I came to the conclusion there was no possible way that I could hide nine months. I just couldn't write off the calender.
>
> I think the biggest pressure was my mom's health. That really pressed me right down. My dad loves my mom a lot and won't want to see her suffer. He would have looked at me as selfish if I decided to keep the baby. When I was driving up to the hospital I said, "This is the last time my baby and I are going to be together," and it bothered me something awful. I felt like I was going to cry. And when I got there and just before the surgery, I just kept saying, "Don't put me under sleep; just give me two more minutes."

---

agreement with Friedlander, Rosen (1990) found in a study of 432 unmarried women aged 18 and under that their male partners had more influence on the decision favoring continuance of the pregnancy.

And nobody was willing to give it to me. I said, "You have signed in a way, June, it is over; it was just about to be done."

*   *   *

First, I thought of marrying the guy, but he got cold feet. I then started to weigh all the odds and ends and thought that I could not go through the pregnancy for nine months and give up the baby. If I went through it my parents would eventually know and it would be hazardous to their health.

Even as I went for a check up for the abortion, I was trying to contemplate some other ways of getting out of it and was trying to have the baby. I was decided and undecided. I thought of keeping it. Financially, it might have been a squeeze but I might have been able to afford it, but mentally the strain would have been too heavy. When I came for my abortion appointment, even then I was not decided. In my mind one time I wanted abortion, other times I hated to give up the life I started.

Women having "great" ambivalence generally experienced quite strong conflicts, which may have lasted until abortion. But they were able to attenuate its intensity before they went in for surgery through adaption to reality. They reconciled with the circumstances and came to terms with the idea that it was not possible to keep the pregnancy.

There was quite a struggle because I was not sure if you consider it a person, and therefore I was killing it. Or it was a blob of protoplasm. I thought of keeping it, but again my parents would have found it. I did not want to hurt them.

I decided on abortion the day I found definitely that I was pregnant. But all along in the back of my mind I kept thinking, "Oh, gee, I don't know whether I should have an abortion or not." But I knew that was the only thing I could do. I would not have it, had it been under completely different circumstances. These thoughts kept occurring in my mind right up to the abortion.

*   *   *

For the first few days I thought about all the different things I could zero in on. Whether or not to have an abortion, whether or not to keep the baby, whether I should moveaway for a year. I thought of keeping the baby, but I knew I couldn't bring it up properly on my own. The best thing seemed to be an abortion.

When I first thought of having an abortion I kept saying no to myself that I shouldn't have one. But then I would say to myself, "Am I doing the right thing; am I killing someone, am I doing the best thing for my baby and me?" Then finally I had straightened out and said, "It is the only thing to do, it is the best way."

"Somewhat" ambivalent women went through the dilemma, but its intensity and regularity were limited. They considered other alternatives but did not allow themselves to dwell upon them too long and soon came to grips with the reality of the situation.

I thought about other alternatives before deciding on abortion. I first considered marriage, but didn't have much choice in that matter. My boyfriend didn't say anything. I knew I could not support the baby. I just couldn't see what else I could do.

I was not sure whether it [abortion] was right thing to do. I couldn't sort of ease my mind on this. Finally, I convinced myself that this was the best thing for me.

*   *   *

I couldn't decide--whether I wanted to have the baby or have an abortion. I didn't want abortion, because I was kind of thinking that it was my baby; it was my or our fault that it had happened.

I had about a week of mental struggle. I was so mixed up that I didn't know what to do. I had to think so fast. I felt sad, because it was my baby and I didn't want to get rid of it. But if I had the baby, it would be hard to give up for adoption. If I kept the baby, it wouldn't be fair to it. When I finally made a decision I figured it would be the best thing for the baby.

Women who reported "no ambivalence" were most likely to consider abortion as their first choice. They appeared resolute and unequivocal about their decision. They took less time making up their minds and did not let themselves be swayed by emotions. They had a full appraisal of their circumstances right from the moment they suspected they were pregnant and decided to have an abortion, largely by their own volition.

> My first choice was abortion. My mother was telling me, "Cindy, you can keep the baby if you want to." I love babies, and I would have kept it, but I didn't want to go through the pregnancy and then give it up. I knew abortion was the only choice and the best choice for me and for the baby.
>
> *   *   *
>
> Abortion was my first choice. I made up my mind for abortion even before I went to see my doctor. I considered keeping the child, but only briefly. I realized that I couldn't support the child on my salary. I didn't think I was ready to accept the responsibility of having a child yet. I don't think marriage was a solution, because it was going to force a couple for getting married.
>
> I always liked children. I work with children. But for me to have a child, I didn't think would have been the right thing to do. I wanted to have an abortion even though I had to go to the states, and I didn't care about the side effects of the operation.

The upshot of the above discussion is that these findings repudiate the claim made by anti-abortion groups that women who seek abortion approach it with little or no qualms as they view abortion as an innocuous surgical procedure. It is also not true that every woman who seeks termination of her pregnancy is psychologically distressed. The findings give credence to the notion that certain extraneous factors in each woman's life largely determine who is likely to be ambivalent and who is not.

SHARING THE SECRET

As is evident, pregnancy evoked in these women a variety of emotional responses ranging from euphoria and curiosity to anxiety and panic. Whatever their reactions, they all eventually came to realize that the pregnancy proved to be a serious personal problem. As well, for a substantial proportion of them, the decision to abort produced added mental stress. Given the pressure of emotional and physical strain both within and without, it would appear that having someone who could provide comfort and support was crucial to them. But to alleviate their stress they would probably have to tell somebody about their pregnancy, either because they needed money or social validation of their decision or because they simply wanted to talk out their anxieties and share their feelings, as this woman states:

I was living by myself at the time I discovered my pregnancy. I thought of all the weird things I would do. I really wanted to talk to somebody and I didn't have anybody around.

Another woman expressed her desperate need for comfort:

When I was pregnant I really wanted somebody to comfort me, someone to love me. That was what I needed most then.

Who Were the Confidants?

Upon discovering pregnancy, all of the women first confided in another person. The sex partners were told by four out of every five women (83 percent) (see table 5.3).[16] This does not seem surprising, since most of the women had stable relationships and less than one-tenth had merely casual sex encounters. The next likely person to have been confided in was their girlfriend (64.3 percent).

---

[16]This finding is in complete agreement with the previous studies by Bracken et al. 1974, Henshaw and Kost 1992, Melamed 1975, Friedlander et al. 1984, and Major et al. 1990.

Table 5.3
Persons Respondents Discussed Their Pregnancies with before Abortion Decision

Persons	N	Percentage
Sex Partner	58	83.0
Girlfriend	45	64.3
Parents	11	15.7
Colleague	5	7.1
Sibling	14	20.0

Totals amount to more than 70 because of multiple responses. Percentages were calculated from the number of respondents in the sample, and not the number of responses.

Among kinsfolk, siblings (mostly sisters) were more trusted than parents, 20 percent and 15 percent respectively.[17] Interestingly, of the eleven parents who had knowledge of their daughters' pregnancies, five discovered it through the siblings or through suspicion. Thus, parents were the least likely to be confided in.[18]

---

[17]Henshaw and Kost (1992) also observed in their nationally representative sample of unmarried minors having an abortion that, generally, the older women were less likely than the younger ones to involve their parents in the abortion decision.

[18]These findings correspond to previous studies that noted that far greater reliance is placed on sex partners or girlfriends than on parents (Greenglass 1976; Lee 1969; Major et al. 1990; Martin 1972; Zimmerman 1977). Major et al. reported that most women told their partners (85 percent) or their friends (66 percent) of their abortion. Similar findings were reported by Henshaw and Kost (1992) in their study based on a nationally representative sample of more than 1,500 unmarried minors who

Least popular among those who knew about the pregnancy were the women's colleagues at work (7.1 percent). The reason for telling them had more to do with inescapable circumstances rather than closeness of relationship. All five of these women had recently moved in the city and had no family members or friends around. They had hardly formed closeness with a female friend. Also, three of them were abandoned by their sexual partners on becoming pregnant, and the remainder did not receive support from the male partners. Indeed, they needed to turn to someone at least to find out where they could obtain abortions.

How Did the Key Persons React?

Reactions of trusted people, especially those valued, to the woman's pregnancy and her decision to have an abortion can be significant for easing her ambivalence or conflict and coping with her abortion experience.

Sex partner's reaction

Close to thirty percent (28.6 percent) of the women found their sex partners very supportive.[19]   These men showed deep commitment throughout the crisis and offered to marry or provide financial help.   They were reassuring and felt fully or partiallyresponsible for the pregnancy. They showed a deep concern for the women's well-being. They actively shared in the decision making and were supportive of the women's decision. The following excerpts illustrate these women's perception of their male partners:

> At first he was shocked when he learned about the
> pregnancy.   He was pretty good as for knowing the dates
> and all that. He was cautious about it and felt terribly bad

---

had had an abortion. The authors found that 89 percent of them consulted their partners. Zimmerman found that 65 percent of the women confided in sex partners. Consistent with Lee's findings, none of the women in this study consulted a social worker, a religious, or any professional counselor.

[19]Major et al. (1985) found that of the 247 women who had had an abortion, 34 percent received support from their partners. The partner's support was assessed by whether he accompanied the woman to the abortion clinic.

that it happened. He asked me what I wanted to do. I told
him, I didn't want to have the child, and he wanted to know
more whether abortion would affect me in anyway,
emotionally or physically. I wasn't even worrying about it.
We talked and talked about it and we were thinking on the
same lines. He was more considerate to me than I was to
myself.

*   *   *

I was very fortunate at the time that my boyfriend was very
much a part of it. He first wanted to marry me, and I didn't
because I thought it was no reason for marriage. He was
concerned. As a matter of fact, he was the one who kept
phoning the doctor. He was more worried than I was. I had
fantastic support. If I had been alone in making the decision
and having to go and find the doctor, I think, I'd probably
have been depressed.

Less than one-tenth (8.6 percent) of the women felt that their
sex partners were a little concerned but were largely uninvolved and
distant. These men showed some concern, but only superficially.
Otherwise, they were financially helpful. They took interest in what
the woman wanted to do and endorsed her decision. Typical of their
reactions are the following excerpts:

He felt very guilty about what he was sort of putting me
through. He was also happy and wanted me to go ahead and
have it, which was sort of bad. To me this was romantic
and magic thing inside that we were going to run away from
and live in some cold water.

*   *   *

He was very understanding. He said it was up to me if I
wanted an abortion. He wanted to be sure that I was sure
what I would do. Marriage was not mentioned. He didn't
want to marry. But he said, "If you want to keep the baby,
I would help you as much as I can."

Nearly one-half of the men (45.7 percent) showed a complete
lack of concern for the woman's predicament.   Their attitude was
one of indifference to the female's anguish, for which they held her
responsible. They did not recognize their own involvement in the
pregnancy's resolution. Upon learning of the pregnancy, these men

reacted with anger and annoyance and decided to terminate the relationship or continued it merely to seek sexual gratification. The following excerpts exemplify these men's total lack of support:

> He was not serious about it at all and didn't care how I felt about losing the baby. He came out saying, "Oh, I'm easy to get along, you can have an abortion." As soon as he found out I was pregnant, the first thing that came in his head was, "What's it that we now have to worry about? We can have intercourse and we don't have to use any methods." He wasn't interested in anything else.
>
> When I told him, he didn't say anything, really. He just asked me what I was going to do now. He took it so mildly and didn't appear much concerned. It didn't even touch him, not even what I was going through. He didn't make any offer to help. I felt I was made to take all the sufferings on my shoulders. I expected he would comfort me and do his best to get me help

Twelve women (17.1 percent) did not tell the men involved in the pregnancy, either because the relationships lacked emotional commitment or because the men had been casual sexual partners.

In summary, judging from the reactions of the male partners, it appears that seven out of ten women (71.4 percent) went through the crisis with little or no support from the man involved in the pregnancy.[20] One thing seems noteworthy. Whenever men shared

---

[20]This finding is contrary to some studies on male partners of abortion patients, which have shown that sizable proportions of them feel guilt and remorse for risking pregnancy. They feel isolated and left out from the decision making and do care about the turmoil their girlfriends experience (see, for instance, Brosseau 1980; Redmond 1985; Rotter 1980; Shostak & McLouth 1984; Smith 1979). However, other investigators confirm the findings of this study. Martin (1972), for instance, found that three-fourths of the women in her study either received negative support or equivocal support--emotional, physical, or financial. Addleson (1973) reported that more than 60 percent of the male partners were not supportive (p. 144).

in the decision making, they either validated the women's decision or they remained neutral. It was the women who ultimately made the decision to have an abortion.[21]

Support of the male partner might have been reassuring to the women that everything would work out fine in the end and that they would see it through together, but it did not relieve their conflict regarding pregnancy and abortion. This may be true because the ambivalence was related to the women's personal moral and religious convictions, which were not susceptible to change.

Girlfriend's reactions

Nearly all the women (95 percent) who discussed the pregnancy and mental conflict with their girlfriends found them warm, understanding, and helpful. They felt that the female peers were reassuring, not punitive or judgmental. While some girlfriends offered strong advice, they did not control the decision. Because 40 percent of the girlfriends had experienced premarital pregnancies and abortions themselves, they could be empathetic and sensitive, as these women explained:

> If I had been alone, I think I would have thought of the end of the world. But this girlfriend of mine was great. She was sort of stabilizing effect on me so that I was not half as upset as I think I would have.
>
> *   *   *
>
> My girlfriend said it could happen to anyone and she gave me a lot of support. I said I was certainly thinking of an abortion and one girlfriend--psychiatric counselor--told me where I could get one in Canada.
>
> *   *   *
>
> I just felt so lonely at the time and I really needed somebody to stand beside me for what I was going through. I felt she was someone I could trust and she turned out to be a very good friend. She was very supportive and understanding. Her sister was in the same situation two years before.

---

[21]In a study of 1000 males who accompanied their pregnant sex partners to an abortion clinic, Shostak and McLouth (1984) concluded that females typically made the final decision (p. 32).

Sibling's reactions

The siblings who were told were older sisters in all but one case, when it was the woman's older brother. Three of the sisters had become pregnant and undergone abortions themselves before marriage. The general response of the siblings was one of initial shock followed by admonition, "See, that's what I have been telling you." These reactions were mostly transient and benign and soon gave way to a display of concern, empathy, and friendly advice favoring abortion. All but one sister kept it a well-guarded secret. This sister informed the parents. Siblings did everything to help the women implement the abortion decision. All fourteen women were unequivocal in their feelings that they were amply helped by their siblings. None of the women felt coerced by their siblings, although they might have been influenced by them in their decision.

Parent's reactions

As mentioned earlier, fifty-nine women did not confide in either parent. The most frequent reason cited was their fear for dire reactions amounting to a total rejection of these women. Their recurring comment was that "They would have thrown me out of the house, or they would have killed or disowned me." Fathers were more feared (33 percent) than mothers (17.2 percent) (see table 5.4). As this woman remarked: "My father would have called me every name under the sun; he is very strict. And my mother would be just mortified." Some women felt that their parents would feel betrayed and hurt. They said that their parents trusted them and believed that they would never compromise with their chastity until marriage. Mothers were just as likely to feel this way as fathers at 39.6 percent and 31.2 percent, respectively. For instance, one woman's father was a social worker whose work dealt with juvenile delinquent girls. She thought her father would be disappointed in her and view her as a "wayward girl--a juvenile delinquent." Another woman said: "My parents had the image of a pure, sweet daughter and marriage in a white gown was a big thing for them."

A third (34.5 percent) of the women felt certain that their parents would have accepted the pregnancy and offered them comfort and support in their predicament, but they tried to avoid hurting their

Table 5.4
Reasons for Not Telling Either Parent of Their Pregnancy
(*Percentage*)

Reasons	Father*	Mother**
Violent and extreme negative reactions	33.3	17.2
Upset, hurt & betrayal	31.2	39.6
Would make them worry, no need to involve them	27.1	34.5
Afraid to be coerced into marriage or full-term pregnancy	8.3	8.6
Not known because parents seperated or divorced or deceased	18.6	1.6

*Percentages are based on forty-eight cases for whom reactions were anticipated by the women. Since eleven women had lost their fathers via death, desertion, or divorce--in many cases even before the women were old enough to know them well--they could not anticipate their fathers' reactions.
**Percentages are based on 58 cases, since one woman had not been living with her mother for quite some time and, therefore, could not reasonably anticipate her reactions to the pregnancy.

parents by keeping their pregnancy a secret. "What they don't know won't hurt them," was their attitude. Mothers were perceived to be more tolerant and accepting than fathers (34.5 percent vs. 27.1

percent).[22] As one woman remarked: "My mother would probably take me under her wings, but my dad is very strict and believes if you have made your bed, you have to lie in it."

Some women were afraid that they would be pressured by their parents into having an abortion, and this fear was attributed equally (8.3 percent) to both parents. In some cases, there was a solid reason for such apprehension, as unmarried sisters who became pregnant had been forced to get married or have an abortion.

It seems, however, that had the women decided to discuss their pregnancy, they were more likely to have done so with their mothers, whom they found less threatening and more tolerant than their fathers. There was another deterrent, however: the mothers would not be able to keep the news from the fathers, as this woman explained: "I wanted to tell my mother, but I knew to tell one meant to tell the other." Interestingly, the eleven women found, much to their surprise, that the mothers who came to know about the pregnancy through the sisters were very helpful, understanding, and comforting.[23] One woman explained:

> My sister had already told my mother. I broke down and was crying. I felt sorry that I had to do this to my mom. She said, "It is okay, don't worry; your father and I are going to stick by you, no matter what." I went upstairs and found she had told my dad. And I didn't want to face my dad after that . . . I felt he shouldn't know about it. Dad

---

[22]In a 1991 nationwide study of 1,500 teenagers who had abortions, Henshaw and Kost (1992) found that the most common reasons the minors gave for not telling their parents were that they wanted to preserve their relationship with their parents and to protect their parents from stress and disappointment. Mothers were much more likely than fathers to be told of their pregnancy and abortion--43 percent vs. 12 percent.

[23]Consistent with the findings of this study, Henshaw and Kost (1992) found in their national survey of over 1,500 unmarried minors having an abortion that the most common reason for not telling their parents about the pregnancy was their fear that their parents would be angry or disappointed. The minors were much more likely to believe that their father would be upset and disappointed about their sexual activity and pregnancy. However, the great majority of parents (mother--87 percent, father--77 percent) were understanding and supported their daughter's decision to have an abortion.

said, "We'll work it out, you don't have to tell anybody. We'll work it out between us and John [her boyfriend]." I really felt much better.

Their parents' reassuring action was quite unexpected for three women. As one of them said:

My mother suspected I was pregnant. She asked me, "Are you pregant?" And I said, "Yes, I am." She said, "If you are not sure don't come out with it." I was scared she'll do something or yell. But she asked me how I felt and said, "Don't get upset, you are not the first one that has done a mistake. Don't forget where your home is." That really made me feel great. I knew she was very upset and crying, but she took it so great. I was very surprised.

Another finding was equally suprising. Most women did not receive any condemnation or disapproval for violating the chastity standards, as most mother knew that their daughters were sexually active but had pretended not to know. However, they feared hostile reactions from their parents upon getting pregnant. This signifies that the double standard still existed, at least in the minds of the women.

Colleague's reactions

The five women who talked about their pregnancy with their colleagues at work did so for a limited purpose. These women already knew that they wanted to have an abortion and therefore did not engage in any discussion or solicit for validation of their decision. They simply wanted to know how they could obtain an abortion.

SUMMARY

Faced with an unwanted pregnancy, an unmarried woman may deny its existence. But she must sooner or later come to grips with the realistic issue of making a decision about the disposition of the pregnancy. Although a majority of the women had their pregnancy confirmed within three weeks of suspicion, a substantial proportion were not prepared to face the reality. They postponed confirmation until four to eight weeks after they recognized the symptoms.

Their immediate reaction to the pregnancy varied from negative to positive to mixed feelings. They were almost evenly divided between those whose immediate reaction was one of unequivocal rejection and those who identified with the pregnancy. Interestingly, although only eleven women consciously desired pregnancy, nearly one-half of the women became involved in it. Thus, one could say that for many of these women the pregnancy was originally unintended, but when it occurred it became a problem pregnancy rather than an unwanted pregnancy.

Abortion was rarely a decision taken lightly. One-half of them considered alternatives before choosing abortion and thus experienced emotional conflicts. Younger women and those who took longer (more than one week) in confirming their pregnancy were more ambivalent. Also, the women who identified with the pregnancy and held conservative attitudes towards abortion experienced a more intense personal dilemma in choosing abortion. The women who considered other alternatives (marriage, unwed motherhood) experienced more conflict than those who elected abortion as their first choice.

Given the pressure of emotional and physical stress occasioned by the unintended problem pregnancy, it would appear that having someone who could provide comfort and support was crucial to these women. Four out of every five women confided in the sex partner; the nex most frequent confidant was a girlfriend. Older sisters were more trusted than the parents. Less than one-third of the sex partners were supportive, leaving seven out of ten women in crisis with little or no support from the man involved in the pregnancy. However, girlfriends were reassuring, understanding, and empathetic. The general response of siblings was one of initial shock and admonition, but this reaction was transient and gave way to a display of concern and support for the women's decision. The fifty-nine women who did not confide in their parents were afraid of negative reactions and hurting parental feelings. Fathers were more feared than mothers. However, the women found, much to their surprise, that mothers who came to know about their pregnancy were very helpful and comforting.

6

Choosing Abortion

It was noted in chapter 5 that for one-half (47.1 percent) of the women the choice of abortion was obvious from the first awareness of the pregnancy. For the other half (52.9 percent), it was a decision made after vacillating and winnowing various alternatives.[1] Evidently, a woman who is displeased about becoming pregnant has three alternatives, besides abortion, to consider: She can carry the pregnancy to term and raise the child as an unwed mother; she can give the baby up for adoption; or she can get married and raise the child. Each alternative involves certain liabilities. No decision is simple for an unmarried woman who does not want to have a baby.

ALTERNATIVES

The women for whom abortion was not the first choice considered raising the child as an unwed mother (34.3 percent) or marriage with the sex partner (18.6 percent).[2] They rejected

---

[1]Cynthia Martin (1972) reported similar findings. Fifty-four percent of her sample women actively considered other alternatives before finally deciding on abortion.

[2]In contrast to raising the child as an unwed mother, marriage appearing as the least popular alternative has been documented by other studies as well (Smith 1973). In a study of unwed mothers by Zelnik and Kantner (1974)

marriage as an unrealistic solution for a variety of reasons. They felt they were not prepared financially or psychologically or that they lacked emotional commitment to the man or did not like the idea of pressuring the man, who might resent them and the child later on. As one woman explained, marital bonds based on a child are fragile and could invite such comments from the man as "I married you because you were pregnant," which could hurt the woman's self-esteem. Most (71 percent) ruled out the possibility of raising a child without a father because it would be burdensome. They said that a child would need a father to share the financial responsibility as well as the day-to-day care. Three women decided against continuing the pregnancy because their personal educational and career goals could be jeopardized by the commitment that child care would impose. Two women felt pressure by their parents to choose abortion. Another two women considered it unfair to bear a child if they were not able to provide the love and attention it would need.

Incidentally, but not surprisingly, none of these women considered having a baby and giving it up for adoption. The reason stated by almost all the women was that relinquishing a baby would cause even greater emotional trauma than abortion. They said that going through a full-term pregnancy would develop a deep emotional attachment to the baby that would be extremely painful to sever. They would prefer to keep the baby if they continued the pregnancy. If they had to surrender the baby for adoption, they feared they would be haunted by the memory for life, as one woman eloquently stated:

> It's hard to give up when you are two or three months pregnant. But I can't imagine to go through the birth and sign papers and say, "Look, someone else can have my baby; he is yours, he is no longer mine." I would think the rest of my life that someone is walking around, someone is bringing up my child the way they wanted to, not the way I would have brought him up . . . I think it is better for a girl to have an abortion than to have to give her baby up for adoption.

---

the proportion of women who married as a result of pregnancy was 15.3 percent, compared to 70 percent who maintained the pregnancies in order to raise the babies themselves. In the Baltimore study of unwed adolescents by Furstenberg (1976), only 20 percent of them married because of their pregnancy.

Some women opposed adoption because they would worry whether or not their children had been adopted into good homes and were being raised properly. They were afraid their children might languish in foster homes, as this woman stated:

> I didn't want anything to do with adoption. I know too many friends of mine whose children have been in foster homes and they have been sent from pillar to post. My cousin, my mother's sister's daughter, was put in a foster home in England . . . and she grew up there and nobody wanted her, because she was not a very attractive child. It is funny that people go shopping for babies; they want a pretty little girl or a pretty little boy.

The anguish and the emotional pain as an aftermath of adoption feared by these women is corroborated by millions of unmarried mothers who relinquished their babies because their circumstances did not allow them to assume parenthood.[3] Many of them have wished in retrospect they had raised the babies themselves. Thus, the most appropriate solution to unintended pregnancies seems to lie not in banning abortions, but in providing needed resources and social support to unmarried women who wish to raise their children.[4]

Why Abortion?

As noted, these women became pregnant because they were unwilling or unable to avoid sexual activities that were not adequately protected. However, whatever their motives, abortion was not the inevitable outcome of every pregnancy. More than one-half of the women were orientated toward the child, which refutes the

---

[3]Sachdev 1989: 19.

[4]Lundberg and Plotnick (1990) measured the influence of state welfare, abortion, and family-planning policies on decisions concerning premarital pregnancy. Using a probability sample of white females (14-21), the authors' analysis shows that higher welfare benefits reduce the likelihood that pregnant adolescents will marry before bearing their children and that restrictive policies on the public funding of abortion will more likely force teenagers to carry the pregnancy.

assumption that women who seek an abortion outright reject motherhood.   Obviously, some women were unambiguously committed to abortion, while others considered other alternatives before deciding on abortion. The specific reasons that motivated these women finally to favor abortion are the focus of this section.

Each woman was asked: "Could you say that under certain circumstances, you would not have had an abortion and instead have delivered the child?" Some women gave more than one reason, but certain reasons predominated, which are shown in table 6.1. As will be seen, the most frequently occurring reason for seeking abortion centered on the man involved in the pregnancy.[5] That is to say, two-thirds of the women attributed their abortion to either the fact that matrimonial commitment from their sex partners was not possible or to the fact that they did not receive from the man the support necessary to have the child and raise it. There were several reasons. Some women were interested in shotgun marriages, but their partners

---

[5]Consistent with the findings of this study, Elizabeth Smith (1973), in her follow-up study of eighty women who had abortions, observed that the two major reasons for single women to have an abortion were lack of marriage and desire to continue education (p. 577). Osofsky and Osofsky (1972) discovered that the most recurring reasons for abortion among their 250 sample women were related to boyfriend and marital status. Greenglass (1976) found in a Toronto study of a mixed sample that single women were generally motivated to have an abortion for social reasons such as financial factors, pressure from others, poor relationship with the man, and social embarrassment for an out-of-wedlock child (p. 77). Similar to this study, Zimmerman (1977) observed that the most common reasons the women in her study gave for abortion were the lack of support from male partners and parents (p. 139). Murphy et al. (1983) also confirmed earlier research. Using sophisticated analysis for predicting the likely outcome in the event of an unplanned pregnancy among 106 sexually active women aged 15-30, the authors concluded that women choosing an abortion were more likely than those who would choose to deliver to perceive lack of material and psychological support for the child from another person such as their mothers or the male partners. The other factor associated with prediction that an unplanned pregnancy would be aborted was the perceived negative consequences for an out-of-wedlock motherhood. See also Bracken et al. 1978b, Fischman 1977.

Table 6.1
Dominant Reasons as Reported by Seventy Women for Seeking Abortion

Dominant Reason	N	Percentage
Fear of parental adverse reaction	7	10.0
Absence of male partner's support or love relationship	25	35.7
Marriage with sex partner not possible	21	30.0
Unprepared for motherhood (educationally, financially, and/or vocationally)	13	18.6
Never liked children	2	2.9
Fear of social disgrace and embarrassment	2	2.8

saw this as a trap and terminated the relationships.[6] In some cases the men offered to marry, but the women turned them down, thinking that their partners might accuse them of using pregnancy as a set-up for marriage or that they might be marrying out of pity rather than love. Ten sex partners were married and living with their spouses or separated and not legally available for a remarriage. One-tenth of the women did not wish to continue the pregnancy because they feared their parents would be emotionally upset and might denounce them, if discovered, as this woman explained:

---

[6]Contrary to popular impression, marriage as an escape from unwed motherhood was more likely to be considered by older women (22-25) than their younger counterparts (18-21) (76 percent vs. 33 percent).

I destroyed the life that I really wanted because of my mother, and that was really selfish. I was more worried about my mother's feelings than my feelings towards the child. I was selfish, because I was worried what she might think of me, she would degrade me, and I would never be the same under her eyes as I did before.

Fear of embarrassment and social disgrace were the reasons given by two women for seeking abortion. The insignificantly small number of women fearing social disgrace reflects the growing tolerant attitude of society toward unwed motherhood. All of these women were describing aspects of the same group of reasons, the central focus of which is the overwhelming prospect of raising a child given their single status and unrealized educational and vocational aspirations.[7]   Only two of these women expressed a complete repugnance for children and motherhood. They described children as a "nuisance," "funny looking creatures," and "a big liability who destroy fun in the life of a couple." Thirteen women did not find the circumstances propitious for assuming motherhood. Thus only one-fifth of the women were categorically committed to having an abortion under any circumstances.[8]

These women's perspective on the reason for abortion did not change when asked whether, if they were to make the decision over again, they do the same. Only two women were not sure that they had made the right decision. That these women would make the same decision again does not imply a lack of regret. It simply means that they fully assessed the motivating factors after the fact the same way they had done when facing the problem pregnancy. In fact, all of these women stressed the words "under similar circumstances" in justifying their decision.

---

[7]Similar to this study, Torres and Forrest (1988) found in a national survey of abortion patients, referred to earlier, that more than three-quarters chose abortion because having a baby would interfere with their job or schooling or they did not want to be a single parent.

[8]This finding that most unmarried women do not view abortion as another method of fertility control was supported by another survey by Ryan & Dunn (1988) of college students (n = 704) from two universities in the southeastern U.S. The results indicated that the majority of these students would rather choose to marry in the event of an unplanned pregnancy than to abort.

ATTITUDES TOWARD ABORTION

A woman's attitude toward abortion may significantly determine how she approaches her decision to seek termination of her pregnancy and how she reacts afterward. As discussed in chapter 3, the attitudes toward abortion the women held prior to the pregnancy were assessed using a self-report measure or a Likert Scale consisting of twenty-six items. The women were classified as having a liberal attitude (25.7 percent receiving the highest one-third of scores), conservative attitude (27.1 percent receiving the lowest one-third of scores) or moderate attitude (47.1 percent receiving the middle one-third of scores).[9] Judging from this percentage distribution, it seems that the women do not represent one extreme position, a finding that agrees with the Canadian and U.S. national surveys.[10] It is generally accepted that a woman's attitude, however disapproving, undergoes a revision when she is herself faced with a problem pregnancy.[11] This phenomenon is synonymous with "situational ethics" implying that individuals become the ultimate and autonomous judge of their life when they wish to take advantage of the situation they are in. This means that persons find it convenient to justify the violation of their norms when they wish to engage in a behavior that they disapproved for others. A few women volunteered the information that they were opposed to abortion under any circumstances until they got pregnant and were confronted with this choice. Because attitudes may differ depending on the circumstances or on "value specific situations" (that is, when the person is not

---

[9]The total numerical scores range from a low of 57 to a high of 118 with larger scores signifying a more permissive attitude toward abortion than the numerically smaller scores The range was split into three equal parts.

[10]Sachdev 1988: 70, 475.

[11]Singh and Williams (1983) examined data from a 1977 national opinion survey of 793 adult respondents regarding their attitudes and behavioral intentions about abortion. The authors found that a sizable proportion of them would approve of abortion for others but would not opt for abortion themselves.

facing the situation herself), one must be cautious in comparing the results between studies on women who have undergone abortion and those conducted on populations that have not.[12]

There was no difference between younger women and their older counterparts in their attitude towards abortion (see Appendix A table 15).[13] Similarly, education did not affect the attitude of these women (see Appendix A table 16).[14] However, the women's attitudes towards abortion were influenced by their religious beliefs. Religiously devout Protestant women were more approving of abortion than devout Catholics. Jews and women with no religious affiliation were more favorable toward abortion than either Protestants or Catholics. However, nonpracticing Catholic women were more liberal than nonpracticing Protestant women. This finding shows it is more important for a Catholic woman to be influenced by religion in her attitude towards abortion than it is for a Protestant woman.[15]

---

[12]Abortion attitudes vary greatly depending on the situation. Surveys on abortion show that hard reasons such as the mother's health, deformed children, incest, and rape are more acceptable for abortion than soft reasons such as financial plight or not wanting more children (Arney & Trescher 1976; Ebaugh and Haney 1985). Similarly, people are less approving of abortion if affective items such as "fetus's right to life" are included in the survey (Peyton et al. 1969: 185).

[13]Previous studies are equivocal as to whether age affects attitude toward abortion (Michelman 1971; Westoff et al. 1969; ASA 1968; Ebaugh and Haney 1985).

[14]Other studies have also noted that in the last few years, especially since the late 1970s, education has lost its impact on abortion attitudes (Ebaugh & Haney 1985; Skerry 1978). However, Szafran & Clagett (1988) disagree with this observation. Convinced by their analysis of the American public attitude toward abortion since 1978, the authors claim that "education continued to be a strong predictor of abortion attitudes" (p. 271).

[15]The only other study that arrived at a similar conclusion was by Westoff et al. (1969). They observed that "whether one is more or less Catholic is of greater significance for attitudes towards abortion than whether one is more or less active in any Protestant denominations" (p. 20). Other investigators support the findings of this study that attitudes toward abortion are positively related to religious devoutness. The association is strongest for Catholic women and weakest for Jewish and non-affiliated women. The attitudes of those who belong to fundamentalist Protestant denominations are more similar to Catholic attitudes (ASA 1968; Ebaugh & Haney 1985; Gabrielson et al. 1971; Granberg & Granberg 1985; Lee 1969;

The women's pre-abortion ambivalence was significantly influenced by their attitudes. The women who were more favorable toward abortion had progressively less conflict about seeking termination (see Appendix A table 17).

Facing the Surgery

Having reached the decision to have the pregnancy terminated, a woman now confronts the reality of the surgery. It is true that any surgical procedure, minor or major, is likely to evoke fear and anxiety, which may be justifiable or may be exaggerated because they stem from misinformation or lack of information about the mechanics of the surgery. These apprehensions may add to the woman's mental stress.

Because the medical fears of women seeking abortion have rarely been investigated by previous studies, it is not known how many women reverse their decisions to abort because of such fears. This study will not answer this question, but it will examine the doubts and apprehensions its respondents experienced and compare them with the women's actual experience with the abortion surgery. The answer to these questions are of immense significance in terms of developing a sound counseling and educational service for abortion patients.

Forty-eight women (68.6 percent) reported having fears and doubts about the procedure (see table 6.2).[16] Two-thirds of them

---

Maxwell 1970; Rossi 1967; Szafran & Clagett 1988). Among U.S. women who obtained an abortion in 1984 and 1985, Henshaw and Silverman (1988) also found that women with no religious affiliation had a higher abortion rate than those who claimed some religious affiliation. Catholics were as likely to seek termination as were non-Catholics. However, Protestants and Jews were less likely to do so.

[16]This finding corresponds very closely to those of Osofsky and Osofsky (1972), who reported that of the 250 abortion patients they studied, two-thirds were either moderately or very fearful of the abortion procedure, while one-third were not at all fearful (p. 55). Kimball (1970), too, observed a wide range of ignorance among his forty patients about the procedure, which contributed to many of their fears and anxieties (p. 295). An English study by Ashton (1980a) noted that 42 percent of the women in his sample were frightened of the procedure.

Table 6.2

Apprehensions and Concerns Regarding Abortion Procedure as Reported by Forty-Eight Women

Apprehensions and Concerns	N*	Percentage*
How is an abortion done?	32	67.0
Will it cause internal damage?	30	62.5
Is it painful?	21	36.5
Does it cause psychological after-effects?	4	8.3
How long does it take?	10	20.8
What do they do with the fetus?	3	6.2
When can I resume sex?	3	6.2
Can it cause death?	8	17.0
When can I resume normal routine?	2	4.1
Will the scars show?	2	4.1
Would the hospital keep my abortion confidential from my parents?	3	6.2
What precautions do I take following abortion?	2	4.1
When do the periods resume?	2	4.1

*The total number of responses exceeds the number of respondents, i.e., 48, who reported fears and doubts because some of them gave more than one answer. Also, the percentages are based on the number of respondents, and not responses.

were completely ignorant about or had a vague idea of the actual surgical procedure, as this woman exemplified:

> I was scared of not knowing what they would do. I wanted to know what they would do inside of me when they would take me in the operating room.

One woman found that instead of assuring and comforting her, the operating physician confirmed her fears. Nevertheless, she did not mind the physician's lack of sensitivity, because she felt that providing an abortion was an obliging act on the part of the medical personnel:

> I was quite scared. The doctor in the hospital told me right off the bat, "Everybody probably has told you how simple it is, but it is not as simple as you might think." That scared me because my girlfriend who had her abortion told me it was relatively simple. Also, my doctor [who confirmed her pregnancy] told me that I will be in and out the same day. So I got concerned about what this doctor had said. None of the doctors explained to me what was to be done. But I didn't expect them to explain it to me, since they were doing me a favor.

In addition to the women's concern for the mechanics, their most common fear (62.5 percent) related to damage that the surgery might cause, resulting in permanent sterility. For some women this concern was strong enough to delay their decision, while others were prepared to take this risk because they could not bring the child into the world:

> I was indecisive because I was wondering if I could have any more kids after that. That was the real reason that kept me from going into it right away.
>
>   *   *   *
>
> I was worried that abortion might damage my inside, but I thought I could always adopt children who did not have homes or are without love. I would like to have a couple of kids of my own, but I felt if my inside was damaged I could probably get the same feelings by adopting some.

Physical pain was the concern of one-third of the women. They did not know if abortions were performed under general or local anesthesia. A little less than one-fifth of the women feared death. The following woman rejected her pregnancy from the moment she suspected it, but the fear of death deterred her from having the abortion surgery. She mustered her courage as she checked into the hospital, but was overtaken by her fears. However, she found it was too late to change her mind:

Abortion was my first choice. But I considered keeping it, because I thought I was going to die. But I checked into the hospital. The next day I chickened out. On the day of the operation I was up four o'clock in the morning running up and down the hall. I told the head nurse, "I'm chicken, and I don't want it. I want to go home. I can't go through with it." The nurse calmed me down and said there was no way out of it now.

Some women were not sure how the abortion would impact on their lives, as this woman asked:

Would I be able to go through with this? What is the first thing I'll think of myself when I wake up? Will I be able to go through this all my life thinking to myself, well, I had an abortion? Will I be able to tell my husband if I was to get married? Is it something I had to live with the rest of my life?

Other concerns related to resumption of periods and sex life, precautions following the abortion, and confidentiality of the records. Two women were concerned that there would be scars on their bodies. They were afraid that their friends would see the scars and thus discover that they had had an abortion. They suggested that a premarital pregnancy was more acceptable among their peers than abortion, as this woman said:

I didn't want anything to show that I had an abortion. If any of my friends found out that I had an abortion, I could just tell them that I miscarriaged it and there would be no way they could prove me wrong. Going through with the pregnancy would be alright in the eyes of my friends. But a lot of my friends considered abortion as murder and I didn't feel that way. They would think I killed my child by going through with the abortion.

Three women wanted to know if the fetus had life and how it was disposed of after it was expelled from the uterus. These women had heard some horrifying stories regarding the expelled fetus.

SUMMARY

The choice of abortion was not simple for a majority of the women. They arrived at a decision after considering various alternatives. Athough one-half of them decided on abortion from the first awareness of pregnancy, no solution was easy for these unmarried women. Marriage appeared to be an unrealistic choice, either because they were not prepared, psychologically or financially, or because they lacked the necessary emotional commitment. Most ruled out the possibility of raising the child as an unwed mother. None of the women considered adoption as an alternative; they thought it would be more emotionally traumatic than any alternative.

The most frequent reason for seeking abortion centered on the man involved in the pregnancy. Two-thirds of the women attributed the abortion decision to the fact that either matrimonial commitment from their sex partners was not possible or they did not receive from the man the support needed to have the child and raise it. More than one-half of the women were orientated towards the child, which refutes the assumption that women who seek an abortion reject motherhood. These women's perspective on the reason for abortion did not change when they were later asked whether they would make the same decision again.

Using a self-report measure or a Likert Scale consisting of twenty-six items, the women were classified as having a liberal attitude (25.7 percent), a conservative attitude (27.1 percent), or a moderate attitude (47.1 percent) toward abortion. Thus, the women did not represent one extreme position. There was no difference between the younger women and their older counterparts in their attitude toward abortion. Education did not affect the attitudes of the women either. However, the women's attitudes were influenced by their religious beliefs. Religiously devout Protestant women were more approving of abortion than active Catholics. However, nonpracticing Catholic women were more liberal than nonpracticing Protestant women. This means it is more important for a Catholic woman to be influenced by religion in her attitude towards abortion than it is for a Protestant woman. The attitude towards abortion influenced the degree of conflict these women experienced before termination. The women with more favorable attitudes had progressively less conflict.

More than two-thirds of the women reported having fears and doubts about the procedure. Their most common fear related to possible damage to the reproductive system. Some women were not sure how the abortion would affect their lives.

7

A Day in the Hospital:
The Final Act

When an unmarried woman comes to the hospital,[1] willy nilly or
determined, for the final act of surgery, she confronts the totally alien
environment of the medical world. The hospital routine, her new role
as a patient, the fears and anxieties of the surgical procedure--all can
be emotionally stressful. At this juncture the attitude of the service
providers is immensely critical in determining how the woman reacts
to the surgical procedure, in both a psychological and a physical
sense.[2] The providers may take a grim view of her conduct, because
she violated the society's moral codes by being pregnant before
marriage and now seeks to erase the evidence of her "guilt" by
terminating the pregnancy. Research shows that the providers
exercise discretion in the way they provide abortion services to

---

[1]In Canada, most abortions are performed in an accredited hospital in
all provinces except Quebec, where abortions are also performed in the
doctor's clinic. Recently, clinics are being opened in a few provinces such
as Nova Scotia, Newfoundland, and Saskatchewan by Dr. Henry
Morgentaler in the wake of the Supreme Court of Canada's ruling of 1988
that declared the federal abortion law unconstitutional.

[2]Greenglass (1976) found in her Canadian study that the women who
view their doctor's attitudes as negative or neutral tend to have adverse
psychological reactions after the abortion. Adverse psychological reactions
were described as feeling guilty, worried, unfeminine, or sad and having
low self-esteem (p. 87).

women of different socioeconomic and personal characteristics.[3] Some investigators of Scottish women's experience report that obtaining an abortion was a matter of luck for them, because of the variation in the physician's responses, depending on their attitudes toward women seeking termination.[4] Conditioned by the negative attitudes in her environment, an unmarried woman can be extremely sensitive to the attitudes of the staff around her. Even the most inadvertent or perfunctory attitude can be interpreted by her as censuring behavior. The following statement by a 22-year-old woman captures the unmarried women's feelings of low self-image and degradation when they seek abortion:

> It was very, very lonely for me. I felt it was like a federal prison and I was there because I did something wrong. I felt that the staff were being nice to me because they had to be. Every time they came near me I just wanted to swallow up myself in shame. It was an awful feeling. I was very ashamed of myself.

STAFF ATTITUDES

This chapter will discuss the attitude of the physicians and nurses of three hospitals as perceived by these women during their stay. It will also examine their experience with the counseling and family planning services they received prior to and after the abortion. A few women offered suggestions, which will also be discussed later in the chapter.

Physician's Attitudes

The women selected one of three categories to describe the attitudes of the doctors in the hospital: negative (i.e., uncaring, moralizing, critical, threatening, humiliating, sarcastic, rejecting), positive (i.e., pleasant, supporting, caring, nonjudgmental), or neutral

---

[3]Nathanson 1985; Tietze, 1979.
[4]Farmer 1973; MacIntyre 1977.

(i.e., indifferent, distant, mechanical). The largest proportion of the women (65.7 percent) perceived the doctors' attitudes as negative or neutral; only one-third saw their attitudes as positive (see table 7.1).

Table 7.1
Attitudes of Doctors and Nurses as Perceived by the Women
(*Percentage*)

Attitude	Doctors %	Nurses %
Negative	44.3 (31)	8.6 (6)
Positive	34.3 (24)	75.7 (53)
Neutral	21.4 (15)	15.7 (11)

One might argue that these women could misinterpret their doctor's attitudes and that therefore what they perceived was probably a misconception of reality. To rule out such a possibility and to ascertain the accuracy of their perceptions, the women were asked to elaborate on the category they chose to describe how the hospital staff regarded them. Typical of the doctor's *negative* attitudes as viewed by the women are the following excerpts:

I had a vaginal infection after my abortion and so I went back to the hospital to have it checked. There was a student doctor and he was very abrupt with me. Then a doctor came in with another student and he kept asking me if I had intercourse and I said, "No," because I didn't. And they asked me about at least five times. They obviously thought I was lying and that annoyed me. Then I asked him when

> I can have sexual intercourse and he said, "Just wait until
> your next period. Do you think you can wait that long?" I
> felt so low and humiliated.
>
> *   *   *
>
> I wanted to have an abortion and a doctor came in and he
> blasted at me, "Oh, so you are in trouble now and you want
> to get rid of it, eh?" I started crying.
>
> *   *   *
>
> I did not like the way this doctor examined me. He was
> rough like I was just another whore. As soon as he entered
> the room and without introducing himself, he said right off
> the bat, "Do you want the pill?" and he started to examine
> me very rough. I felt like I was being raped. I was very
> upset and cried in fact in front of him.

Those who saw the doctors as *neutral* felt that they were not hostile
or threatening but that they did not seem interested or concerned
either. The comment most commonly used by these women was "so-
so."

A few of the women described the doctors' attitudes as
positive. They felt they had been treated like other patients who came
to the hospital for other ailments. These women had expected that
they would be segregated and kept out of sight from the rest of the
patients. The following excerpts exemplify the positive attitudes of
doctors as perceived by these women:

> They seemed to be nice; they were generally interested in
> what I had to say, especially when I was talking about my
> nerve.
>
> *   *   *
>
> The doctor was nice. My voice was shaking and he said, "I
> know you are nervous; you don't have to be, you are among
> friends." I was sort of groping for someone to tell me,
> "Well, don't worry."

Nurse's Attitudes

Nurses were viewed as far less negative in their attitudes
toward these women than doctors. Far more women (75.7 percent)
viewed the nurses' attitudes toward them as positive than they did the

doctors' (see table 7.1). They described the nurses as committed, supporting, empathetic, nonjudgmental, and concerned. A few excerpts illustrate this view:

> I had expected a terrible time and to be looked down upon. I was surprised at how kind the nurses were, in spite of the fact that they must be getting sick and tired of seeing young people in good number for abortion. They had a high degree of professionalism and were above personal beliefs.
>
> *   *   *
>
> They all seemed very nice, very kind and considerate. It was as if I was there for another operation--to have my tooth pulled out, something that seemed not very different.
>
> *   *   *
>
> They were very comforting, motherly types and very, very helpful. They were so non-committal and easy going. I sometimes wondered if they knew what they were doing.

Those who perceived the nurses as having *negative* attitudes toward the unmarried women comprised less than one-tenth. They described them as hostile, moralizing, and stigmatizing. They thought the nurses were more accepting of abortion patients if they were married women than if they were single. Generally, these attitudes were characteristic of older nurses.[5] Their most typical comments were:

> The younger nurses were nice. They were talking to me if I wanted an abortion or not. But the older nurses looked down upon you. Some of them were cranky and didn't pay any attention to you. Their attitude was, "Oh, you can wait."
>
> *   *   *

---

[5]Confirming this finding, Brown et al. (1971) observed in their survey of nurses at the University of Washington Hospital that "there was a gradient of increasing support from single to married to widowed to separated-widowed nurses for abortion . . ." (p. 1416).

My girlfriend came to visit me and a nurse remarked of her,
"Is she one of them?" meaning who get busted and get
abortions.

*   *   *

Nurses didn't consider you a sick patient as they did the
other patients, because they thought you were getting an
abortion and there was nothing to it; you were going to live.

One-sixth of the women (15.7 percent) considered the nurses'
attitudes as *neutral*, that is, indifferent, mechanical, and uninvolved,
but nonjudgmental and strictly perfunctory.   Typical of their
comments are the following:

It was their job. They were businesslike. They were not
pleasant, but not pushing either. They knew they didn't like
to do what they were doing.
*   *   *
They were not rude, but were not friendly either.

Previous investigations on the physicians' and nurses' attitudes toward
their participation in the abortion surgery support the findings of this
study. They consistently reported resentment and hostility of doctors
toward abortion patients, because of their dissatisfaction with this type
of work. They found that the doctors in their studies experienced
anxiety and guilt feelings attributable to ambivalence regarding their
medical role of saving lives.[6]   A well-known and oft-quoted
psychiatrist, Kummer (1967), provides a psychoanalytic reason for the
doctors' and nurses' negative attitudes toward women requesting
abortion. He believes that as abortionists, doctors engage in an act
that is contrary to the mandate of the healing profession and thus
activate their "deeply buried, hostile impulses." In one sense, they
blame the woman for their discomfort with the abortion surgery.
Their hostility and uncaring attitude is simply their way of retaliating
against her.[7]

---

   [6]See, for instance, Char and McDermott 1972; Greenglass 1976; Kane
et al. 1973; Martin 1972.
   [7]Ullman (1972) found in his study of 598 women who had an abortion
at New York Hospital that they complained "they were talked at, treated like

ABORTION COUNSELING

Forty-six women (65.7 percent) received counseling before the abortion from the social worker of the hospital or of the referral agency. The remaining women either missed contact with the social worker or found the counseling service unavailable at two of the three hospitals. Counseling was generally limited, consisting merely of procedural information regarding the functioning of the abortion committees and their decision-making process. Counseling at the referral agency involved providing names of the hospitals and doctors who performed abortion. Contact with the social worker was usually very brief, lasting a few minutes. Not surprisingly, the women did not find counseling to be a helpful and supportive experience. They felt that the social worker was doing a routine task and wished that she had permitted an interpersonal exchange and encouraged them to share their feelings, fears, and doubts, as these women said:

I don't think it was counseling; I think it was a routine thing. She didn't talk about abortion or how I felt.

    *   *   *

I wish I had more time to be able to sit down and tell her exactly about my feelings. I don't think she would understand you unless she understood the whole story.

    *   *   *

It was not really counseling. I just saw her very briefly and she sort of explained to me about the abortion committee and what would happen if I was approved, that sort of thing.

Some women were upset because the social worker was presumptuous, judgmental, moralizing, and condescending. Her attitude reflected insensitivity and contempt for the unmarried women seeking abortion:

She told me, "Now that it is going to be over, think of the positive things." I felt as if I had done something wrong.

    *   *   *

---

numbers rather than people and kept waiting too long and felt the professional staff condemned them" (p. 485).

> She said, "How come you didn't use your diaphragm? You
> should have protected yourself. Why did you get yourself
> into this mess when you knew you were risking a
> pregnancy?"
>
> *   *   *
>
> This counselor was mad at the other patient for having got
> pregnant four times in a row and when I went in she
> chuckled with me, "You are not going to try it again, are
> you?"

Statements like these conveyed condemnation and admonition, which
were likely to evoke anxiety and feelings of rejection. The women
reacted with anger or guilt feelings for being "bad or immoral girls"
or with a sense of humiliation. Some women were shocked to
encounter negative and punitive attitudes from the social worker,
which was in sharp contrast to their expectation. Judging from the
intonation of their voices and other nonverbal manifestations, it was
evident that many of these women resented the social worker. Some
women were subdued in expressing their feelings, while others were
quite vocal in ventilating their sentiments:

> She made me feel really bad that I didn't take birth control
> pills. She looked at me as if she regarded me as a very
> ignorant, stupid little girl who was irresponsible and now
> they had to go to all the trouble to provide her an abortion.
>
> *   *   *
>
> She gave me a lecture, "Why didn't you use anything?
> Didn't you know, you were eighteen?" I felt very bitter and
> against her. With the treatment like that, I felt I shouldn't
> have come there at all. I knew I did a wrong thing by not
> using birth control methods and now her lecture.

Another woman who found her social worker insensitive and
moralizing was quite blunt in expressing her feelings:

> The social worker was a bitch. She didn't care how I felt.
> Her attitude was, "Use protection or marry the guy."

Only seven women (18.5 percent) claimed positive encounter
with their social workers. Four of them had received counseling
from the referral agency. The women in this category felt the

counselor was supportive, concerned, reassuring, and nonjudgmental. A few of their comments on how "great" the counselors were are as follows:

> The counseling was extremely helpful. The social worker was great. She was the first person who put me at ease and reassured me that not to worry about it. She didn't ask me why I wanted an abortion. I was really surprised. I thought she was going to give me a big lecture like you must be careful next time and I had been a bad girl, etc.
>
>   *   *   *
>
> The counselor was very helpful in relieving my fears about abortion and she planned every thing for me including her visit to me before the operation, which I thought was very good.

Post-Abortion Counseling

None of the women sought and received counseling after the abortion. When asked if they wanted counseling sometime following abortion, fifty-eight women (83 percent) replied in the negative and twelve (17 percent) stated that they could have used the service, if available.

The reasons given by the fifty-eight women for not wanting to have counseling were as follows. Twenty women (34.5 percent) stated that they did not need counseling because abortion had had no adverse effects on them. Another thirty-five (60.3 percent) were able to share their feelings and experiences with their close friends, who provided the needed support. Three women were not interested in post-abortion counseling because they were trying to forget the entire experience and did not want to talk about it. The fact that only a very small number of them wanted to repress their abortion experience refutes the impression that the women who undergo abortion develop resistance to sharing their experience for fear of getting upset. Therefore they are usually not available to follow-up studies. On the contrary, a large majority of them (77.3 percent) did express a need for someone with whom to discuss their experience and feelings after abortion. Although none of the fifty-eight women gave their dissatisfaction with pre-abortion counseling as the reason for their disinterest in professional counseling, it is possible that had their experience with the social worker been satisfying, their enthusiasm for professional counseling might have been more clearly evident.

Clearly then, most women experienced a judgmental, moralizing, and hostile environment in the hospitals, which illuminated stigma associated with abortion among unmarried women. Although this study did not plan to assess the impact of such negative experience on the women's psychological reactions, a few researchers have provided evidence that the attitude and behavior of the service providers affect the nature of the woman's psychological adjustment afterward.[8]

In this study, nurses were the only key hospital staff who treated the women with dignity and courtesy and provided comfort and support. If these women were anxious and nervous during their stay at the hospital, it was natural. To begin with, an unwanted pregnancy presented an emotional crisis of some sort and required contact with a physician for its termination. Then the doctor's negative and stigmatizing attitude heightened their anxiety and sensitivity. In an attempt to underline the significance of the hospital environment in affecting the emotional and physical health of a woman, these women offered certain suggestions toward creating a benign and less threatening experience for unmarried abortion patients.

By far the most frequent suggestion made was the improvement of the hospital clinic atmosphere, which they felt was highly impersonal and threatening. They stated that the abortion patients were treated like assembly-line commodities. Each woman was given a number, which was called aloud by the nurse. The receptionist, located in the middle of the large clinic area, answered calls regarding abortion appointments; the identity of the callers could be heard by the patients in the clinic. The obvious lack of anonymity was threatening to the women and evoked anxiety in them over the possibility that they might have been exposed to someone who knew them. Further, there were not enough magazines to occupy them and hide their embarrassment and nervousness while they were waiting. They stated that the patients simply stared at each other, which was quite embarrassing, and there was nothing to divert their attention. Besides, the waiting period before seeing a doctor was too long and

[8]Greenglass 1976; Nathanson 1980, 1985.

wearying, as all patients scheduled for abortion that day were required to present themselves at the same time. Typical experiences are illustrated by these comments:

> I felt like I was a guinea pig, like a welfare client. You are always paranoid in such situations. I had to wait in the clinic for an incredible amount of time from 9:00 to 12:00 noon, just waiting to see a doctor. You are really tired, nervous and tense and they make you sit there. You are not even allowed to smoke unless you go out.
>
>   *   *   *
>
> Calling on the phone for an appointment was the worst part, but coming to the clinic was terrible. I hated that I had to get a number, line up and fill out a questionnaire. That made me feel bad the first time that I had done really a bad thing.
>
>   *   *   *
>
> They just wanted to get you through just as fast as possible. Their attitude was, "Here are all these girls who got themselves pregnant and they come to us for help."

The lack of clear instructions explaining all the steps involved was quite confusing and annoying. The women arrived at the hospitals without any idea of the length of stay, the mechanics of the surgery, the pain involved, and the precautions to take before and after surgery. One woman's comments were illustrative:

> On the telephone they said very little; they tell you to come on Friday at 9:00 a.m. They don't tell you that it was just a preliminary examination and the abortion will be done some other day. That's why my friend went down with her suitcase with everything thinking she was going into the hospital the same day.

The women had infrequent and limited contact with the service providers, which they interpreted as a rebuff and a penalty for having an abortion. There was no follow-up visit by the doctor during their stay in the hospital after the surgery, providing little opportunity for the women to seek clarification regarding their fears and doubts in the aftermath of the surgery. Nurses also maintained a limited contact with them, which further reinforced their feelings of isolation and stigmatization. As these women were sensitive to even a slight hint of censuring, the casual or negative attitudes of the service providers served to intensify their anxiety and self-doubts. In such a state of mind, the need for communication with the service providers is quite obvious, as these women stated:

> You are lonely there. Not many people come to visit you unless you are close to your parents. So if nurses more often come and talk with you and ask you how you are feeling and joke around, that'll be nice. You are feeling guilty most likely anyway and you are scared, too.
>
> *   *   *
>
> I wanted the doctor to talk to me just to reassure me that I was not going to die.

There was no attempt to involve the male partners in counseling, the prototypical attitude of social work practitioners toward the male. It has been assumed that males are not interested in the decision making and are insensitive to the mental anguish and dilemma an unmarried woman experiences.[9] Some women thought that their sex partners should have been encouraged to participate in the interviews, which would give them some understanding of the stress and emotions women face when confronted with an unwanted pregnancy and abortion:

> I think the guy should be involved and brought into the counseling. Then he understands what goes on in the girl's mind. Lots of guys just think you can just go and get an abortion and that is it.

In view of these women's feelings toward the impersonal and mechanical atmosphere of the hospital, one wonders why there has been and still is stiff resistance to recognizing free-standing clinics for providing abortion, the type Dr. Henry Morgentaler has been advocating and operating in some parts of Canada. The Supreme Court of Canada, in its ruling on January 28, 1988, abolished the federal abortion law, thereby removing all restrictions on abortions performed in accredited hospitals. In the U.S., two-thirds of

---

[9]Sachdev 1991b.

procedures are performed in free-standing abortion clinics.[10] In contrast to hospitals, clinics provide a supportive, nonthreatening, empathetic, and caring environment to women in addition to offering medically safe and prompt abortion services. Despite women's unequivocal preference for the clinics and their demonstrated effectiveness, the provincial governments of Canada continue to recognize only publicly funded hospitals as legitimate medical facilities for performing abortions. Only the governments of Ontario and Quebec reimburse patients for the medical costs of abortions obtained in a doctor's clinic.

Contraceptive Pill: The Hospital Policy

It was the policy of all three hospitals to put women on contraceptive pills and to provide them with a month's supply before they left the hospital.[11] It was not first explored with the woman whether she was planning to return to active sex life and whether the oral contraceptive was, in fact, the best method of contraception control for all women. The women gave a strong impression that the contraceptive method was disseminated indiscriminately to them without giving them an opportunity to explore fully their pattern of sexual life and the choice of the contraceptive that was best suited to their need. Worse still, it was presumed that all the women were definitely going to be sexually active and therefore needed protection. One woman stated:

> Every girl got the pills at the time of leaving the hospital and the same pill was given to everybody on mass scale, regardless of their physical condition. One girl had a blood clot.

---

[10]Henshaw 1991.

[11]It could not be confirmed with the hospitals whether they indeed had such a policy, but a clear impression was gained from the statements of these women that all three hospitals pursued an aggressive practice of recommending the contraceptive pill to unmarried women who had had an abortion.

Another woman could not refuse to take the pills, although she clearly had no need for them at that moment:

> I am not having sex and I don't feel like taking the pills. [Why are you on the pill?] The doctor told me that I was supposed to take them, that's all. They told me when you leave this place, you are going to start taking birth control pills.

Sometimes the approach used to persuade the reluctant woman to accept the birth control pills was one of intimidation, which made them feel humiliated and downgraded, as one woman explained, while wiping off her tears:

> When I told the doctor that I didn't want these pills, he got very mad at me. I told him I wasn't going to have sex, but he wanted me to have the pills anyway. He said, "Do you want this to happen again to you? I hope you don't go out and do this again." He gave me the pills and made sure that I took them. I felt sort of looked down upon.

Another woman described how the doctor was insensitive toward and resentful of unmarried women for getting pregnant and then seeking an abortion. She felt extremely degraded by the doctor's statement:

> The doctor gave me the birth control pills and said, "This is how you prevent yourself. We don't want you to end up here again." When he said that, it made me feel very bad. I felt really low then.

SUMMARY

Given the stress of the unwanted pregnancy and the fears regarding the surgery, the attitude of the service providers is immensely critical, especially if the woman is unmarried, in determining how she reacts to the abortion afterwards, in both a psychological and a physical sense. Conditioned by the negative attitudes in her environment, an unmarried woman can be extremely sensitive to the attitudes of the staff around her. Most women (65.7 percent) in this study found the doctors' attitude negative (moralizing, uncaring, threatening) or neutral (indifferent or mechanical); only one-third (34.3 percent) saw their attitudes as positive. Nurses were far less negative in their attitudes toward these women. Three-fourths described the nurses as committed, supporting, empathetic and nonjudgmental. Some investigators suggest that doctors feel resentment toward women seeking abortion because of the doctors' dissatisfaction with this kind of work.

Forty-six women (65.7 percent) received counseling before the abortion. Contact with the counselor was usually very brief, and counseling was generally limited to procedural information. Not surprisingly, the women did not find the counseling to be a helpful experience. Some women found the social worker presumptuous, moralizing, and condescending. None of the women sought and received counseling after the abortion. However, 83 percent of the women said that they did not need post-abortion counseling, either because they did not experience any adverse effects of the abortion or they had close friends to share their experiences. Nevertheless, three-fourths of the women did acknowledge the desirability of having someone with whom to discuss their feelings.

From the detailed accounts of these women, it is clear that most women experienced hostile and negative environments in the hospitals. In an attempt to underline the significance of the hospital environment in affecting the emotional and physical health of a woman, these women offered certain suggestions toward creating a benign experience for unmarried abortion patients. They emphasized that the abortion services should be offered in an environment that is friendly, supportive, and caring. They resented the approach used by some doctors to impose contraceptive devices on the unmarried women. They felt that patients should be involved in the selection of a birth control method suited to their needs and circumstances.

8

After Abortion

"It wasn't what I had expected."

As has been noted all the women found their pregnancy unacceptable and eventually decided to seek its termination. It seems obvious that their desire to escape unwanted parenthood transcended the concerns these women had regarding the medical and psychological risks of the surgical procedure. One thing is clear, that the extraordinary trouble women go through to achieve abortion shows that they must reach a critical point of internal and external stresses.

But what happens after the pregnancy is terminated? Is their actual experience with the surgery different from what they feared? How does the abortion affect the women psychologically? How do they process and reconcile with the experience? How does abortion affect the women's sexual and contraceptive behavior?

EXPERIENCE WITH THE SURGICAL PROCEDURE

Nearly two-thirds (64.3 percent) of the women said that they were amazed that the surgery was very simple and was not nearly so frightful as they had thought. The relatively painless procedure, performed in a short time, was by far the biggest surprise for these women. Illustrative of their reactions are the following excerpts:

I didn't realize how easy it was . . . I had thought a long, drawn stay at the hospital for a few days. I could not believe it was so quick. I was just in and out.

*   *   *

I thought there would be more pain. I just had slight cramps afterward. It went really fast. It wasn't horrible as I had thought.

*   *   *

I thought it will hurt and I will come out bleeding to death. I thought it will be ugly. When I came out I felt great physically.

Abortion did not make them disabled or incapacitated, as they had feared. To their utter surprise, they could spring back into daily activities soon after the abortion, as this woman remarked:

I expected to come out of it aching sore and feeling completely sick. As soon as I got out of this [anesthesia], I was in the happiest mood in the world. I couldn't believe it was the same night. I was walking all over the hospital until the nurse told me to get back into bed. I felt ready to go home.

Fifteen women (35.7 percent) were not surprised by the relatively painless and simple surgical procedure, as they had had information on what goes on in the surgery. For instance, four had read quite extensively on the subject; eight received detailed explanation of the mechanics of the surgery from their gynecologist or nurses or from a woman who had had an abortion. Three women had worked in a hospital as a nurse's aide and were thus familiar with the technique. These women were not anxious about the procedure itself, which underscores the need for detailed instructions regarding the procedure prior to the surgery. Lack of information can contribute to misconceptions and exaggerated fears, which may complicate the dilemma of needing an abortion.

ABORTION IMPACT

Immediate Psychological Reactions

"I was glad it was over."

Soon after the abortion most women (78.6 percent) felt relief and euphoria. This is understandable, because these women were under a heavy stress occasioned by the unwanted pregnancy and its termination delivered them from a heavy burden. They expressed satisfaction in these words: "I felt great, as if I had been reborn;" "I felt free and a new life;" "I felt elated and total freedom." Having reversed the pregnancy, they were able to rid themselves of the painful dilemma, as one woman explained:

> As I regained consciousness I felt relieved that I was no longer pregnant. It was a nice feeling to have it all over, because it was a problem and now this was out of my way. I was totally transformed from my former state of depression.

"Oh God, they have done it."

Less than one-fifth (18.6 percent) of the women felt depressed or felt there was a void in their lives.[1] They felt they had lost something that they wished to retrieve. They regretted their decision, which was irreversible. They experienced intense feelings of estrangement and blamed themselves for the decision to have an abortion. For some, the pregnancy had represented a hope for a firm matrimonial commitment by their male partner. The following excerpts will illustrate these feelings:

---

[1] In agreement with these findings, other investigators also noted that immediately following abortion a majority of the unmarried women (between 57 and 78 percent) felt relief and satisfaction and that the remainder, a minority, felt depressive moods (Lazarus 1985; Lemkau 1991; Major et al. 1985; McCoy 1968; Mueller & Major 1989; Niswander & Patterson 1967; Osofsky & Osofsky 1972; Patt et al. 1969; Smith 1973).

After my abortion I realized that something I had wasn't
there, neither the one who created it. Even if I hated him,
I still loved him. I just felt alone--completely alone. Even
when I had a fight with Bill, I knew I had someone. Right
after the abortion, everything was gone, every hope was
gone. [R cried.]

        *   *   *

I wanted to erase everything. I wanted to go back and not
have it. Right after my abortion I was really depressed and
I cried. I was not myself at all. I was always snapping at
my family and was not nice with them at all. I just wanted
to be alone to put things in perspective. I hated myself. I
was sort of wishing I could turn back the clock and be the
way I was before, just really a good girl.

"I didn't know if I did the right thing."

Two women felt both sad and pleased. They experienced a
sense of loss and emptiness but were also relieved that abortion
delivered them from the distress caused by the unwanted pregnancy.
They felt reprieved because their pregnancy was problematic and felt
sad because abortion had moral implications. Their mixed feelings
are exemplified by these excerpts:

Right after the abortion, I felt relieved of the burden which
is not a good word to use, because it sounds like I hate kids.
I would say I had mixed feelings of relief and maybe a bit of
sadness that something that I had was now gone.

        *   *   *

Afterward, I felt relieved that everything was over and done
with. But still, there was something at the back of my mind
asking if I did the right moral thing. I felt depressed for the
fact that I might have killed something real, something alive
at that stage. I wanted to cry.

Long-Term Psychological Reactions

It has been suggested that, after the crisis is ended, the
euphoria experienced within hours of the termination begins to
recede, giving way to more sober moods or other emotional responses

such as guilt and depression. The women in this study reported that their sense of relief and satisfaction lasted anywhere from a week to as long as five weeks (34.3 percent and 65.7 percent of the women, respectively). How did these women feel after the initial reactions faded away? In other words, did they feel guilt or depression as a consequence of the abortion? How long did these feelings last, and how did the women resolve these feelings?

Each woman was asked if she experienced, at any time since the abortion, symptoms relating to guilt or depressive reactions and how often she had these feelings. As explained in chapter 3, each woman was presented with a card that listed the symptoms indicative of guilt or depressive reactions in three steps of severity: severe, moderate, and mild (see Appendix B). This method ensured that they all understood uniformaly the behavioral and emotional symptoms of these reactions.[2]

Table 8.1 shows that four-fifths of the women reported slight or no feeling of guilt or depression and one-fifth suffered moderate to severe reactions sometime since the abortion.[3] To permit the reader to appreciate the relative intensity of the psychological reactions, the following excerpts are provided to typify each category. The symptomology of guilt and depressive reactions are described in three steps of severity in Appendix B and will not be repeated here.

---

[2] In reporting the data, the guilt and depressive reactions are combined, because the description of their symptomatology is much the same, except for the moral element, which may or may not be present in depressive reactions. It is worthy of note that the psychiatric measurement of conscious guilt when expressed in psychosomatic symptoms borders closely on depressive reactions. Because of the overlap of symptoms, several authors have either used the terms interchangeably or lumped them together (Callahan 1970: 71).

[3] A few authors who reviewed the literature on the effects of abortion have concluded that negative post-abortion emotional reactions range from less than 10 percent to almost 50 percent depending on whether the single women obtained therapeutic or illegal abortions or obtained them on request or under restrictive conditions. Less than 10 percent reflect women with severe reactions, while 50 percent and more women report moderate and transient feelings (Adler et al. 1990; Ashton 1980b; Burnell & Norfleet 1987; Lemkau 1988).

Table 8.1
**Degree of Guilt or Depressive Reactions as Reported
by Seventy Women**

Degree of Reactions	N	Percentage
Severe	6(1)*	10.0
Moderate	6(1)	10.0
Mild	26(9)	50.0
None	21	30.0

*The numbers in parantheses represent those women who indicated depressive reactions.

"Severe" guilt reactions

A twenty-year-old bank teller gave a very emotional account of her feelings:

I know I'm guilty, because that was my own decision. I was the one who was pregnant, nobody else. As soon as I'm by myself, I think of losing my baby I created [tears welled up in R's eyes]. It is just like cutting off on your own that belongs to you and somebody else. I also often thought if my father, who passed away long ago, would have been alive he would have been the person I would mostly have hurt because he loves children. Maybe he wouldn't even forgive me. Often I think he hears me; I know he is there all the time and I wish he could tell me what he feels like, what he thinks of me now.
I don't date. I have seen a boy once I used to go out with four years ago. I know I can't see him again because he is against abortion. I don't know what the other guy is going to say about it. That is what scares me. I don't know if he might say, "You are no worse than anybody else" or "You are just a tramp." When somebody talks about it or I

read about abortion, or a guy at work says, "My wife had a baby," that time I feel more upset.

"Severe" depressive reactions

A 21-year-old woman working as a waitress was tearful when she talked about her feelings three and a half months after the abortion:

> It bothers me, because I still miss the baby. Sometimes I lay in bed at night and feel real empty. I remember the first time after the abortion I laid down on the bed and all of a sudden I couldn't figure out why it was so different. I was depressed. There was something gone. Like I felt as if you are home all the time and suddenly everyone is gone.
> I never felt alone when I was pregnant. I always felt I was with somebody and I almost talked to him already kind of good feelings and all of a sudden he is gone. I wonder what happened to him. Did they pack him down in a plastic bag and take him down to the boiler room? I felt sick thinking about it.
> [How often did these feelings occur?] When I first came out I must have felt it strong every minute, every second of the day for a month or longer. I was a nervous wreck thinking about it all the time. Then I started to forget a little more. There is something that haunts me if that was going to be my only baby.
> When I see a pregnant lady sometimes it hurts. All of a sudden I go, "Oh, it is not there." You see her [the pregnant woman] walking along with a great big smile on her face. She is the happiest person on the earth and even sometimes you think to yourself, "What would she think if she knew what I did." She would think terribly low of me. All of a sudden out of the blue I'm really depressed.

"Moderate" guilt reactions

Deeply saddened, a 23-year-old teacher talked very touchingly how she felt when she saw in her vaginal bleeding what appeared to be the endometrial lining, four days after the abortion. She thought the tissues were residues of the fetus:

I still regret the fact that I had to do this sort of thing. The thought of abortion, I think, will always bother me. Before, I felt these feelings more often than I do now. I'm trying to forget about it, but it's still there.

One thing that did happen after the abortion was that on Thursday [four days later] I went to the washroom and there was a fetus and I thoroughly examined it. I held it on a piece of Kleenex and it started to stick to the Kleenex. I kept saying to myself, "Don't do that, you are hurting it," even though it was dead already [R's voice choked]. I started thinking that it could have been a person; it could have possibly been loved by somebody else who could have taken care of it. I thought as if it was almost still alive. That really shocked me.

For about a week I had it wrapped up in that Kleenex and in the cabinet underneath the sink. I couldn't bring myself to throw it in the garbage or do anything like that. And then every time I came into the washroom I knew it would be there and I wouldn't dare open the door of the cabinet.

After about a week I worked up enough nerve to take another look at it. But by this time it was all sticking to the Kleenex and I just didn't want to start tearing it apart. So I ended up putting it in the garbage. It sounds so horrible, saying it that way. It really affected me.

"Moderate" depressive reactions

An 18-year-old working as a waitress described her feelings of grief and self-reproach:

I feel guilty, because it was a baby and I was just thinking of myself and my life, when in fact it was my fault that I got pregnant.

When I watch commercials on T.V. and see little babies, it bothers me. I constantly wonder what it was, boy or girl, and think, ah, it is nice to have them, they are so sweet. Then I start thinking to myself, "You don't even deserve to think like that."

The idea that I have murdered a baby sometimes pops up in my mind. I sometimes get weird feelings that there might be something wrong with the babies I'll have in the future and that I may be punished for this.

I think when it will be my first pregnancy [after marriage], I'll never really feel that good again, because I'll know this is not the first time I have ever been pregnant. Eventually, it is going to bother me, and make me wonder more about this [aborted] baby.

"Mild" guilt reactions

A 24-year-old woman described her feelings, which lasted two months.

I felt a bit guilty for about 2 months for doing this to something living, but I don't feel any more. I have dreamt a few times after the abortion. I saw that I have a child with me and was playing with it and then the child just disappeared. Then something would happen to me. Somebody was always trying to kill me. I had this dream quite often.

It is very emotional to go through a pregnancy and abortion, because like you are destroying something and you know you are. It just makes you feel guilty about it. I think it does, because you know you are meant to have babies. But when you look at it the other way--that I didn't really want the baby right now, because it was too hard to raise.

ARE PSYCHOLOGICAL REACTIONS INFLUENCED BY WOMEN'S ATTITUDES TOWARD PREGNANCY AND ABORTION?

The study shows that the women who had greater difficulty in making the decision, who identified with the fetus as a real person or "my baby," and who fantasized about the unborn child were more likely to experience psychological problems of guilt or depression after abortion (see Appendix A tables 18 and 19).[4] Similarly, the women's attitude toward abortion also influenced the degree of psychological problems in the aftermath of abortion. Those who were liberal in accepting abortion were less troubled by guilt or depressive reactions afterward (see Appendix A table 20).

How Did They Cope with the Abortion Experience?

The two most significant findings, which are worthy of emphasis, are these: first, serious psychological consequences of abortion were rare among this group of women, and those who suffered serious reactions were not impaired or inhibited in their day-to-day functioning.[5]   Second, all the women, whatever their reactions, eventually began to experience attenuation of their symptoms; how soon a woman was completely able to resolve her experience depended upon her coping ability.[6] The latter finding

---

[4]This observation is consistent with results of other surveys on the impact of abortion and pregnancy. These surveys found that women who had difficulty in choosing abortion were more likely to experience negative emotions (guilt and depression) after the abortion. Women who experienced a difficult decision were those who intended their pregnancy or attached more meaning to it. See Adler 1975; Adler et al. 1990; Ashton 1980b; Bracken 1978; Eisen & Zellman 1984; Kummer 1967; Lemkau 1988; Lodl et al. 1985; Major and Cozzarelli 1992; Osofsky and Osofsky 1972; Peck and Marcus 1966; Senay 1970; Shusterman 1979; Smith 1973; Wallerstein et al. 1972.

[5]These conclusions are in complete accord with those reached by reviews of the literature on the after-effects of abortion. See chapter 2.

[6]Cohen and Roth (1984) evaluated reactions of 55 women (aged 14-42) who had had an abortion and confirmed that their response to the abortion impact depended upon their coping styles. Consistent with this finding, Armsworth (1991) found in her review of the literature that the two factors related to the abortion experience were perceived support from the male partner and parents and a woman's coping processes. Lodl et al. (1985) reached a similar conclusion from a review of the literature that lack of social support and inadequate coping skills contribute to emotional distress post-abortion. Another review of the literature by Major and Cozzarelli (1992) confirmed that self blame for pregnancy, perceived social (i.e., male partner and parental) support, and specific coping styles are the likely factors that determine a woman's adjustment to abortion. Using a series of

became evident first from the frequency of reactions to the abortion and then from the specific thinking and behaving patterns each woman used in adapting to these feelings. Following are the various coping strategies the disturbed women used, according to their pattern of adaptation to traumatic life situations.

Suppression

Over one-half (55 percent) of the women made conscious efforts to avoid any thoughts of the pregnancy and abortion and to prevent morbid feelings associated with these events. The technique most often used was to involve themselves deeply in various activities, thus diverting their minds from these subjects. If the thoughts escaped into their minds, they either denied having those experiences or distanced themselves as spectators. These thoughts, at times may have been disturbing, but their intensity and frequency were progressively less with time. A few excerpts illustrate the process of suppression:

> The feelings of guilt and sadness are still with me today, but not as great as they were just after the abortion. Before, I had these feelings more often than I do now. I just try to keep myself really occupied, so I won't really have time to sit down and think about it. I get out of the apartment, write report cards and things like these which have been pretty well the only things on my mind. My grandfather is not feeling too well, so I think about that; my girlfriend is going to get married and I have been busy trying to help her.
>
> *   *   *
>
> I didn't want to think that I had a child inside me, or if it was a boy or girl, something like that. I didn't think about my religion, though I agree with my religion when they say no abortion. I knew if I started thinking about it, I would feel sad and would change my mind. When I see a child I

---

path analyses, Major et al. (1990) have shown that perceived social support has no direct effects on adjustment, but operates through increasing feelings of self-efficacy which enhances adjustments to abortion. Robbins & DeLamater (1985), however, noted in their sample of 228 white women that, though male partner support contributed to positive reactions to abortion, involvement or support of parents did not make a difference.

think about my abortion and that makes me feel sad and depressed. I don't want to think about it and say to myself, "It's no good to think about the child and all that." So I keep these thoughts out of my mind.

Rationalization

Rationalization was another manipulative strategy employed by one-fifth (20.4 percent) of the women to relieve their stress caused by guilt or depressive reactions to the abortion. They justified their decisions to have an abortion, thinking that it was for the "sake of the child or the parents, or the career, or for preserving the relationship with the male partner." Typical of this coping strategy are the following statements:

I wonder what it would have been--a girl or a boy. Then I look at it that I couldn't support it or if I had to give it up, it would have hurt me more. I wouldn't want the child to live on the street, not being able to feed it or clothe it. You see some of the kids who run around the neighborhood, look like they don't even have pants. I just couldn't have my child like that. I know I am irresponsible and if I can't look after myself how can I look after somebody else?

*   *   *

I still think about it and its moral question and it still bothers me. I just convince myself that I had to have the abortion for my mother's sake.

Intellectualization

One-fourth (24.5 percent) of the women handled the abortion experience through intellectualizing its emotional impact. They did think about the abortion and could talk about it, but only in analytical and logical terms, and would not associate feelings with the event, as these comments exemplify:

I still think about the abortion. It is part of my life. But when the thought of abortion crosses my mind, it does not make me feel sad, because then the logical mind takes over and says, well, this has happened.

*   *   *

I had mixed feelings of relief and a bit of sadness that something that I had was now gone. I had these feelings, maybe a week or two. After that there was no feeling, as if I never had the abortion. If the subject is discussed or if I see a car bumper sticker, "Abortion is murder," I tell myself that although it had a life of its own, I'm the one who has to contend with it and live with it.

How Do These Findings Compare with Other Studies?

Despite variation in the quality of the data, the sampling and measurement procedures, and the incidence reported by previous authors, one consistent conclusion can be drawn from these studies: Serious psychological reactions to abortion are low and transient.[7] A few authors recognized the psychic health and defense structure of a woman as important factors in limiting the psychological impact of abortion.[8] They observed in their samples that the women who were mentally healthy could manage the stress of the unwanted pregnancy and abortion with little or no difficulty; however, those who were psychologically weak were vulnerable to adverse emotional reactions regardless of the option they followed to resolve the pregnancy dilemma. However, other investigators do not view the psychological health of the woman as significant in managing the impact of abortion and contend that the ill effects of abortion, like any stressful events in life, fade as a natural consequence of time until a woman is completely adjusted.

It was evident from this study that, of the women who experienced psychological reactions, eight out of ten (81.6 percent) had completely or considerably adjusted six months to one year following the abortion. They were troubled on occasion when the

---

[7]See, for instance, Brody et al. 1971; Callahan 1970; Ekblad 1955; Ford et al. 1972; Hamilton 1966; Ingham & Simms 1972; Kretzchmar & Norris 1967; Levene & Rigney 1970; McCoy 1968; Monsour and Stewart 1973; Niswander & Patterson 1967; Osofsky & Osofsky 1972; Patt et al. 1969; Peck 1968; Perez-Reyes and Falk 1973; Simon et al. 1967; Sloane 1969; Smith 1973; Wallerstein et al. 1972; Walters 1969.

[8]See Ford et al. 1971; Lee 1969; Simon et al. 1967; Walter 1970. Cohen & Roth (1984) found that women who actively confront the problem are better able to resolve the abortion experience.

sight of a baby or pregnant woman or a discussion of the subject would trigger their memories. Only less than one-fifth (18.4 percent) of the women seemed to have been unable to resolve their adverse reactions at the time of the interview. It is hard to say with certitude what changed the emotional states of these women, time or their coping abilities. It might be that, as the cliche goes, time is a great healer of emotional trauma in life and that one's coping abilities catalyze the effects of time. It also stands to reason that socioenvironmental factors may intervene in the "healing" process, such as a woman's attitude toward abortion, her reaction to the pregnancy, pre-abortion ambivalence, support from key people in her life and their attitudes toward abortion, and post-abortion counseling. The following excerpts illustrate how the women who suffered guilt or depressive reaction after abortion were increasingly less troubled with time:

> For a while, I used to have guilt feelings just about every day. Now I feel about a couple of times a week. I sort of had got it out of my system when one day my friend, a girl I worked with, called me and said she was getting an abortion. That brought back my feelings.
>
> *   *   *
>
> Much of my guilt feelings are gone now. It's very gradual and I feel less and less emotional pain. But when I see a little baby I wonder if mine was like that; was it a boy or girl, was it blond or dark?
>
> *   *   *
>
> I was very depressed for the first couple of weeks. It's only in the past week that I'm starting to feel better. I still think about it and its moral aspects, and it still bothers me. But it does not depress me like it did after my abortion.

Relationship with the Sex Partner

"It was not fair, because it was me who became pregnant, had the abortion, spent all my money and he was completely unaware of all this."

This statement by a 22-year-old student nurse sums up the feelings of these women toward their male partners after the abortion. As noted in chapter 5, most women experienced deterioration in their relationship with the male partner at the onset of the pregnancy because the demand it placed on the male for commitment. The women found the sex partners uncaring and insensitive to their needs. Fragile as it was, the pair relationship suffered further setback following the abortion, because it demanded more involvement and support than the male partner could provide. To assess the impact of abortion on the pair relationships, the women's feelings toward the man and their marriage plans, if any, were examined as they occurred before becoming pregnant, after discovering the pregnancy, and following the abortion. The three indicators were used to determine whether the pair relationship was changed and how it was changed after each event. Tables 8.2, 8.3, and 8.4 depict changes in these behavior patterns.

Frequency of Dating

It will be noted in table 8.2 that there was a progressive diminution in the couples' commitment after the experience of pregnancy and abortion. One-third of the women who had been going out regularly or fairly regularly had their relationships dissolved after the onset of the pregnancy. Another ten percent of the women broke off the relationships following the abortion, bringing the total number of breakups to 43 percent.[9] These women felt a strong dislike for the man, because he came across as being insensitive and indifferent to their physical and emotional pain. The women felt that as they were equal participants in the sexual activity, it was unfair that they had to make the decision alone and endure the hardships. Some women held the man responsible for their decision to have an abortion, because he remained largely uncaring and uninvolved with the woman's predicament.   The following excerpts illustrate

---

[9]A gradual deterioration of pair relationships was also observed by Shostak and McLouth (1984) in their study referred to earlier. While 3 percent of the men ended the relationship on the day of the abortion, one-quarter in their follow-up study broke up after the abortion (table 6.1).

Table 8.2
Frequency of Dating with Sex Partner Pre- and Post-Pregnancy and Post-Abortion

Frequency of Dating	Pre-Pregnancy		Post-Pregnancy		Post-Abortion	
	N	%	N	%	N	%
No more than now and then	6	8.6	6	8.5	2	2.8
Going together regularly	49	70.0	34	48.5	34	48.5
Going together fairly regularly	12	17.1	4	5.7	1	1.4
Never since first time	3	4.3	3	4.3	3	4.3
Broke off	-	-	23	33.0	30	43.0

poignantly the resentment and hostility of these women toward the male partners, who showed an utter lack of concern, sensitivity, and feelings:

> When I told him I was pregnant and asked him what he thought about it, he said, "It is fine, I can get along, you go and have an abortion, if you want to." From that day, I couldn't take it. He really turned me off. He always said he loved me and wanted a child, yet he didn't care if I had an abortion. Well, how much care is that?
>
> He called me after I came back from the hospital. He asked me how I felt. I said, "How can you care what I feel now; you never cared before how I felt." I said, "Fine myself, but I feel awful just to talk to you." I really hated him.
>
>   *   *   *
>
> I went out with him a few times, after everything was over. He was sort of quiet and all of a sudden he brought up the subject and asked me, "What happened?" He wondered what I had gone through with it. I told him it was enough for him to make me face it alone rather than ask me a stupid question like that. It upset me so much, that I refused to see him again. He became interested in me only when it was too late.
>
>   *   *   *
>
> He didn't come to see me in the hospital nor did he call me. He always made excuses why he couldn't come to the hospital, like, "One time I went to the florist, the shop was closed," or "There was no flowers." That really turned me off.

Feelings toward the Sex Partner

Table 8.3 reveals a continuous weakening of the women's emotional involvement with their sex partners from the onset of the pregnancy. It is significant to note that more women reported lack of love at the occurrence of the pregnancy than they did after the abortion. Of the women who loved or had a feeling of love before the pregnancy, almost one-fifth (18.6 percent) fewer women claimed such feelings upon becoming pregnant. However, the drop in the proportion of women having such feelings was slight (7.2 percent)

Table 8.3
Women's Feelings toward Their Sex Partner Pre- and Post-Pregnancy and Post-Abortion

Feelings toward sex partner	Pre-Pregnancy		Post-Pregnancy		Post-Abortion	
	N	%	N	%	N	%
Loved him or thought I was in love with him	48	68.6	35	50.0	30	42.8
Liked him a lot	15	21.4	8	11.4	7	10.0
Just liked him and had casual acquaintance	7	10.0	8	11.4	3	4.3
Resented him or I didn't care much	-	-	19	27.2	24	34.3
Not certain	-	-	-	-	6	8.6

after the abortion. Similarly, the proportion of women who "liked him a lot" before the pregnancy dropped 10 percent post-pregnancy, but there was no significant change in the number of women feeling this way post-abortion. The reason that the pregnancy precipitated a sudden drop in the number of women claiming love relationship may be that the intervention of an unwanted pregnancy exerted a far greater demand on the couple for commitment and intimacy than did the abortion. Abortion, in fact, was an anti-climax to the stress brought on by the pregnancy. Finally, as many as 43 percent of the women either resented the man or felt indifferent toward him after the abortion. Sometimes the feelings of resentment were very intense, as the following excerpts illustrate:

> I hated him. He was not nice to me when I was pregnant. [When I called him about the pregnancy] he told me, "Don't bother me and all that." I mean, when you want somebody there and he is not there [R cried] you can never forget the hurt right away.
>
> *   *   *
>
> Until the time I had the abortion, I loved him. When I decided to have an abortion, I actually started hating him. [Why?] I blamed him more than I blamed myself. I started hating him, not because I got pregnant--that was great; I always thought that I would have his baby, but because I had to have an abortion. I just couldn't stand him any more.

Sometimes their hatred towards the male partner generalized towards all men. This woman explained the reason why she lost interest in men in general and wished for a while that the world would be a better place to live if there were no men:

> I blamed him a little and so I didn't want to marry him, though he wanted to, because he gave me a rough time. I hated all men for a time. I always depended on my boyfriend. There were lots of frictions; sometimes I would feel sick and he wouldn't understand why I was feeling sick. I felt if there were no men in the world this wouldn't have happened to me. I wanted to live all by myself and never have to worry about men any more.

To Marry or Not To Marry

That the abortion adversely affected relationships with sex partners is further evident in the women's marriage commitments, which were progressively altered after the pregnancy and then following the abortion. As shown in table 8.4, the proportion of women who changed their minds and did not want to marry the male partner increased by almost one-tenth after the pregnancy and by one-fifth after the abortion. The number of those who had doubts about the male partner decreased by one-tenth after the pregnancy but increased by more than 10 percent following the abortion. Part of the explanation for why more women were interested in marriage after the pregnancy than after the abortion   seems to be that marriage offered an acceptable way to avoid single parenthood, which they all thought too onerous and problematic. But when they felt marriage to the male partner was neither possible nor a viable solution, they no longer felt the pressure or the genuine interest in marriage once the problem pregnancy was terminated.

In summary, from the three measures of relationships, it was evident that within the period covered by the study, abortion did prove disruptive to the women's relationships with their male partners,[10] but its effects were less adverse than those of the unwanted pregnancy.[11]

---

[10]These findings are quite compatible with those of other studies that reported that 14 percent of the couples broke off their relationships subsequent to abortion because the male partners were perceived to have lacked the emotional commitment and concern (Hamilton 1966; Lee 1969). Some studies reported a higher incidence of breakup, between 25 and 44 percent, which is probably due to the longer interval before follow-up, which in some cases was up to two years (Greenglass 1976; Monsour & Stewart 1973; Smith 1973). Whether or not a relationship will survive the impact of abortion also seems to depend upon the closeness to the partner. A relationship with strong ties before pregnancy and the procedure is more likely to weather stresses and tensions than a weak and casual relationship (see Milling 1973).

[11]Robbins (1979) also found that given strong ties to one's partner termination of a pregnancy places no greater strain on the relationship of aborters than that of women who choose to deliver.

Table 8.4
Women's Desire for Marriage to the Sex Partner as Considered by the Women Pre- and Post-Pregnancy and Post-Abortion

Feelings toward Sex Partner	Pre-Pregnancy		Post-Pregnancy		Post-Abortion	
	N	%	N	%	N	%
Didn't want to marry	31	44.3	37	52.9	43	61.4
Wanted to marry	31	44.3	32	45.7	18	25.6
Not certain	8	11.4	1	1.4	9	13.0

Sexuality

As in other areas of abortion, contradictory evidence exists about the effect of abortion on women's sex drive. Previous studies are polarized, with some contending adverse effect[12] while others maintain the opposite viewpoint.[13] One potential source of difficulty in assessing the influence of abortion on women's sexual life lies in the nature of female sexuality, which is relatively complex and orientated in diverse directions. Sexual response in a woman more than in a man is influenced by a variety of factors--psychological, social, emotional, and biological.[14] It is also affected by her self-image and her feelings and attitudes toward the sex partner and sexuality.[15] Research shows that a woman's sexual life is more affected by being in love or thoughts of being in love than is a man's.[16] Furthermore, the studies available do not offer tangible criteria to assess satisfactorily the effect of abortion on women's sexual response. The present study makes no pretence that the indicators used to determine changes in the sexual desire of its respondents have met the level of sophistication needed. However, it is fair to say that they represent an improvement over the existing methodology. Reliance is placed mainly on three indicators that assess changes in the women's sexual desire after abortion.

First, symptomatology of depressive and guilt reactions included a statement on the women's feeling toward sex and men following abortion that read in three degrees of severity: "I felt a complete loss of interest in sex and men;" "I felt a fair degree of loss of interest in sex and men;" "I felt a slight loss of interest in sex and men" (see Appendix B). Each woman was asked to check a statement appropriate to her situation. They were also asked to skip the statement if the abortion did not affect their usual interest in sex. This information provided their *affective responses* to sex, responses that lasted for varying periods of time subsequent to abortion.

---

[12]See, for instance, Deutsch 1945; Freundt 1973; Hamilton 1966; White 1966.

[13]See, for instance, Gebhard et al. 1958; Patt et al. 1969; Walter 1970.

[14]Hyde 1990; Katchadourian 1989; Masters, Johnson & Kolodny 1992.

[15]Chilman 1974, 1979, 1980; Masters & Johnson 1970.

[16]Katchadourian 1989; Masters, Johnson & Kolodny 1992.

Second, each woman was asked to check the appropriate category to indicate what degree of pleasure in sex she had usually experienced prior to the pregnancy. The same question was repeated later in the interview to identify her sexual response following her abortion. The difference between the two responses provided some evidence on her *behavioral response* in sex (see table 8.5).

Third, any statement a woman made elsewhere in the interview that offered a clue to her sex-related behavior and attitude constituted a third indicator, which was used to supplement the information obtained by the first two indicators.

Affective Responses in Sex

Based on the statements checked, close to three-fourths (73 percent) of the women reported no effect on their usual sex interest. More than one-fourth (27.1 percent) of the women reported slight to complete loss of interest in sex and men following the abortion, with a heavy preponderance in the category of fair to complete loss. These feelings lasted from a few weeks to as long as five months.[17] Women with "complete" loss of interest developed an abhorrence of sex and resentment toward men that lasted for a few months. They could not think of getting interested in sex again. Women with "fair" loss of interest disliked having sex, but not for very long. Although they resumed sexual activity, they were not completely free from the fear of pregnancy and therefore did not enjoy sex for a few weeks. Women who reported "slight" loss of interest resumed sex after a few weeks and could enjoy it, but only if they were protected contraceptively. To illustrate the relative degree of their loss of interest in sex, a few comments are provided:

---

[17]A Canadian study by Greenglass (1976) found that 80 percent of the single women in her sample resumed sex "on an average of 6.84 weeks after the abortion" (p. 117). The findings of another study by Belsey (1976) reported 74 percent of the women (same percentage as in this study) having satisfactory sex relations post-abortion. Ashton (1980b) reported a higher proportion (98 percent) of women resuming sex eight weeks after the abortion. Using data collected during the mid 1970s in the San Francisco Bay Area, Miller (1992) found that of 65 women who had had an induced abortion three years prior to the interview, 76 percent (almost identical to this study) reported that the abortion did not affect their feelings about their sexuality, and 22 percent reported that they felt "sexless."

Table 8.5
Degree of Enjoyment in Sex Relations Pre-Pregnancy and Post-Abortion

Degree of Enjoyment	Pre-Pregnancy		Post-Abortion	
	N	%	N	%*
Extremely enjoyable	36	51.3	27	60.0
Somewhat enjoyable	24	34.3	16	35.6
Not too enjoyable	6	8.7	1	2.2
Not enjoyable at all	3	4.3	-	-
Depends	1	1.4	1	2.2
Never since abortion	-	-	25	35.7

*Percentages are based on the number of cases who were sexually active since abortion and not on the total number of responses and therefore exceed 100.0.

"Complete" loss of interest:

I hated all men at the time and I didn't have much trust in them. For five months I didn't have sex at all.
*   *   *
I said to myself, I'll not have sex again, not until I'm married. I got out of the mess and there is no way I wanted to get back into another mess.
*   *   *
For a few months after my abortion, I didn't like him to touch me. I was afraid I might get started again.

"Fair" loss of interest:

> After my abortion, I didn't feel like having sex. When I came back from the hospital, he [the boyfriend] came to see me again, but this time I thought there would be no intercourse. When I had sex afterwards, the abortion was on my mind and I didn't enjoy it. I was saying to myself, "How come I did it?" I again promised myself I'll never do it again.
>
> * * *
>
> I didn't feel like having sex then; I couldn't be bothered, at least not for some time.

"Slight" loss of interest:

> After the abortion, I didn't feel like doing it for a couple of weeks. Then I started doing it. I won't be enjoying it if I were not on the pills.

Behavioral Responses in Sex

Forty-five women, nearly two-thirds (64.3 percent) had resumed sex relations at follow-up. Of the twenty-five women who had not engaged in sex relations, only two women had completely lost desire for sex relations as a result of the abortion, a state that persisted ten to fourteen weeks after the abortion.[18] Ten women did not resume sexual intercourse because they had not completely recovered medically and had been advised to abstain. Six women had not dated anyone seriously thus far. Another three women were afraid of getting pregnant and wanted to go on the pill before resuming sex relations. Four women stated they had weak sexual urges and were never interested in sex. One of them said: "To be truthful, I don't think I ever had interest in sex. I had only one intercourse and it never turned me on." Another woman said: "I had a fear of sex from the time I was old enough to know about it."

---

[18]Confirming these findings, Ashton (1980b) reported that 90 percent of the women who had sex partners had resumed sex relations eight weeks after the abortion.

A comparison of the sexual experience of the forty-five women prior to the pregnancy and post-abortion makes it quite clear that these women by and large had greater enjoyment of sex after the abortion than prior to the abortion (see table 8.5). More women (10 percent) found sexual intercourse pleasurable after abortion. More significantly, eight out of nineteen women who reported fair to complete loss of interest in sex and men immediately after the abortion found the sex act enjoyable after they resumed sexual activity, and only one woman found it not too enjoyable. The rest had not returned to sexual activity. One should, however, not credit abortion for their enhanced sex experience. The fact that these women were able to enjoy sex after the abortion was attributed to the quality of their pair relationship, which was trusting and non-exploitative. All of these women were involved with a new sex partner who was considerate and caring in sexual interaction. Three women found sex acts more enjoyable because they were using the most effective method of birth control, the pill, and were therefore relieved from the fear of pregnancy. A few excerpts will make this point clear:

> He is really gentle. I trust him. If you love somebody you feel more comfortable and then you can really confide in the guy.
>
> *   *   *
>
> It was not a true sexual intercourse because the man I had sex with before abortion was the kind of person who was selfish in sexual intercourse. He won't hug or kiss, be affectionate or do other things before sex relations. He was not a particularly affectionate or loving type. He was just concerned to relieve himself, whether I reached orgasm or not.
>
> *   *   *
>
> Now I reach orgasm practically every time I have sex. I never had an orgasm before. This guy takes lot more care in what he is doing. He just makes sure I have one [an orgasm].

Judging from these women's sexual feelings and practice, it can be concluded that very few of them experienced sexual apathy after abortion which lasted for a limited duration. Given a caring interpersonal relationship in which the male partner was sensitive and concerned, all women were capable of returning to the level of sexual desire and pleasure they had maintained before pregnancy. Indeed, important as the relationships are, it makes one wonder how these women were able to forge an ideal relationship with a man after the abortion which was quite in contrast to their earlier experiences. One plausible, though impressionistic, explanation may be that the abortion had a maturing effect on these women which enabled them to be more discrete and careful in committing themselves in a relationship that is not exploitative and egocentrist. Having faced a crisis situation which required them to make decisions and go through with them on their own helped these women gain self confidence and a sense of empowerment. These feelings enhanced their ability to handle interpersonal relationships with greater responsibility and a sense of purpose. They tended to look on their abortions as having taught them a lesson so that they could reevaluate themselves and their needs and become a somewhat different person, as is illustrated by these comments: "I've become wiser and more careful when I go out with a man and with whom I go out;" "I've grown pretty fast. I was a dumb, mixed-up kid, denying realities; now I've learned to be more responsible and more able to make decisions;" "The abortion taught me a lesson, though an expensive one. I do not jump in bed with any guy as I used to do." Some women who continued their relationships with the same boyfriends felt that the abortion experience brought them closer to each other and increased their communication which improved their sex relations, as one woman stated: "I usually feel great about life now; my boyfriend and I are closer now and he is really more understanding of what I have gone through. We share our lives a lot differently now and I never enjoyed sex before as I do now." Other investigators have also referred to a growth experience from abortion reported by the women they studied.[19] In the absence of a long-term followup of these women it is hard to say how long these women were able to maintain the new perspective and transformation they acquired as a result of the abortion experience.

---

[19]Monsour & Stewart 1973; Patt et al. 1969; Smith 1973; Zimmerman 1977.

Contraceptive Use

Each of the forty-five women who had became sexually active again was asked what kind of birth control method she used and how frequently she used it after her abortion. All of them said that they were practicing contraception regularly, compared with one-third (34.3 percent) before the abortion. The pill was the method of choice by all but two women, who relied on condom or foam.[20] Both of them had tried the contraceptive pill but abandoned it because of side effects. Interestingly, six of the women who had not yet returned to sexual activity were also taking the pill regularly because, as one woman put it, "You never know." Another woman who was on the pill expressed a similar reason, but more cogently:

> I have gone out [since abortion] with a couple of guys but there is nobody that I care about right now. I think I might as well stay on the pill. I think it is a safer thing to do, just in case something ever does happen again. Then I won't have the fear of getting pregnant. I do not want to make the same mistake again.

"I do not want to make the same mistake again" was the resolve that motivated all forty-three sexually active women to stay on the most effective method of birth control, the pill. Their determination reflected unequivocally in the following statements: "Now, I'll never quit taking them;" "I have been on them right after

---

[20]Studies from North American and other countries confirm that contraceptive use increases manyfold after abortion among both married and unmarried women. Most women choose more effective methods--the pill, the IUD, and sterilization. These studies uniformly report that the practice rate before the abortion, which was about 30 percent, increased to 70 or 84 percent afterward. The current use of contraceptives is consistently higher among the abortion group than for all women, suggesting that induced abortion is a key in motivating to regulate fertility through nonsurgical methods of birth control. See Cobliner 1970; Freeman et al. 1981; Monsour & Stewart 1973; Martin 1972; Perez-Reyes & Falk 1973; Sachdev 1988; Smith 1973. Henshaw (1986) observed the trend among abortion patients that the percentage of those not using any contraceptives before the first abortion was 70 percent, compared to 9 percent of the women who failed to use a method after the abortion.

my abortion;" "Since the day of my abortion, I'm taking one every day, never miss it;" "I won't go off them until after I marry." Just how the experience with the unwanted pregnancy and abortion made these women contraceptively vigil and sophisticated is evident from the fact that nearly one-third of them had never used any birth control method prior to their pregnancy and that among the users three-fifths had relied on the male methods, condom or withdrawal. Their determination to stay on the pill contradicts the claim by anti-abortion lobbies that experience with abortion encourages the women to view the surgical method as an easy alternative to contraceptive use. On the contrary, even the women who rejected the pill before pregnancy because of the fear of side effects found this method of birth control acceptable after the abortion, as this woman's statement exemplifies:

> [Before pregnancy] I didn't want to use the pill because of its side effects. I read a lot about the pill and my mom who works at the hospital also told me that it caused problems. [After abortion] I now feel that I don't want to be in the same situation and the pill is the best method to avoid the same situation. You are liable to forget using the other methods. I don't want to take any chance with them.

SUMMARY

All the women found their pregnancy unacceptable and eventually decided to seek its termination. The relatively painless procedure performed in a short time surprised two-thirds of the women. The remainder expected it to go as it did. Soon after the abortion most women (78.6 percent) felt relief and satisfaction, which lasted from one week to five weeks. Thirteen women (18.6 percent) felt a distressing emptiness. Long-term (up to one year in this study) psychological reactions of guilt or depression were rare. Four-fifths of the women reported slight or no such reactions. Only one-fifth suffered moderate to severe reactions sometime after the abortion. However, regardless of the severity of the reactions, these symptoms tended to dissipate. The length of time each woman took to resolve the abortion experience depended on her coping abilities. The strategies most often used were suppression, rationalization, and intellectualization. The women who had greater difficulty in making the decision, who identified with the pregnancy, and who had less favorable attitudes toward abortion were more likely to experience psychological problems. The psychological reactions were determined on the basis of symptomatology of remorse and depression in behavioral and affective terms, explained in three steps of severity. Despite variation in the quality of the data, the sampling, and the measurement procedures used in previous investigations, the results of this study corroborate their findings.

Abortion adversely affected the relationships of most of these women with the men involved in the pregnancy. The pair relationship was assessed by the frequency of dating, feelings toward the man, and the women's desire to marry him. The post-abortion patterns were contrasted to those reported prior to and following the pregnancy.

Judging from the women's affective and behavioral responses, it seemed that the effect of abortion on their sex desire was minimal and transient. Only one-fourth (27 percent) reported a loss of interest in sex and men lasting from a few weeks to as long as five months. On the other hand, of the two-thirds of the women (64.3 percent) who resumed sexual activity, 10 percent more women found the sex act enjoyable after abortion. The improved sexual experience was attributable largely to a new freedom from the fear of pregnancy because most women were practicing the most effective methods of birth control.

9

Epilogue

NOW WHAT WAS I SAYING?

The study shows that although abortions have been legally available in Canada, only a few (13 percent) of the women sampled used abortion as a primary method of contraception. Most women considered abortion when other alternatives to an unwanted parenthood did not appear viable. The study also reveals that first-trimester abortion did not affect most women adversely and that almost all of them had assimilated the abortion experience by six months to one year after the procedure. A few women (10 percent) who suffered severe psychological reactions of guilt and depression were not impaired, and their symptoms eventually began to dissipate. The abortion effects were largely influenced by the women's identification with the pregnancy, moral and religious views of abortion, difficulty in deciding about termination, the degree of support from key people (such as the male partner or parents), and their ability to cope with life stresses. These findings are supported by recent reviews of previous scientific studies on abortion (see chapter 1). In point of fact, the psychological responses to abortion are far less serious than those experienced by women bringing their unwanted pregnancy to term and relinquishing the child for adoption. In my study of seventy-eight birth mothers selected randomly from a social agency in a Canadian province, 95 percent reported grief and loss after they signed their consent to adoption and two-thirds (67.7 percent) continued to experience these feelings five to fifteen years after relinquishment.[1] These findings were confirmed by the U.S. study I conducted in 1989-90. This study involved a much larger sample (n=364) of birth mothers who were contacted in thirty-nine states through a mail questionnaire. It showed that nearly 90 percent felt guilt and grief in the aftermath of adoption and that these feelings lasted for ten or more years.[2]

Studies of women who are denied abortion suggest that they suffer greater psychological disturbances such as emotional stress than those who are granted abortion.[3] Some investigators have noticed an improvement in the mental health (measured by the degree of depression and feelings of hostility) of the women who had an abortion compared to those who were compelled to deliver a child.[4] The consequences of an unwanted pregnancy on the development of the children born to women who are refused abortion are equally serious.   Studies, mostly on Scandinavian and Czechoslovakian (Prague) children show that the children not wanted by the mother run the risk of greater behavioral and developmental problems and poorer school performance than those born of an accepted pregnancy.[5]

The accounts of the women in this study as well as in previous studies strongly suggest that they do not want an abortion, but need one when confronted with an unwanted pregnancy. The protagonists on either side of the abortion controversy agree on the same goal of reducing or eliminating the need for abortion. While the anti-abortion activists seek legal means to ban abortion altogether, the pro-choicers stress preventing unwanted/unintended pregnancies through the availability of contraceptives and sex education and thereby averting the need for abortions.   The anti-abortion groups contend that unrestricted abortions encourage irresponsible sex among young unmarried women, weakening their resolve about contraception, and pose threats to traditional family values. However, research evidence refutes this claim.   Diamond (1981) conducted a comprehensive review of the data from Hawaii and Canada and found that, compared

---

[1]Sachdev 1989.

[2]Sachdev 1991a.

[3]See, Hook 1963, 1975; Pare and Raven 1970; Shainess 1970.

[4]Illsley & Hall 1976; Lipper et al. 1973; McCance et al. 1973.

[5]See, David et al. 1988; Matejcek et al. 1980, 1985;   Forssman and Thuwe 1966; Pare and Raven 1970.

to the period prior to the legalization of abortion, no significant changes had occurred during the three years following the law change in the mean age at first intercourse, the level of contraceptive use, the rates of illegitimacy, or the marital status of those who chose to abort or deliver. The author concludes, "if a marked shift in reproductive behavior continues to develop, it is likely to be for reasons other than a change in the law" (p. 205).

The abortion opponents advocate abstinence for young unmarrieds and maintain that sex can wait. Obviously, returning to Puritanical sex norms is not realistic, given the biological, psychosocial, demographic, and cultural normative forces in our society that encourage sexual activity, whether unrestrictive abortions are available or not. The reality is that adolescents are engaging in sex relations in higher proportions than ever and at an earlier age,[6] and they are getting pregnant in record numbers against their will because of imperfect contraceptive technology.[7] The demographic

---

[6]For an excellent analysis of factors associated with early initiation of adolescent sexual activity and its incidence, see Forrest and Singh 1990; Miller and Moore 1990; Sachdev 1981; Sonenstein et al. 1991; Smith 1991. Also, see *Time*, September 1991, p. 58.

[7]Teenagers in the United States have a higher rate of pregnancy, childbirth, and abortion than in most developed countries, even though the levels of adolescent sexual activity are almost similar. Women in their 20s and those older are no exception. This difference is attributed to a low level of contraceptive use in the United States, compared with that in most of these other countries, especially the use of the two most effective methods, the pill and the IUD. Westoff (1988), having compared the fertility rates among women in Western industrialized countries, concluded that American women under age 25 are far more likely to become pregnant than are comparable young women in other developed countries because they are less likely to use contraceptives. According to the author, American women have fewer birth control options than their European counterparts. Also, see Jones et al. 1986, 1988; Potts 1988. For a detailed account of adolescent sexual behavior, see Forrest & Singh 1990; Miller & Moore 1990; Robinson 1991; Sonenstein et al. 1991.

In Canada, while the marital fertility rate (per 1,000 women 15-44) dropped by 40 percent between 1974 and 1982, the fertility rate among unmarried teenagers under 20 increased 36 percent during the same period. Putting it differently, never-married women aged 15-19 accounted for 80 percent of all live births in 1989, compared to 34 percent in 1976. In addition, the pregnancy rate (live births plus abortions) among never-

profile of young women provides added reason for concern about their exposure to unintended pregnancies. Even if the rate of sexual activity among young women remains unchanged, there will be a greater number reporting sexual relationships because more women are being added to the reproductive age cohort. Thus, more women will be at risk of pregnancy. Unfortunately, even the risk of HIV infection does not seem to have slowed down the pace of sexual activity among the vast majority or to have made them contraceptively vigilant.[8] Young people seem to have a feeling of invulnerability,

---

married women jumped by 29 percent in 1980 and 57 percent in 1986 from 1975 (Statistics Canada, Catalogue #89-509, 1989; *Health Reports*, 1989, 1990).

[8]In a national probability sample of secondary school students in the United States, Anderson et al. (1990) found that nearly all students were fairly knowledgeable about the risk of HIV infection. However, only one-third of them always used condoms during sex acts. Females were less likely to say they always used condoms than were male students. Forty percent of all students had ever had two or more sex partners. According to NBC News (September 5,1992) about 8,000 teenagers become sexually active everyday and only one-quarter use condoms. Other studies have also indicated that, while high-risk groups, male homosexuals, and intravenous drug users have modified their behavior in the wake of the AIDS epidemic, there is less evidence of behavior changes among adolescents. See Becker and Joseph 1988; Bowen et al. 1990; Smith 1991; Sonenstein, Pleck, and Ku 1989; *Evening Telegram*, December 1, 1991; *Time*, September 1991: 58-59.

A survey of fifty-one Canadian colleges and universities showed that nearly all of the students knew that having sex with multiple partners increases the risk of acquiring AIDS, yet one in five men and one in twelve women have had ten or more partners, and only 16 percent of the women and 25 percent of the men said they always used condoms. Among the women, those with the most partners were the least likely to use condoms consistently (MacDonald et al. 1990). In high-risk areas of San Francisco, Catania et al. (1992) found that only 9 percent of unmarried heterosexual men and women said they always used condoms; 45 percent and 30 percent respectively said they sometimes used condoms, and 46 percent and 61 percent respectively never did so. In contrast, 48 percent of homosexual men surveyed said they always used condoms, and just 10 percent never did. Heterosexual men and women who had had one partner in the past year were twice as likely as those with two or more partners to always use condoms. In one of the largest U.S. sexual surveys, Catania et al. (1992)

which makes them prone to risk-taking. Kristine Luker suggests in her book *Taking Chances: Abortion and the Decision Not to Contracept* that some women view pregnancy as risk-taking like other risks in life, such as "failing to fasten safety belts in cars, cigarette smoking and risk-taking in sports" (1975: 62).[9] There is a possibility that more and more women who are users of contraceptive devices will experience unwanted pregnancies. Widely publicized risks for the pill and IUD have led many women to reject these methods and to switch to less effective methods of contraception.[10]

Undoubtedly, contraceptive methods that must be used during the sex act are not conducive to success because of the human factors involved in their consistent use and the cooperation these methods

---

found that among those with multiple sex partners, only 17 percent used condoms all of the time. Among those with high-risk sexual partners the condom use was only 13 percent regularly. Women and low-income people were most likely to have risky sexual partners and about 70 percent of them reported no condom use. The authors used a national probability sample involving 10,630 heterosexual Americans who were questioned by telephone. The authors concluded that current HIV prevention programs have failed to reach high-risk populations and a large segment of heterosexuals deny a personal risk (Catania et al. 1992). In the 1988 National Survey of Adolescent Males, Ku et al. (1992) found that 65 pecent of sexually active teenage males had never used condoms or used them irregularly. The authors concluded that the frequency of condom use was significantly decreased among teenage males who had sex more often, had more partners, and had contracted a sexually transmitted disease (p. 131).

That sexually active adolescents are more prone to risk-taking was also evident from another study of junior high school students in Rhode Island. Researchers noted that male students who were sexually active were less knowledgeable and less fearful about HIV and more likely to engage in risky behavior in the future than their counterparts who were abstinent. Less extreme patterns were found among sexually active female students of the same ages. See Brown, DiClemento & Beausolil 1992.

[9]Friedlander et al. (1984) concluded from their own study as well as from the literature that contraceptive risk-taking is associated with external locus of control (i.e., external forces or chance determine outcomes of unprotected sex). Also, see Dixon et al. 1984.

[10]For a comprehensive analysis of American women's contraceptive choices and behavior see Rindfuss, Swicegard & Bumpass 1989. Also, see Mosher 1990; Silverman, Torres & Forrest 1987; and *Globe and Mail*, April 7, 1990: D1.

require between sex partners. Although motivation and personal factors are important in the effective use of preventative methods, undesired pregnancies do not always result from lack of motivation. There are social, cultural, and societal factors that restrict the availability of birth control devices and information to the target population. The U.S. National Academy of Sciences in its report, *Developing New Contraceptives: Obstacles and Opportunities*, released in January 1990, observed that, although the contraceptive use has increased among sexually active young people in the last few years, the incidence of contraceptive failure and its discontinuance has also been high.[11] In addition, the currently available methods of birth control are not suited to many women because of religious, economic, cultural, or health reasons. Available methods also do not meet women's needs at different stages of their lives and in the different contexts in which sex takes place. In view of this, some experts maintain that even if all sexually active single women are exposed to contraceptive information and devices, a considerable number of them are at risk of becoming pregnant when they do not

---

[11]The Academy estimated that 1.6 to 2 million accidental pregnancies occurred in the United States in 1987, which could be attributed to contraceptive failure; about half of these pregnancies end in abortion each year (Mastroianni, Donaldson & Kane 1990). Former U.S. Surgeon General Koop reported to the U.S. Congress in March 1989 that of approximately 55 million women of reproductive age 32 million were sexually active and 88 percent of them practice birth control. However, many did not use methods regularly or use less effective methods, exposing a substantial number of them, approximately 23 million, to the risk of unintended pregnancy (Committee on Government Operations 1989: 220). Kost, Forrest & Harlap (1991) put the estimates of sexually active American women at 38.8 million (two-thirds of their population); 90 percent of them use a birth control method at some time. However, these women are at risk of having five unintended births during their reproductive lifetime. Unintended pregnancies are particularly prevelant among young single women. Between 1983 and 1988, 87 percent of all births to 15-19-year-old never-married women and 69 percent of all births to 20-24-year-old never-married women were reported as unwanted or mistimed (Pratt et al. 1984: 31). In a study of birth control in southern Ontario, Canada, Delmore et al. (1991) found that while sexually active adolescents obtain the most effective method, the pill, many do not comply with its continued or proper use.

want to.[12] Further support of their pessimism is provided by the large number of unwanted/unintended pregnancies that regularly occur among married women who do not face the same paradoxical circumstances and structural obstacles as do young unmarried women.[13] Teitze and Henshaw (1986) reviewed the international data on abortion and estimated that in the absence of contraceptive methods each women would require an average of nine or ten abortions in her lifetime. On the other hand, if the couples used 95 percent effective contraceptives, seven out of ten women would require one abortion sometime in their lives.

As noted in this study as well as by other investigators, adoption or a "quickie marriage" cause an unmarried woman more personal and emotional hazards than termination of a pregnancy. Thus, faced with an unwanted pregnancy, many a woman will resort to the only option, the induced abortion as a back-up measure. What is needed is not more restrictive or encumbered abortion laws, but greater understanding of the women who are faced with the dilemma of choosing an abortion and, more important, improved contraceptive techniques that are noncoital, safe, effective, convenient, inexpensive, and reversible and that are suited to a variety of circumstances. Only such an "ideal" contraceptive method can offer hopes of reducing the

---

[12]See Cutright 1971; Sandberg & Jacobs 1971. Two comprehensive analyses of contraceptive failure rates among married and unmarried women reveal that the probability of unintended pregnancies is considerably high even under conditions of perfect use (Trussell & Kost 1987). Having corrected for underreporting of abortion in the previous reviews, Jones and Forrest (1989) reported revised contraceptive failure rates that indicated that, depending on the method used, between 6 percent and 26 percent of couples experience an accidental pregnancy in the first year of use.

[13]According to the former Surgeon General's testimony referred to earlier, of the more than 6 million pregnancies annually, approximately 54 percent are unintended. Also, see Bachrach 1984; Greenglass 1976; Hepworth 1975; Mosher & Pratt 1990; Williams & Pratt 1990. A more recent analysis of the 1988 data for the National Survey of Family Growth shows that 57 percent of all pregnancies conceived in 1987 were unintended (Forrest and Singh 1990). In a startling report published in the *British Medical Journal*, the author observed that despite increased contraceptive use, the incidence of unintended pregnancies has risen among English women from 27 percent in 1984 to 31 percent in 1989, even among those using the pill. The author attributes the phenomenon to "gaps in knowledge about birth control, even among users" (Fleissig 1991).

demand for abortion. However, such a contraceptive continues to elude scientists. Since the advent of the pill and the IUD in the 1960s only modest efforts have been made toward new methods. In the past few years an array of new contraceptive devices have been tested, including injectables (e.g., DepoProvera), transdermal patches, NORPLANT, a five-year subdermal implant, and a contraceptive vaccine that can immunize a woman for several months. But the development of these methods has so far been limited to a few human trials because of poor funding for research, strict federal regulations, and conservative public attitudes.[14] A new oral contraceptive pill known as Centchroman has been tested on humans in India.[15] This is the first nonhormonal pill of its kind considered safe, effective and free from the side effects usually associated with hormonal pills. To be taken only once a week, the pill works post-coitally too, if taken within 24 hours following intercourse. The pill is now available in India, but it could be years before this drug would be permitted by the U.S. Food and Drug Administration and the regulatory agency in Canada for use by North American women. Some of the newer methods such as NORPLANT are running into stiff opposition from some groups. Surprisingly, among the critics are feminist groups who charge that these contraceptives are potentially hazardous to women's health and that their long-term safety is not yet demonstrated or not publicized.[16] Besides, none of these devices, if developed,

---

[14]Mastroianni, Donaldson & Kane 1990. In October 1992, the U.S. Food and Drug Adminstration gave approval to Depo-Provera for use as a contraceptive that would prevent pregnancy for three months after its injection. Already used in ninety countries, the drug is highly effective. Despite the euphoria among some women's groups, the contraceptive is not without its side effects, including weight gain and menstrual irregularities. It can also make women tired, weak, dizzy, and nervous, and can cause headaches and abdominal pain. Besides, the drug is linked to cancer of the cervix and breast, and it is not recommended for long-term use for some women. Indeed, the inventors of the drug claim that its potential benefits outweigh the risks.

[15]*Times of India*, February 15, 1992.

[16]NORPLANT is becoming available in clinics and private medical offices across the United States and in more than ninety other countries. Its initial reports reveal that side-effects of NORPLANT are similar to those of the pill (*Chatelaine*, April 1991: 28). In many cases the side-effects of a drug or contraceptive are not fully known until after their use for years as

is capable of serving the needs of all women in different circumstances. For example, young single women who engage in sex sporadically may not feel the need to "stay prepared." Not surprisingly, much of the research efforts have been concentrated on females' contraceptives rather than males'. This attitude reflects the traditional view of society, which regards the woman as the gatekeeper and the controlling agent. The man is willing to go as far as a woman lets him go, and it is her responsibility to say "no." As it has always been the woman and not the man who bears the brunt of nonmarital sexual activity, society continues to believe that the woman must take responsibility for contraception if she does not want to become pregnant.

New Abortion Pill: A Medical Breakthrough

The most viable alternative to abortion is a pill, known as RU 486, that induces an abortion without surgery in pregnancies of less than seven weeks. The drug, developed by a French company, is taken twice a day for seven days and blocks progestin, causing the fertilized egg to dislodge or preventing its implantation, and the pregnancy is terminated. RU 486 is dramatically different from existing contraceptives or the morning-after pill in that it is clearly an abortifacient that does not prevent fertilization but induces the termination of pregnancy. Also, women who take RU 486 as a morning-after pill suffer less nausea and vomiting than women given the standard post-coital contraceptive, a large dose of birth control pills. Some suggest that the drug acts at the time of ovulation and before implantation. RU 486 in combination with prostoglandin is

---

in the case of the oral pill and IUD. A new study published in the Journal of the American Medical Association suggests that barrier methods such as condoms and diaphragms increase the risks for developing preeclampsia, which causes maternal and fetal complications (*USA Today*, December 9, 1989). NORPLANT, which is considered the most revolutionary contraceptive since the birth control pill, has already fallen into disrepute because some conservatives are trying to use coercive means to enforce its use among poor women, for example, in the states of Louisiana, California, and Kansas (*New York Times*, October 18, 1991). While American women gained a new contraceptive option, NORPLANT is priced out of reach of low-income women.

widely used in France with a success rate of 96 percent and is commercially available in China, Britain and at least eleven countries in Europe, but not in North America.[17]

The testing of the pill has not begun in the United States, but it is already raising the hackles of the anti-abortion groups, among others. The abortion opponents have threatened boycotts worldwide against the manufacturer of the pill. They charge that RU 486 is no different from surgical abortion, as it indiscriminately takes life after it has begun. They argue that, although the pill may do away with abortion clinics, it will not do away with abortions, because life begins at the moment of fertilization. By this definition, women who have intrauterine devices (IUDs), which work by preventing egg implantation are also having an abortion. Is it not better if a woman prevents a pregnancy with a morning-after pill than if she terminates it later?

If the pill goes on the market, it could make many surgical procedures obsolete. Early tests results show that the pill has few side effects, mainly for women with cardiac problems and for those over 35.[18] Because it is taken early in pregnancy or before a woman knows that she is pregnant, it raises fewer moral dilemmas.[19] It can eliminate an agonizing problem that confronts women who worry they might be pregnant, and it can do away with the emotional stress associated with a visit to an abortion clinic or hospital. Also, replacing early surgical abortions could result in substantial saving of taxpayers' monies. It is unfair to deny women a possible medical advance which makes the reproductive decisions truly a private matter of the woman, not of the government or others intervening in that

---

[17]Klistch 1991; *Plain Dealer*, October 29, 1989; *Pro-Choice News*, Summer 1991: 8; Digest (1990), *Family Planning Perspectives*, 22 (3): 134-35. RU 486 is banned from use in the United States and Canada.

[18]Klitsch 1991: 275. The pill has other potential virtues. It may prove useful in the treatment of Glaucoma, and breast and adrenal cancer (*Globe and Mail*, Editorial, October 9, 1992).

[19]Studies done on French and British women show that 88 percent to 94 percent of the women who obtained a medical abortion (by taking RU 486) were satisfied, and even some women who had had both types preferred the medical abortion to a surgical abortion (Klitsch 1991: 277).

decision.[20]   It holds the promise of an "ideal" contraceptive and could end the abortion wars. Given the stiff resistance from abortion foes, it seems women will have to wait a little longer before they win freedom in reproductive choices.

Pregnancy Counseling

As long as women need abortions, any punitive measures would only exacerbate their emotional problems. Studies have shown that neither fears of pregnancy or sexually transmitted diseases nor denial of legalized abortion deter women from engaging in pre-marital sex relations.[21] Equally true, an absence of abortion laws does not encourage women to beat down the doors of abortion clinics, as demonstrated in Canada (see chapter 1). Because abortion is not treated like any other surgical procedure and it is opposed by religious and political leaders, a visit to an abortion clinic or hospital induces a lot of emotional stress.   This finding underscores the importance of pregnancy counseling as a means of ensuring women a supportive environment and a sympathetic handling of their problems.[22]

A medical practice that confines the parameters of its concerns to the female reproductive system represents an unsound and circumscribed abortion service and is not truly therapeutic. Given the social climate where abortion is still condemned, an unwanted pregnancy and the decision to have an abortion can present an acute emotional crisis and a serious personal dilemma for many unmarried women. An undesired pregnancy can be especially overwhelming if it coincides with adolescence, a period characterized by sexual,

---

[20]The way RU 486 is administered under controlled conditions in Britain does not make the reproductive choice for women totally free from the intrusion of health professionals and institutions. Women who want the pill must obtain written permission from two doctors. The abortion pill is administered in approved clinics or hospitals under medical supervision, and women are not allowed to take the pills home. The use of the pill under controlled environments will not make abortions casual, easier, or less morally difficult, as is feared by anti-abortion groups. The pill is merely a technique that will make abortions safer.

[21]Lindemann 1974; Schofield 1965.

[22]Sachdev 1985.

physical, and emotional changes. Many of these women live within a social network that is critically deficient, which further restricts opportunities to share in the decision making and to seek objective, dispassionate advice and support. Young single women are particularly vulnerable to the intense emotional trauma of an unwanted pregnancy as they generally lack the needed emotional support and participation from the male partner.

The primary objective of counseling is to recognize and understand the nature of the woman's dilemma and help her reach the best decision possible by providing factual information. The counselor enables the woman to canvass each alternative with its attendant liabilities, keeping in view her psychosocial milieu and value system so that the choice made is deliberate, rational, and the least undesirable. If an abortion is her choice of action, it is crucial that the woman is helped with her dilemma so that she can approach the abortion with the least doubts and anxiety. Feelings of ambivalence can be gauged by exploring her feelings about abortion itself and about the fetus. The resolution of a woman's pre-abortion ambivalence is significant in light of the research findings that adverse psychological reactions of guilt and depression in the aftermath of abortion are highly likely to occur among those with unresolved feelings and negative emotions.

In fact, the resolution of the problem pregnancy is only the short-term goal of abortion counseling, which should also emphasis as its long-term objective of preventing future undesired pregnancy and abortion. Given the heightened concern over the incidence of repeat abortions among young unmarried women, contraceptive counseling constitutes another significant component in the abortion service. The demand for an abortion generally represents failure-- contraceptive, societal, or personal. Obtaining and successfully using a contraceptive method involves a complex set of variables. A counselor should thoroughly evaluate the nature of the relationship of the woman with her sex partner, her attitudes toward contraception, the circumstances under which her sexual activity takes place, and the psychosocial factors affecting her contraceptive practice. Family planning is more than writing a prescription; it involves discussion of various methods of conception control and assisting the woman to choose one best suited for her age, her religious scruples, her ability to implement contraceptive responsibility, and her current sexual activity.

Working with the Male Partner

Effective contraception is a deliberate and cooperative act involving mutual planning and support. If a woman's partner is still in the picture, he should be involved in the decision making. By encouraging his involvement, the counselor is emphasizing that reproductive responsibility is as mutual as sexual activity. The counselor can also use this opportunity to effect a constructive and more meaningful relationship between the couple, which is crucial for emotional support for the woman during her stressful period. This orientation is consistent with the emerging relationship-centered focus of family planning services.[23] The male's active involvement and encouragement is particularly important if the couple chooses female-orientated contraception, a strong possibility in most cases. Studies show that most males do not take effective precautions against pregnancy and view contraception as the female responsibility.[24]

---

[23]Figley & Scroggins 1978.

[24]Even if there were a more convenient contraceptive method than condoms, men might be unwilling to use it because they wish never to be concerned with the procreative consequences of unprotected sex, which, after all, happen in someone else's body. Gough (1979) asked 151 randomly selected men living in the San Francisco Bay Area, if they would use a contraceptive pill for males if one were available. No more than a little over one-half (55.6 percent) said yes. Freeman et al. (1980) studied 730 male and female high school students and found that males were less likely to recognize the risk of pregnancy, had less information about contraception, and fewer attitudes that supported contraceptive use than females. Pleck et al. (1990) analyzed the National Survey of Adolescent Males conducted in 1988, the first survey of its kind to assess the sexual and contraceptive behavior of adolescent males in the United States. The authors found that males who indicated their intentions to use condoms tended to believe that males are repsonsible for contraception, that condom use would be appreicated by one's partner, that condoms involve little reduction in sexual pleasure, and that condoms would reduce the risk of AIDS. Based on these findings, it can be argued that condom use could be promoted among sexually active males by emphasizing male responsibility and the benefits to males of this contraceptive method.

It is possible that with the advent of the pill and IUD, which gave women tools for choice and their sexual freedom, the women bargained more than they had asked for, since the contraceptive technologies exposed women to health hazards and provided men with a convenient rationalization

Studies have also shown that the male partner's support and encouragement significantly contribute to the initiation and maintenance of contraception among young females.[25]

The male's involvement in counseling also serves the useful purpose of providing an opportunity for him to gain an appreciation of the emotional stress that a woman experiences. There is disagreement among investigators as to the male partner's reaction to the woman's experience with abortion. This study shows that in most cases the women's boyfriends considered abortion to be a woman's concern and were indifferent to their experience. However, other investigators observed that many male partners of women who underwent abortions usually felt upset and worried about the woman's situation and resented being excluded from the actual decision.[26] It seems that the male consort's reactions depend, in large part, upon the nature of the dyadic relationship.

As has been noted, the most common contraceptive methods used by unmarried women are the condom and withdrawal, which put the onus on the male to prevent pregnancy. In such situations, a woman's vulnerability to pregnancy is linked to her ability to persuade the man to use protective devices and to his responsiveness to her persuasion. Thus, the counselor may teach the woman assertiveness as a valuable social skill to enable her to exert a greater influence in sexual and contraceptive decisions. Fox (1977) found that women with a feminist orientation are more successful in obtaining compliance from their sex partners in contraceptive use than more conventional women. Jorgenson et al. (1980) also observed in their sample of 150 clinic patients aged 12 to 17 that the female's active involvement in sexual decisions was directly related to the male's responsibility for contraception.

---

for shifting the responsibility to the woman to prevent conception as well as to deal with the conception she failed to prevent (see Collins 1985 and Greer 1984 for their thought-provoking analysis of the impact of contraceptive and reproductive technologies on the relations between women and men and the social control of women's reproductive functions).

[25]See Cvetkovich & Grote 1982; Herold & Goodwin 1980; Niemela et al. 1981.

[26]Brosseau 1980; Shostak & McLouth 1984.

Attitude Toward Sexuality

Because the act of contraception is intimately linked with sexuality, it is imperative that a counselor explore the woman's attitude toward sexuality, her sexual behavior, and how she views her responsibility. As noted in chapter 4 there are a variety of nonsexual needs that propel women toward sexual relations in addition to the physical drive to release sexual tension or libidinal energy. The counselor needs the skill and training to understand the woman's underlying motives of sexual and reproductive behavior. Only by discussing with the woman the reasons and responsibility for her sexual behavior and helping her find more constructive ways of self-expression and dealing with interpersonal relationships can a counselor help the woman become reproductively discriminating.

There is compelling research evidence that women who have a positive attitude toward themselves and accept their sexuality and personal responsibility are more likely to prepare themselves contraceptively.[27] It stands to reason that women who view their sexual behavior as unacceptable are likely to feel guilty about it, as deliberate and conscious use of contraceptive methods implies admission that they are sexually active. Such denial serves to prevent only contraception, not sex.

Abortion counseling does not end with the resolution of the pregnancy dilemma but continues even after a woman has made the decisive choice of carrying the pregnancy to term or ending it via abortion. In the former case, the counselor may refer the woman to a family and child welfare agency that provides follow-up and management of such cases with support, assistance, and guidance throughout the gestation period and following childbirth. If the woman chooses the abortion option, it is vitally important that the counselor discuss the mechanics of the surgical procedure, its

---

[27]See Brandt et al. 1978; Cvetkovich et al. 1975, 1982; Dembo & Lundell 1979; Fisher 1978; Winter 1988. Research findings also suggest that sexual self-concept improves with age, which partially explains why younger teenagers are less effective in contraceptive use (in terms of frequency and the choice of the most effective methods). Because of their developmental limitations, most adolescent females lack the adequate reasoning, decision-making abilities, and cognitive maturity that are required to be effective contraceptive users (see Elkind 1967; Ginsburg & Opper 1988; Struder & Thornton 1989).

physical, emotional, and sexual after-effects, the post-operative precautions, and the hospital protocols.[28] Questions such as those regarding physical pain and sterility should be fully discussed prior to the procedure. It has been noted in this study as well as other investigations that even the determined woman experiences nagging doubts and eerie feelings regarding the abortion surgery, which essentially emanate from misinformation or a complete absence of information about the technique. The significance of dealing with surgery-related fears becomes abundantly clear when one considers the impersonal nature of the hospital environment and the not-very-supportive attitude of the health-care personnel toward premaritally pregnant women. Given such circumstances, at times these women feel too threatened to bring up their doubts with the health-care staff.

Post-Abortion Counseling

If the knowledge of what happens during abortion surgery is important, it is equally important to know what to expect psychologically and emotionally following surgery. This study as well as others have consistently shown that, while severe psychopathology is rare after first trimester abortion, many women experience negative psychological reactions of guilt or depression, although these reactions are mild and transient. To be sure, follow-up counseling may not be required by some women, because they have a supportive psychosocial milieu. But for those women having difficulty in resolving their pregnancy and abortion experience, post-abortion counseling can be of benefit. As this study suggests those women who approach abortion with ambivalence, lack psychological strength and a supportive network, identify with their pregnancy, have an unfavorable attitude toward abortion, or feel coerced into accepting an abortion and those whose pregnancy is terminated by saline procedure are highly susceptible to psychological trauma. These women make highly suitable candidates for follow-up counseling.

---

[28]Some investigators found in their studies that women who were less adequately prepared for the procedure were at greater risk of emotional distress afterward (Belsey et al. 1977; Lemkau 1991; Strassberg & Moore 1985).

Psychological disturbances are not the only basis for post-abortion counseling. Contraceptive and sex counseling can form an important component of follow-up with women who have undergone an abortion. In fact, once a woman is relieved from the anxiety brought about by her pregnancy, she is more likely to accept rationally contraceptive advice. During this phase, a counselor should also deal with a woman's attitudes toward sex and men in general, which may be adversely affected by guilt, as possible reactions to abortion. A woman may begin to distrust all men and to view sex as dangerous.

It is ironic that the people who oppose abortion also oppose sex education and contraceptive information for teenagers. Most young people lack information on reproductive system and sexual anatomy and functioning. Their primary source of information or misinformation is peers and "girlie" magazines, which create misconceptions of them and their roles as men and women. Too often program initiatives in this area are hampered by anti-abortion activists' disagreement with the definition, objectives, and contents of the curriculum. They also argue that sex education should be provided by parents and the schools should not be involved. However, most parents support the idea of sex education programs in the schools because of their limited knowledge and discomfort in discussing sex-related matters with their children. According to a national survey of Canada and a Gallup Poll in 1984, 83 percent of Canadian adults supported the teaching of sex education in schools.[29] While parents overwhelmingly endorse a high-school based sex education program, their support for making birth control devices available to teenagers is considerably weaker. In a survey done in Calgary, Alberta, in 1979-80, while eight out of ten parents with school-going children favored such educational programs, only one-half (53.5 percent) of them supported the idea of making contraceptives accessible to teenagers.[30] The American surveys provide similar findings. The 1986 survey of adult Americans showed that 85 percent were in favor of sex education in school curriculum. This proportion was up from 76 percent in 1975 and from 69 percent in 1965 favoring such instruction.[31] They also

---

[29]*Tellus*, September 1984: 25.

[30]Meikle et al. 1985: 103.

[31]Kenney et al. 1989.

support making birth control information available in school health clinics, but only a minority believe that clinics should dispense contraceptive devices.   Those who are opposed to providing contraceptives to adolescents argue that the ready availability of contraceptive methods will encourage sexual experimentation. Research evidence does not support this assertion.   On the other hand, research studies have consistently shown that adolescents who receive sex education or contraceptive information at home are more likely to postpone sexual activity to a later age, to use contraceptives, and to have fewer sex partners.[32]

---

[32]See Eisen & Zellman 1987; Furstenberg et al. 1985; Inazu & Fox 1980; Kirby 1984; Kirby et al. 1991; Rosoff 1989; Shah & Zelnik 1981; Spanier 1977; Yarber & Greer 1986. These authors reported that sex and contraceptive information in the schools had little impact on the student's premarital sexual behavior. In some metropolitan areas birth rates declined among sexually active teens who were exposed to sex education (Zelnik & Kim 1982).   A Johns Hopkins University study of the effectiveness of school based health clinics (Zabin et al. 1986) showed that schools in which health clinics made referrals and dispensed contraceptives reported an increase in the percentage of virgin females visiting the program, an increase in contraceptive use, and a significant reduction in pregnancy rates. After twenty-eight months, pregnancy rates had decreased 30 percent at experimental schools versus a 53 percent increase at control schools. Kirby et al. (1991) designed a study to assess the impact of reproductive health programs of six school-based clinics in different states on sexual and contraceptive behavior of students. The authors found that in the two-year period following the introduction of the program, "the clinics neither hastened the onset of sexual activity nor increased its frequency" (p. 6). In four of the six school clinics that provided "contraceptives or vouchers to obtain contraceptives without charge, contraceptive use increased that helped prevent a small number of pregnancies" (p. 16).   More recently, using a quasi-experimental design Kirby et al. (1991) evaluated a sexuality education curriculum (called Reducing the Risk) among 758 students in thirteen high schools in rural and urban areas of California. The investigators measured the impact immediately after the exposure, six months later, and eighteen months later and found that, while the program increased participants' knowledge of contraceptives and parent-child communication, it did not significantly affect frequency of sexual intercourse among sexually experienced students. The authors also noted that the sexuality education did not significantly increase the use of contraceptives among sexually active students, a findig which was inconsistent with their earlier study, referred to above. The authors attributed this contradiction to the small sample size

in the California study.

Similar findings were reported by Dryfoos (1988), who extensively reviewed impact-evaluation data available during the three-year period since the school-based health clinic programs were introduced. These clinics provided sex education, contraceptive services, and counseling to students of junior and senior high school. The author noted consistency in the studies that reported delay in the initiation of sexual activity and increased use of contraceptives among young people. The studies were also consistent in refuting the anti-abortion argument that such programs would encourage promiscuity and increase the rates of sexual activity among students. A reproductive-health consultation program emphasizing abstinence and contraception among teenage males demonstrated that highly explicit contraception instruction did not encourage early initiation of sexual activity. On the contrary, the evidence suggests that the young males felt reduced pressure to become sexually active and that the consultation promoted the use of contraceptives. The authors obtained samples of adolescent males aged 15-18 from four health clinics in four northwest states (Danielson et al. 1990).

In an effort to determine the specific content of sex education that may influence the sexual attitudes and contraceptive activity among young people, a few studies documented skills to avoid intercourse and good values as having an effect on sexual and contraceptive behavior, rather than dissemination of sex education, contraceptive information, and methods alone. Eisen, Zellman & McAlister (1990) evaluated the outcomes of school-based education and contraceptive education programs that emphasized values and personal responsibility and found substantial delays in the initiation of sexual activity among adolescent men and increased use of effective contraceptives. More recently, Ku et al. (1992) reported similar findings. Using a nationally representative sample of never-married men aged 15-19 in the United States, the authors observed that the receipt of AIDS education and sex education with emphasis on skills needed to resist sexual intercourse resulted in modest but significant decreases in the numbers of sexual partners and the frequency of intercourse and promoted safer sex in the year prior to the survey. Similarly, Olsen et al. (1992) demonstrated the use of three sex education programs: Values and Choices, Teen Aid, and Sex Respect, which were "received very positively by secondary school students" (p. 369). These programs stressed abstinence until marriage, responsibility, importance of planning for the future, consequences of teenage pregnancy, and how to resist peer pressure. Having extensively evaluated several sexuality education curriculums in high schools in the United States, Kirby et al. (1991b) concluded that knowledge alone is not a complete soution to inadequate contraceptive use among

Counseling Effectiveness

A few studies   show that counseling can be effective in
encouraging women to return for post-abortion check-ups and thus
reduce the incidence of complications. Counseled women also choose
the most effective methods of birth control. They also approach
abortion with less apprehension and anxiety and react more positively
to the abortion afterward, with fewer emotional disturbances. Group
discussion provides a helpful opportunity to seek support, share ideas,
and resolve abortion-related conflicts.[33]

Some experts in the field suggest that it is not so much the
counseling techniques and procedures that contribute to positive
behavior change in clients as the personal attributes and suitability of
the counselor.[34]   They contend that specific techniques and skills,
while important, do not occur independent of the inherent qualities of
the change agent. They further observe that the personal ingredients
of the counselor cut across therapists and all types of interventative
modalities.   Among counselors' personal traits, the quality of
relationship with the client, empathy, and genuineness have been
identified as comprising the major therapeutic force. The experience
of women who have received counseling at clinics run by Dr. Henry
Morgentaler in Canada and by CARAL (Canadian Abortion Rights
Action League) and Planned Parenthood in Canada and the United
States attests to the caring and personal interest of the counselors.

---

sexually experienced students unless contents emphasize specific values and
attitudes. See also Bennett 1988; Fine 1988; Koop 1988. These authors
contend that the contraceptive approach that ignores good values,
commitment, and sexuality in the context of marriage offers merely a
mechanical and bureaucratic solution and does not effectively discourage
unmarried teenagers from initiating sexual activity. Some studies report that
parental discussion of sexual matters is associated with influence on sexual
opinions, beliefs, and attitudes that play an important role in delaying sexual
activity, increasing contraceptive use, and reducing the chances for out-of-
wedlock pregnancy (see Hansen, Myers & Ginsburg 1987; Sanders & Mullis
1988).

[33]See, for instance, Bernstein and Tinkham 1971; Bracken et al. 1973;
Burnell et al. 1972; Dauber et al. 1972; Kaminsky & Sheckter 1979; Leiter
1972.

[34]See Bergin & Lambert 1978; Kaminsky & Sheckter 1979; Shulman
1989; Truax & Carkhuff 1967; Truax & Mitchell 1971; Zilbergeld 1983.

They have found the counselors very helpful in providing corrective emotional experiences and a psychologically safe atmosphere conducive to free expression. It is, however, unfortunate that these clinics, which have been providing women with the much needed pre- and post-abortion counseling as well as preventative services are under constant, relentless attack from the anti-abortion movement. Its supporters are trying to undo what women have achieved under the *Roe v. Wade* decision and to recriminalize the abortion procedure in Canada. They continue to be on the offensive with moralistic rhetorics, refusing to accept that the woman should be allowed to make the choice between her needs and the developing fetus in accordance with her moral dictates and religious beliefs.

Unfortunately, there is no prospect for truce on the abortion battle in the near future because, as Kristine Luker (1984) argues, the opposition to abortion is based not so much on the religious values of pro-life activists but on their broader commitment to the dogmatic view of women's traditional role as childbearer. In their view women should give higher priority to family than to a career, which does not take into account the new social order or the possibility of new technology that would enable women to accomplish abortion in the privacy of their homes or the new techniques of transplanting fertilized eggs into another womb. According to Lynn Shepler (1991), the traditional view of women has been strengthened by the masculine values that do not recognize the importance of women's health and well-being, including women's capacity for sexual expression, as a positive moral good. She further argues that the anti-women view can be traced to Christian teachings on abortion and contraception. The indifference to the women's well-being, she argues, is reflected in Supreme Court rulings that fail to address the question of the risks of death and disability from state-imposed childbearing. The Court's reference to maternal health arises from its concern for the compelling interest of the state rather than for the right or interest of an individual woman, so that the state can regulate women's access to abortion. There is further evidence that political leaders show a total disregard for women's well-being. While strong commitments are being made to protect potential life from the moment of conception through constitutional amendments, little has been done to increase the level of support for improved contraceptive technology, which is the only way to relieve women from the threat of involuntary childbearing. Abraham Lincoln's advice seems

pertinent here: "The dogmas of the quiet past are inadequate to the
stormy present. . . . As our case is new, so must we think anew and
act anew . . . we must disenthral ourselves."

Appendix A

Table A 1
Legal Abortions, rates per 1,000 Women Aged 15-44 Years, Selected Countries

Country	Rate per 1,000 women
China	38.8
Hungary	38.2
United States[1]	27.3
Sweden[2]	21.0
Japan	18.6
Denmark	18.3
Norway	16.8
Israel	16.2
Italy	15.3
England & Wales	14.2
New Zealand	11.4
Canada[3]	14.8
Scotland	8.3
Netherlands	5.1

1. relates to 1988
2. personal communication, relates to 1989.
3. relates to 1990
Source: Statistics Canada, *Health Reports* 1990, vol. 2(3), p. 234-38.

Table A 2
Legal Abortions by Age of Woman, United States, 1973-88

Age[1]	1973	1974	1976	1978	1980	1982	1984	1985	1986	1987	1988
Total Abortions (Millions)	0.744	0.898	1.179	1.409	1.553	1.573	1.577	1.588	1.574	1.559	1.590
Percent Increase from prior year	n/a	20.7	14.0	7.1	3.8	-0.2	0.1	0.8	-0.9	-1.0	2.1
Percentage											
Under 15 years	1.6	1.5	1.3	1.1	1.0	0.9	1.1	1.1	1.0	0.9	0.9
15-19 "	31.2	31.0	30.8	29.7	28.4	26.6	25.3	25.1	24.7	24.5	24.7
18-19 "	--	--	17.8	17.7	16.8	15.9	15.1	14.7	14.2	14.2	14.7
20-24 "	32.3	31.9	33.3	34.7	35.4	35.0	34.9	34.5	33.8	33.2	32.7
25-29 "	17.4	18.1	18.7	18.9	19.6	20.7	21.1	21.2	21.6	21.6	21.8
30-34 "	9.7	10.0	9.3	9.5	9.8	10.7	11.1	11.4	11.8	12.3	12.4
35-39 "	5.5	5.4	4.8	4.6	4.3	4.7	5.2	5.4	5.8	6.0	6.0
over 40 "	2.3	2.1	1.8	1.5	1.3	1.4	1.3	1.3	1.3	1.5	1.5

241

Table A 2 (continued)

Rates/1,000 women[1]

Total (15-44 yrs)	16.3	19.3	24.2	27.7	29.3	28.8	28.1	28.0	27.4	26.9	27.3
Under 15 years[2]	5.6	6.4	7.6	7.5	8.4	8.3	9.3	9.2	9.2	8.8	8.6
15-19 "	22.8	26.9	34.3	33.7	42.9	42.9	43.2	43.8	42.2	42.2	44.0
18-19 "	--	--	49.3	58.4	61.0	60.0	61.5	63.0	61.9	61.0	63.5
less than 20*	23.9	28.2	35.8	41.1	44.4	44.4	45.0	45.7	44.4	43.8	45.5
20-24 years	26.2	30.4	39.6	47.2	51.4	51.2	51.8	52.3	52.2	52.5	54.2
25-29 "	16.4	19.6	24.1	28.4	30.8	31.5	30.9	30.9	30.9	30.8	31.8
30-34 "	10.9	13.0	15.0	16.4	17.1	17.7	17.8	17.8	17.9	17.9	18.1
35-39 "	7.1	8.4	9.3	9.8	9.3	9.3	9.5	9.7	9.7	9.8	9.9
over 40 "	2.9	3.3	3.7	3.6	3.5	3.3	2.9	2.9	2.8	2.9	3.0

Rate/100 live births plus abortions
(percentage of total known pregnancies[3] terminated by abortion)

Under 15 years	--	--	--	40.9	42.7	42.9	45.9	45.7	43.8	41.0	39.1
15-17 "	--	--	--	39.7	42.4	42.0	42.5	43.2	42.9	42.0	40.9
18-19 "	--	--	--	39.3	40.1	40.5	40.9	41.0	40.7	40.2	40.6
less than 20	25.6	29.0	35.8	39.6	41.2	41.2	41.2	42.1	41.8	41.0	40.7
20-24 years	17.6	20.0	25.0	28.7	30.1	30.6	31.3	31.5	31.5	31.3	31.3
25-29 "	13.2	15.4	18.6	20.8	21.8	22.3	22.0	22.0	22.0	21.6	21.7
30-34 "	18.7	21.7	23.1	23.5	23.3	23.2	22.1	21.8	21.5	21.1	20.6
35-39 "	28.3	32.8	36.6	38.6	37.2	34.2	32.8	32.2	31.9	30.4	29.1
over 40 "	39.7	44.4	50.2	51.6	51.7	51.4	49.4	49.4	46.2	45.3	43.9

1.By reported age at abortions.
2.Per 1,000 women aged 14
3.Legal abortions plus live births

*Rates for women aged 19 or less are computed per 1,000 women aged 15-19 years.

Source: S. K. Henshaw and J. Van Vorts, eds. *Abortion Factbook, 1992 Edition: Readings, Trends, and State and Local Data to 1988.* New York: The Alan Guttmacher Institute, 1992.

Table A 3
Age Specific Therapeutic Abortion Rates (per 1,000 women of same age), Canada 1974-90

Year	18-19	15-19[1]	20-24	25-29	30-34	35-39	40-44	all ages[2] (15-44)	Rate per 100 live births[2] (15-44)
1974	16.6	13.6	14.1	9.7	7.1	5.2	2.5	10.4	14.9
1975	16.7	13.7	13.8	10.0	6.8	4.9	2.4	11.2	14.9
1976	18.2	14.6	15.1	10.9	7.4	5.0	2.5	11.4	16.3
1977	19.2	15.3	15.9	11.2	7.5	4.9	2.4	11.8	16.5
1978	21.1	16.3	17.2	11.9	7.8	5.0	2.4	12.3	18.6
1979	21.7	17.0	18.1	12.2	7.9	4.8	2.1	12.3	19.1
1980	21.8	16.9	18.2	12.1	7.9	4.5	2.1	12.2	19.4
1981	21.1	16.2	18.0	11.9	7.7	4.4	1.9	12.3	19.3
1982	21.1	16.2	18.5	12.0	7.9	4.5	1.9	11.6	20.2
1983	18.8	14.7	17.3	11.2	7.5	4.4	1.7	11.4	18.6
1984	18.8	14.7	17.5	11.5	7.5	4.5	1.6	11.4	18.4
1985	19.7	14.5	17.8	11.5	7.6	4.5	1.7	11.3	18.4
1986	20.5	15.0	18.2	11.6	7.8	4.5	1.6	11.2	18.6
1987	21.1	15.1	18.6	12.0	7.8	4.6	1.6	11.3	18.9

1988	21.9	15.5	19.9	12.7	8.1	4.8	1.7	11.6	19.3
1989	22.9	16.3	21.4	13.8	8.8	5.4	1.8	12.6	20.2
1990	22.5	15.9	21.9	14.0	9.1	5.4	1.7	14.8	23.2

1. Also includes abortions to women of age under 15 years
2. Based on the total of therapeutic abortions that include hospital and clinic abortions in Quebec (for 1978 and the following years) and in the provinces of Newfoundland, Nova Scotia, Manitoba and British Columbia for the year 1990.

Source: *Health Reports*, suppl. 9, 1991; Therapeutic Abortions 1989, 90, Statistics Canada

Table A 4

Percentage Distribution of Abortions by Selected Sociodemographic Characteristics, Canada, 1974-90

Characteristics	1974	1976	1978	1980	1982	1984	1986	1987	1988	1989	1990
Total Abortions	52,435	58,712	66,710	72,099	75,071	69,499	69,572	70,023	72,693	79,315	94,108
Age											
Under 15 years	1.2	1.2	1.0	0.9	0.8	0.7	0.6	0.6	0.6	0.6	0.6
15-19 "	30.3	29.5	29.5	28.8	26.0	22.9	21.7	21.3	21.3	20.8	19.8
20-24 "	29.3	29.6	30.9	31.8	32.8	33.5	32.9	31.8	31.6	30.8	30.4
25-29 "	18.5	19.8	19.3	19.6	20.4	21.3	21.8	22.5	22.8	23.2	23.4
30-34 "	10.7	10.9	11.3	11.6	12.2	12.7	13.7	14.0	14.0	14.4	15.2
35-39 "	6.8	6.1	5.7	5.3	5.9	6.9	7.3	7.5	7.5	8.0	8.3
40-44 "	3.0	2.6	2.1	1.8	1.8	1.8	1.9	2.1	2.1	2.1	2.2
over 44 "	0.3	0.3	0.3	0.2	0.2	0.2	0.1	0.2	0.4	0.1	0.1
Marital Status											
Single	58.2	58.4	61.3	65.2	65.3	66.6	67.5	67.3	67.2	65.2	65.2
Married	31.3	30.7	27.3	23.7	23.0	22.0	21.4	21.8	22.2	22.5	22.8
Other and Unknown	10.6	10.9	11.4	11.0	11.7	11.4	11.1	10.9	10.6	12.3	12.0

Gestation Weeks

Under 9 weeks	20.8	24.1	24.7	24.7	25.9	29.5	30.7	33.2	36.6	36.1	32.6
9-12 "	58.0	59.0	59.9	61.4	61.0	58.5	57.1	55.3	53.1	53.8	55.1
13-16 "	14.0	11.8	11.1	10.4	9.7	8.6	8.7	8.0	7.4	7.5	7.8
17-20 "	6.0	5.0	4.1	3.4	3.2	3.1	3.0	3.2	2.7	2.4	2.2
over 20	1.2	0.2	0.2	0.2	0.2	0.3	0.4	0.4	0.2	0.2	1.9
No. of Previous Deliveries											
0	57.2	57.6	59.7	62.4	61.7	59.7	58.1	57.3	55.4	53.5	52.7
1	14.3	15.0	15.7	15.7	16.4	17.6	18.7	19.5	18.5	19.0	19.7
2	14.2	14.7	13.9	13.1	13.4	14.1	14.7	14.9	14.5	14.8	15.5
3 or more	13.0	10.6	8.3	6.9	6.2	6.3	6.2	6.4	6.4	6.8	6.9
Unknown	1.4	2.0	2.3	1.9	2.3	2.3	2.3	1.9	5.2	5.9	5.2
Previous Induced Abortions											
0	91.0	87.4	84.4	82.6	79.9	77.9	73.2	76.3	72.1	70.4	70.0
1	7.0	8.8	11.0	12.8	14.5	15.7	19.7	17.0	17.2	17.8	19.1
2 or more	1.0	1.2	1.9	2.5	3.0	3.8	4.5	4.5	4.6	5.1	5.7
Unknown	2.0	2.7	2.7	2.1	2.5	2.6	2.5	2.2	6.1	6.7	5.2

Table A 4 (Continued)

Previous Deliveries - Percent to Total Cases for Selected Years

Marital Status	1974 0	1974 1+	1974 Unkn	1977 0	1977 1+	1977 Unkn	1980 0	1980 1+	1980 Unkn
Single	87.0	12.0	1.0	84.9	13.0	2.1	83.9	13.9	2.2
Married	16.0	83.0	1.0	17.9	80.3	1.8	19.4	79.3	1.3
Other and Unknown	22.0	76.0	1.0	25.6	72.6	1.8	27.4	70.9	1.6

Marital Status	1981 0	1981 1+	1981 Unkn	1982 0	1982 1+	1982 Unkn	1984 0	1984 1+	1984 Unkn
Single	82.9	14.8	2.3	82.5	15.3	2.4	NA	NA	NA
Married	18.5	80.0	1.5	19.5	78.6	1.9	17.8	80.3	3.9
Other and Unknown	28.5	69.5	2.0	29.5	68.4	2.1	NA	NA	NA

NA = Information not available

Source: *Health Reports*, suppl. 9, 1991; Therapeutic Abortions 1989, 90, Statistics Canada
Paul Sachdev, ed. *International Handbook on Abortion.* Wesport, CT: Greenwood Press, Table 5.1

Table A 5

Attitudes toward Abortion under All, Some, or No Circumstances, Canada, 1975-90
(*Percentage*)

	Should abortion be legal under any circumstances, legal under certain circumstances or illegal in all circumstances?					
	1975[1]	1978[1]	1983[1]	1988[2]	1990[3]
Legal under any circumstances	23	16	23	29	27
Legal only under certain circumstances	60	69*	59	60	59
Illegal in all circumstances	16	14	17	10	12
Don't know, no response	1	1	1	1	2

*Higher percentage of support compared with 1975 and 1978 polls was due to the question ordering effect.
1. Paul Sachdev, ed. *International Handbook on Abortion.* Wesport, CT: Greenwood Press, Table 5.1.
2. Decima Research Ltd. (*Globe and Mail*, May 6, 1988)
3. *Evening Telegram*, January 15, 1990

249

Table A 6

Comparison of Eligible Women Unavailable to the Study with Those Interviewed, by Select Demographic Characteristics
(*Percentage*)

Characteristics	N=	Sample Women 70	Women Not Available 44
Age			
18-19		27.1	25.2
20-21		30.0	28.6
22-23		22.9	24.8
24-25		20.0	21.4
Mean Age		21.0	21.7
Religion			
Protestant		52.8	50.2
Roman Catholic		30.0	29.1
Jewish		1.4	2.0
Other		1.5	9.6
None		14.3	8.1
Educational status			
Some high school		35.7	37.0
High school graduate		30.0	28.0
Some college		30.0	33.0
College graduate		4.3	2.0
Occupation			
Professional		13.0	14.2
Secretarial and related work		45.0	42.8
Semi and unskilled work		16.0	10.0
Students		16.0	19.3
Unemployed		10.0	11.6
Not stated		-	2.0

Table A 7
Contraceptive Use Status by Age among Seventy Women

Age	Contraceptive Use Status			
	Every time	Most of the time	Occasional	Never
18-21				
%=100	30.0	10.0	25.0	35.0
n=40	(12)	(4)	(10)	(14)
22-25				
%=100	36.7	13.3	26.7	23.3
n=30	(11)	(4)	(8)	(7)
N=70				

$X^2 = 6.56$, df = 3, P < .10

Table A 8
Contraceptive Use Status and Level of Education among Seventy Women

Educational Level	Contraceptive Use Status			
	Every time	Most of the time	Occasional	Never
Some high school or completed high school				
% = 100	28.2	13.0	24.0	34.8
n=4	(13)	(6)	(11)	(16)
Some college or college graduate				
% = 100	41.7	8.3	29.2	20.8
n=24	(10)	(2)	(7)	(5)
N=70				

$X^2 = 2.36$, df $= 3$, NS

252

Table A 9
Contraceptive Use Status and Level of Religious Commitment among Sixty-Eight Women

Degree of Religious Commitment	Contraceptive Use Status				
	Every time[*]	Most of the time[*]	Occasional[#]	Never[#]
Protestant				
Active %=100	33.3	4.2	37.5	25.0
n=24	(8)	(1)	(9)	(6)
Inactive %=100	23.1	15.4	7.7	53.8
n=13	(3)	(2)	(1)	(7)
Roman Catholic				
Active %=100	28.6	7.1	35.7	28.6
n=14	(4)	(1)	(5)	(4)
Inactive %=100	28.6	43.0	14.2	14.2
n=7	(2)	(3)	(1)	(1)

253

Table A 9 (continued)

None	% = 100	60.0	10.0	--	30.0
	n = 10	(6)	(1)	(--)	(3)
	N = 68				

*,# Combined for test. $X^2 = 5.60$, df = 4, NS.

Two women were excluded from this analysis--one was Jewish and the second indicated "other" religion--because their number was too small to constitute a religious category.

Table A 10
Degree of Commitment and Contraceptive Use

Regularity of Use	Degree of Commitment		
	More than One Year	Between Six and Twelve Months	Less Than Six Months
Every time Users*	37.2 (16)	37.5 (3)	26.3 (5)
Most of the Time Users*	11.6 (5)	--	10.5 (2)
Occasional Users	32.6 (14)	12.5 (1)	15.8 (3)
Never Users	18.6 (8)	50.0 (4)	47.4 (9)

*Combined for test, $X^2 = 7.41$, df = 4, P < . 10

Table A 11
Degree of Pre-Abortion Ambivalence by Age

Age	Degree of pre-abortion ambivalence			
	Extreme[*]	Great[*]	Somewhat[#]	None[#]
18-21				
%=100	22.5	27.5	7.5	42.5
n=40	(9)	(11)	(3)	(17)
22-25				
%=100	16.7	10.0	16.6	56.7
n=30	(5)	(3)	(5)	(17)
N=70				

$X^2 = 3.89$, df = 1, p< .05

*# Combined for test.

256

Table A 12
Women's Dominant Reactions to Pregnancy and Degree of Ambivalence

Dominant reaction to Pregnancy	Degree of Ambivalence[#]	
	Extreme to Great	Somewhat to None
Positive		
% = 100	90.5	9.5
n = 21	(19)	(2)
Negative[*]		
% = 100	10.0	90.0
n = 30	(3)	(27)
Indifferent[*]		
% = 100	--	100.0
n = 8	--	(8)
Mixed		
% = 100	54.5	45.5
n = 11	(6)	(5)
N = 70		

$$X^2 = 39.59, \quad df = 1, \quad P < .001$$

* # combined for test because of empty cells.

Table A 13
First Alternative and Pre-Abortion Ambivalence

First choice	Degree of Ambivalence*	
	Extreme to Great	Somewhat to None
Abortion		
% = 100	9.1	90.9
n = 33	(3)	(30)
Carrying the pregnancy to term or marriage		
% = 100	67.5	32.4
n = 37	(25)	(12)
N = 70		

$$X^2 = 24.68, \quad df=1, \quad P < .001$$

*Categories were combined because of zero frequencies in some cells.

258

Table A 14
Degree of Male Partner's Support and Pre-Abortion Ambivalence

Degree of Support	Degree of Ambivalence			
	Extreme	Great	Somewhat	None
Supportive				
% = 100	19.2	15.4	7.7	57.7
n = 26	(5)	(4)	(2)	(15)
Not supportive at all				
% = 100	18.8	22.0	15.5	43.7
n = 32	(6)	(7)	(5)	(14)
N = 58				

$X^2 = 1.618$, df = 3   NS

The total number of respondents shown in the table are the fifty-eight who confided in their sexual partners.

Table A 15
Age and Abortion Attitude among Seventy Women

Age	Attitude toward Abortion		
	Liberal	Moderate	Conservative
18-21			
%=100	22.5	50.0	27.5
n=40	(9)	(20)	(11)
22-26			
%=100	30.0	43.3	26.7
n=30	(9)	(13)	(8)
N=70			

$X^2 = 0.532$, df=2, NS

Table A 16
Education and Abortion Attitude among Seventy Women

Education	Attitude toward Abortion		
	Liberal	Moderate	Conservative
Some high school to high school graduate			
% = 100	24.0	47.8	28.2
n = 46	(11)	(22)	(13)
Some college to college graduate			
% = 100	29.0	46.0	25.0
n = 24	(7)	(11)	(6)
N = 70			

$X^2 = 0.238$, df=2, NS

Table A 17

Relationship between Abortion Attitude and Degree of Ambivalence among Seventy Women

Attitude toward abortion	Degree of Ambivalence[*]	
	Extreme to Great	Somewhat to None
Liberal		
% = 100	27.8	72.2
n = 18	(5)	(13)
Moderate		
% = 100	30.3	69.7
n = 33	(10)	(23)
Conservative		
% = 100	68.4	31.6
n = 19	(13)	(6)
N = 70		

$$X^2 = 8.82, \quad df = 2, \quad P < .05$$

[*]Categories were dichotomized because of zero frequencies in some cells.

Table A 18
Pre-Abortion Ambivalence and Post-Abortion Reactions

Degree of pre-abortion ambivalence[1]	Degree of Post-Abortion Reactions				
	Severe	Moderate	Mild	Never	
Great to extreme ambivalence					
% = 100	21.4	14.3	60.7	3.6	
n = 28	(6)	(4)	(17)	(1)	
None to somewhat ambivalence					
% = 100	2.4	7.1	43.0	47.6	
n = 42	(1)	(3)	(18)	(20)	
N = 70					

$X^2 = 18.89$, df = 3, P < .001

1. Categories combined since some cells had zero frequencies.

Table A 19
Reaction to Pregnancy and Post-Abortion Reactions

Reactions to pregnancy[1]	Degree of Post-Abortion Reactions			
	Severe	Moderate	Mild	Never
Positive to mixed				
%=100	15.6	18.8	59.4	6.2
n=32	(5)	(6)	(19)	(2)
Negative to indifferent				
%=100	5.3	2.7	42.1	50.0
n=42	(2)	(1)	(16)	(19)
N=70				

$X^2 = 18.499$, df $= 3$, P $< .001$

1. Categories combined since some cells had very small frequencies.

264

Table A 20
Attitude toward Abortion and Post-Abortion Reactions

Attitude toward abortion[1]	Degree of Post-Abortion Reactions			
	Severe	Moderate	Mild	Never
Conservative				
% = 100	26.5	10.5	42.0	21.0
n = 19	(5)	(2)	(8)	(4)
Moderate				
% = 100	3.0	12.0	61.0	24.0
n = 33	(1)	(4)	(20)	(8)
Liberal				
% = 100	5.5	5.5	39.0	50.0
n = 18	(1)	(1)	(7)	(9)
N = 70				

$X^2 = 12.249$, df $= 6$, P $< .07$

Figure A 1
Abortions per 100 Live Births, 1980-1990

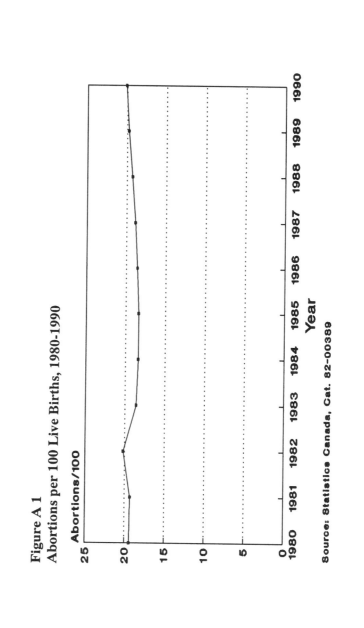

Source: Statistics Canada, Cat. 82-00389

Appendix B

GUILT AND DEPRESSIVE REACTION SCALE IN THREE
STEPS OF SEVERITY

81.   Experience with aborted women show that some of them
       experience feelings of guilt or remorse in its varying degree
       because of their having an abortion, while others don't.
       Please look at this (HAND R CARD 6) which explains the
       term "guilt reactions", in three steps of severity. You might
       have experienced these signs and feelings on other occasions
       in relation to other events in your life.   But here I'm
       interested in the **guilt reactions you might or might not have
       experienced as a result of your abortion**. Could you tell me
       that ever since you had your abortion have you experienced
       guilt reactions-

       __regularly __mostly __occasionally __rarely ___never
                                                              (TOQ.82)

81a.   Now look at your card again and indicate or underline
       your feelings based on the symptoms and signs that
       apply most to you.

CARD 6

You feel tremendous grief, shame (or embarrassment) and
regret; you blame yourself or others very harshly; feel
practically all the time that you are no good person; feel you
have committed a blunder and are the world's worse sinner;
feel anguished and mean "Why did I do it"; you are constantly
bothered by thoughts about pregnancy and abortion; feel
extremely angry at self and others; think very low of yourself;
you dream most of the time or have occasional nightmares
around abortion and hurt child; have constant fear of
punishment; may have recurring thought that people are
looking at you and condemning you; feel a tremendous loss;
feel a complete loss of interest in sex and men.

You feel overall grief and regret; you blame yourself or others somewhat harshly; feel you are not good enough; feel troubled that you have committed a big mistake; feel quite upset that you can't do anything right; very frequently bothered by thoughts around pregnancy and abortion; feel very angry at self or others; think low of yourself; sometimes you see dreams concerning abortion; sometimes you fear reprisal; may have quite frequent thoughts that people are looking at you and condemning you; feel some loss; a fair degree of loss of interest in sex and men.

You feel slight grief and somewhat regret; you occasionally blame yourself or others; feel very infrequently you are a no good person; feel you have not done it quite right; feel slightly and occasionally upset; occasionally bothered by thoughts concerning pregnancy and abortion; feel somewhat angry at self or others; may have occasional dreams about abortion and pregnancy; you occasionally and temporarily feel some loss; slight loss of interest in sex.

82. Experience with aborted women show that some of them experience depressed or blue moods in its varying degree because of their having an abortion, while others don't. Please look at this (HAND R CARD 7) which explains the term "depressed or blue moods", on a three point scale. You might have experienced these signs and feelings on other occasions in relation to other events in your life. But here I'm interested in the **changes in your feelings and moods you might or might not have experienced as a consequence of your having an abortion.** Could you tell me that ever since you had your abortion did you feel depressed or blue moods-

__regularly __mostly _occasionally __rarely __never
(TOQ.83)

82a. Now look at your card again and indicate or underline the symptoms that applied most to you.

CARD 7

You feel "blue" and sad all the time since the abortion; feel you couldn't bear to live another day; you blame yourself very harshly for the whole thing; don;t find interest in anything; are indifferent toward members of your family; cry and sob almost all the time; feel extremely mixed up; you push yourself too hard to do anything; feel too tired to do anything; stay in bed or sit alone most of the time and don't feel like seeing other people; don't feel like eating or eat much more than usual; have very disturbed sleep than usual or difficulty in getting to sleep or no sleep at all on certain nights; get headaches sometimes severely and are more constipated than usual or might have diarrhea; complete loss of interest in sex and men; you get mad at or annoyed with almost anything now; you think all or most of the time about abortion.

You get "blue" moods most of the time since the abortion decision; feel you are no good and blame yourself; occasionally you feel you are better off dead; cry much of the time; you find it very difficult to make decisions in almost every activity; you have to push yourself very hard to do anything; have strong wish to avoid people or postpone many usual activities because they now seem "flat" to you; appetite much worse than before or eat much more than usual; have quite restless sleep than usual or sleep more than usual; occasional headaches and constipation; feel decrease in desire for sex and men; feel general tiredness; feel annoyed with or get mad at many things or people since abortion decision; you think about abortion a lot.

You feel occasional "blue" moods but more than usual; feel mad at yourself and feel it was your fault; some loss of satisfaction in things you used to do; like to cry; might feel somewhat mixed up and can't make decisions as quickly as you used to; it takes then extra effort to get started at doing something; prefer more than usual passive activities like sitting at home or sleeping; you postpone certain things because they are no longer interesting; occasionally you think about abortion; eat little than usual; do not sleep as well as you used to; slight loss of spontaneous interest in sex and men; you feel "worn out" more frequently than you used to.

Appendix C

LIKERT SCALE FOR ABORTION ATTITUDES

45.   Now I'd like to give you this pencil and paper and have you
       fill these out by yourself. These are several statements you
       hear people make about abortion. Please read the statements
       and respond to all of them on the basis of **your own** true
       feelings that you had any time **before** you became pregnant.
       I would like to know the extent to which you agree or
       disagree with **each** statement. Please check ( ) whether you
       strongly agree, agree, neither agree nor disagree, disagree or
       strongly disagree, with it.   (HAND R CARD 3)

                              CARD 6

---

                        1.   Strongly agree
                        2.   Agree
                        3.   Neither agree nor disagree
                        4.   Disagree
                        5.   Strongly disagree
                        6.   Don't know (BUT TRY)

1.   It is strictly up to the woman to decide whether she
      wants to have a baby or wants to abort.___(#)
2.   Abortion is taking of innocent and unborn human life
      and thus a crime against God and man.___(#)
3.   Abortion is justified when it is necessary to save the
      mother's life.___(#)
4.   Abortion should be legalized as simply another type of
      birth control.___(#)
5.   Abortion leaves a woman with a great many guilt
      feelings.___(#)
6.   Abortion should be legalized so that it could be
      obtained with proper medical attention.___(#)
7.   Abortion is a better choice than giving birth to a child
      you don't want and cannot care for properly.___(#)
8.   Abortion should be permitted when the baby would
                   probably be deformed.___(#)
9.   Abortion should be permitted in case of rape.___(#)

10. Abortion should be forbidden because it would lead to greater premarital sexual activity.___(#)

11. Woman has a right to her sexual and procreative freedom.___(#)

12. Abortion should be permitted in cases of incest, that is, where a woman becomes pregnant by a blood relative.___(#)

13. Abortion should be legally available to anyone who really wants it.___(#)

14. If a woman fools around and gets pregnant it's her own fault and she should not be able to get an abortion.___(#)

15. Laws should be stricter than what they are now and should discourage abortion.___(#)

16. Abortion should be permitted any stage of the pregnancy.___(#)

17. Abortion can damage a woman's internal physical system.___(#)

18. Abortion should not be permitted on pregnancy beyond the twelfth week.___(#)

19. Abortion is not justified in any circumstances.___(#)

20. Women who have abortions run the risk of developing psychological and emotional problems afterwards._(#)

21. I believe new human individual begins at conception and has a right to life.___(#)

22. I feel one should be careful beforehand and not take the life of a baby afterwards.___(#)

23. Abortion is an emotional issue.___(#)

24. Abortion is a moral and ethical issue.___(#)

25. Abortion is merely just a medical and physiological issue.___(#)

26. Abortion should be justifiable in the interest of over all well-being of those already born.___(#)

References

Abrahamse, A., Morrison, P. & Waite, L. 1988. Teenagers willing to consider single parenthood: Who is at greatest risk? *Family Planning Perspectives*, 20 (1): 13-18.

Addleson, F. 1973. Induced abortion: source of guilt or growth? *American Journal of Orthopsychiatry*, 43 (October): 815-22.

Adler, N. 1975. Emotional responses of women following therapeutic abortion. *American Journal of Orthopsychiatry*, 45 (3): 446-454.

------. 1979. Abortion: A social-psychological perspective. *Journal of Social Issues*, 35(1): 100-117.

Adler, N. & Dolcini, P. 1986. Psychological issues in abortion for adolescents. In V. Melton, ed. *Adolescent Abortion: Psychological and Legal Issues*. Lincoln: University of Nebraska Press: 74-95.

Adler, N. & Hendrick, S. 1991. Relationships between contraceptive behavior and love attitudes, sex attitudes and self-esteem. *Journal of Counseling and Development*, 70 (2): 302-8.

Adler, N., David, H., Major, B., Roth, S., Russo, N. & Wyatt, G. 1990. Psychological responses after abortion. *Science*, 248 (April): 41-44.

Anderson, E. 1966. Psychiatric indications for the termination of pregnancy. *World Medical Journal*, 13 (May-June).

Anderson, J., Kann, L., Holtzman, D., Arday, S., Truman, B. & Kolbe, L. 1990. HIV/AIDS knowledge and sexual behavior among high school students. *Family Planning Perspectives*, 22(6): 252-255.

Anderson, P., McPherson, K., Beeching, N., Weinberg, J. & Vessey, M. 1978. Sexual behavior and contraceptive practice of undergraduates at Oxford University. *Journal of Biosocial Science*, 10: 277-86.

Apkom, C., Amechi, K. & Davis, D. 1976. Prior sexual behavior of teenagers attending rap sessions for the first time. *Family Planning Perspectives*, 8: 203-6.

Aren, P. 1961. On legal abortion in Sweden. *Acta Obstetrica et Gynaecologica Scandinavica*, Supplement 1, 38: 1-75.

Aren, P. & Amark, C. 1961. The prognosis in cases in which legal abortion has been granted but not carried out. *Acta Psychiatra Neurologica Scandanavia*, (1961): 203-78.

Areny, W. & Trescher, L. 1976. Trends in attitudes toward abortion, 1972-1975. *Family Planning Perspectives*, 8: 117-24.

Armsworth, M. 1991. Psychological response to abortion. *Journal of Counseling and Development*, 69 (4): 377-79.

Arnstein, H. 1971. The emotional scars of abortion. *Ladies Home Journal*, May 1971: 121-92.

ASA Survey of Public Opinion on Abortion in New York. 1968. *Association for the Study of Abortion, Newsletter*, 3: 2-3.

Asher, J. 1972. Abortion counseling. *American Journal of Public Health*, 62 (May): 686-88.

Ashton, J. 1980a. Components of delay amongst women obtaining termination of pregnancy. *Journal of Biosocial Science*, 12: 261-73.

------. 1980b. Experiences of women referred to National Health Service abortions. *Journal of Biosocial Science*, 12: 201-210.

------. 1980c. Patterns of discussion and decision making amongst abortion patients. *Journal of Biosocial Science*, 12: 247-59.

------. 1980d. Sex education and contraceptive practice among abortion patients. *Journal of Biosocial Science*, 12: 211-17.

------. 1980e. The psychosocial outcome of induced abortion. *British Journal of Obstetrics and Gynecology*, 87 (December): 1115-22.

Athanasiou, R., Oppel, W., Michelson, L., Unger, T. & Yager, M. 1973. Psychiatric sequalae to term birth and induced early and late abortion: A longitudinal study. *Family Planning Perspectives*, 5: 227-31.

Aug, R. & Bright, T. 1970. A study of wed and unwed motherhood in adolescents and young adults. *Journal of the American Academy of Child Psychiatry*, 9 (October): 577-94.

Ayd, F. 1969. The teenager and contraception. *Pediatrics Clinics of North America*, 16 (May): 355-61.

Bachrach, C. 1984. Contraceptive practice among American women, 1973-1983. *Family Planning Perspective*, 16: 253-59.

Bacon, H. 1969. Psychiatric aspects of therapeutic abortion. *Canadian Mental Health*, 17: 18-21.

Balsara, N. 1990. MPs expected to approve abortion bill. *Globe and Mail*, May 28: D1.

Bandura, A. 1969. *Principles of Behavior Modification*. New York: Holt, Rinehart & Winston, Inc.

Barglow, P., Bornstein, M., Exum, D., Wright, M. & Visotsky, H. 1968. Some psychiatric aspects of illegitimate pregnancy in early adolescence. *American Journal of Orthopsychiatry*, 38 (July): 672-87.

Barnard, C. 1990. *The Long-Term Psychological Effects of Abortion*. Portsmouth, NH: Institute for Pregnancy Loss.

Barnes, A., Cohen, E., Stoeckle, J. & McGuire, M. 1971. Therapeutic abortion: medical and social sequels. *Annals of Internal Medicine*, 75 (6): 881-86.

Barnett, J., Papini, D. & Gbur, E. 1991. Familial correlates of sexually active pregnant and non-pregnant adolescents. *Adolescence*, 26 (102): 457-72.

Barrett, M. 1980. Sexual experience, birth control usage and sex education of unmarried Canadian university students: changes between 1968 and 1978. *Archives of Sexual Behavior*, 9 (5): 367-90.

Bauman, K. 1971. Selected aspects of the contraceptive practices of unmarried university students. *Medical Aspects of Human Sexuality*, August: 76-89.

Beck, A. 1967. *Depression: Clinical, Experimental and Theoretical Aspects*. New York: Harper & Row Publishers, 1967.

Beck, M., Newman, S. & Lewit, S. 1969. Abortion: a national public and mental health problem - past, present and proposed research. *American Journal of Public Health*, 59 (December): 21-35.

Becker, M. & Joseph, J. 1988. AIDS and behavior change to reduce risk: a review. *American Journal of Public Health*, 78: 394-401.

Belsey, E. 1976. Psychological consequences of abortion. *Family Planning Association Newsletter*, 60 (April): 60-65.

Belsey, E., Greer, H., Lal, S., Lewis, S. & Beard, R. 1977. Predictive factors in emotional responses to abortion: King's termination study. *Social Science and medicine*, 11: 71-82.

Belsky, J. 1992. Medically indigent women seeking abortion prior to legalization in New York City, 1969-1970. *Family Planning Perspectives*, 24 (3): 129-34.

Bennett, W. 1988. Sex and the education of our children. *Curriculum Review*, 27: 70-130.

Berger, C., Jacques, J., Brender, W., Gold, D. & Andres, D. 1984. Contraceptive knowledge and use of birth control as a function of sex guilt. In P. Caplan, ed. *Feminist Psychology in Transition*. Toronto: Eden Press Women's publications.

Bergin, A. & Lambert, M. 1978. The evaluation of therapeutic outcomes. In S. Garfield and A. Bergin, eds. *Handbook of Psychotherapy and Behavior Changes*. 2d ed. New York: John Wiley & Sons.

Beric, B., et al. 1974. Cited in Emily C. Moore. *International Inventory of Information on Induced Abortion*. International Institute for the Study of Human Reproduction, Columbia University: 533.

Berkman, P. 1969. Spouseless motherhood, psychological stress, and physical morbidity. *Journal of Health and Social Behavior*, 10: 323-34.

Bernstein, N. & Tinkham, C. 1971. Group therapy following abortion. *Nervous and Mental Diseases*, 152 (5): 303-14.

Bhatia, M., Bohra, N., Kaur, N. & Goyal, U. 1990. Post-abortion psychological sequelae. *Journal of Family Welfare*, 36 (4): 67-74.

Bibby, R. & Posterski, D. 1985. *The Emerging Generation*. Toronto: Irwin Publishing.

Blomberg, S. 1980. Influence of maternal distress during pregnancy on postnatal development. *Acta Psychiatrica Scandinavica*, 62: 405-17.

Blos, P. 1969. Three typical constellations in female delinquency. In O. Pollack & A. Friedman, eds. *Family Dynamics and Female Sexual Delinquency*. Palo Alto, CA: Science and Behavior.

Bluford, R. & Petres, R. 1973. *The Unwanted Pregnancy*. New York: Harper & Row Publishers.

Blum, R., Resnick, M. & Spark, T. 1990. Factors associated with the use of court bypass by minors to obtain abortions. *Family Planning Perspectives*, 22 (4): 158-60.

Blumenthal, S. 1991. Psychiatric consequences of abortion: Overview of research findings. In Nada L. Stotland, ed. *Psychiatric Aspects of Abortion*. Washington, DC: American Psychiatric Press, Inc.: 17-37.

Blumer, H. 1969. *Symbolic Interactionism*. Englewood Cliffs, NJ: Prentice-Hall.

Bolter, S. 1962. The Psychiatrist's role in therapeutic abortion: the unwilling accomplice. *The American Journal of Psychiatry*, 119: 321-16.

Bott, E. 1959. *Family and Social Network*. London: Tavistock Publications.

Bouvier, L. 1972. Catholics and contraception. *Journal of Marriage and the Family*, August: 514-21.

Bowen, S., Aral, S., Magder, L., Reed, D., Dratman, C. & Wasser, S. 1990. Risk behaviors for HIV infection in clients of Pennsylvania family planning clinics. *Family Planning Perspectives*, 22 (2): 62-64.

Bowerman, C., Irish, D. & Pope, H. 1963-66. *Unwed Motherhood: Personal and Social Consequences*. Chapel Hill, NC: University of North Carolina, Institute for Research in Social Science.

Boyce, R. & Osborn, R. 1970. Therapeutic abortion in a Canadian city. The Canadian Medical Association Journal, 103 (September 12): 461-65.

Bracken, M. 1978. A causal model of psychosomatic reactions to vacuum aspiration abortion. *Social Psychiatry*, 13: 135-45.

Bracken, M., Grossman, G. & Hachamovitch, M. 1972. Contraceptive practice among New York abortion patients. *American Journal of Obstetrics and Gynecology*, 114 (December): 967-77.

Bracken, M., Hachamovitch, M. & Grossman, G. 1974. The decision to abort and psychological sequelae. *Journal of Nervous and Mental Diseases*, 158 (2): 155-61.

Bracken, M. & Kasl, S. 1975. Delay in seeking induced abortion: a review and theoretical analysis. *American Journal of Obstetrics and Gynecology*, 121: 1008-19.

Bracken, M., Klerman, L. & Bracken, M. 1978a. Coping with pregnancy resolution among never-married women. *American Journal of Orthopsychiatry*, 48: 320-33.

------. 1978b. Abortion, adoption, and motherhood: An empirical study of decision making during pregnancy. *American Journal of Obstetrics and Gynecology*, 130 (3): 251-55.

Bracken, M., Grossman, G., Hachamovitch, M., Sussman, D. & Schieir, D. 1973. Abortion counseling: An experimental study of three techniques. *American Journal of Obstetrics and Gynecology*, 117: 10-20.

Brandt, C., Kane, F. & Moan, C. 1978. Pregnant adolescents: Some psychosocial factors. *Psychosomatics*, 19: 790-93.

Brekke, B. 1966. Cited in R. White. Induced abortions: A survey of their psychiatric implications, complications and indications. *Texas Reports on Biology and Medicine*, 24 (Winter): 535.

Brody, H., Meikle, S. & Gerritse, R. 1971. Therapeutic abortion: A prospective study. *American Journal of Obstetrics and Gynecology*, 109 (February): 347-53.

Brosseau, K. 1980. Utilizing male partners of adolescent abortion patients as change agents. Ph.D. Dissertation, University of Colorado at Boulder.

Brown, B. 1989. Nothing new in latest courtroom battle over abortion. *Evening Telegram*, July 13: 7.

Brown, L., DiClemento, R. & Beausolil, N. 1992. Comparison of human immunodeficiency virus related knowledge, attitudes, intentions and behaviors among sexually active and abstinent young adolescents. *Journal of Adolescent Health*, 13: 140-46.

Brown, N., Thompson, D., Bulger, R. & Laws, H. 1971. How do nurses feel about euthanasia and abortion. *American Journal of Nursing*, 71 (July): 1413-16.

Burnell, G. & Norfleet, M. 1987. Women's self-reported responses to abortion. *Journal of Psychology*, 121 (1): 71-76.

Burnell, G., Sworsky, W. & Harrington, R. 1972. Post-abortion group therapy. *American Journal of Psychiatry*, 129 (2): 220-23.

Cahn, J. 1978. The influence of others on teenagers' use of birth control. Ph.D. dissertation, City University of New York.

Calderone, M., ed. 1958. *Abortion in the United States*. New York: Hoeber-Harper.

Callahan, D. 1970. *Abortion: Law, Choice and Morality*. New York: Macmillan Company, 1970.

Campbell, N., Franco, K. & Jurs, S. 1988. Abortion in adolescence. *Adolescence*, 23: 813-23.

Canadian Gallup Poll Ltd. 1985. Gallup poll reveals Canadian attitudes. *Tellus, Journal of Planned Parenthood Association of Canada*, Autumn: 6-8.

Cappen, E. 1964. Cited in J. Rheingold. *The Fear of Being a Woman*. New York: Grune & Straton.

Carson, S. 1974. Adolescence. *Weekend Magazine*, September 7: 4-7. Cartoof, V., & Klerman, L. 1986. Parental consent for abortion: Impact of the Massachusetts law. *American Journal of Public Health*, 76: 397.

Casper, L. 1990. Does family interaction prevent adolescent pregnancy? *Family Planning Perspectives*, 22 (3): 109-14.

Catania, J. et al. 1992a. Condom use in multi-ethnic neighborhoods of San Francisco: The population based AMEN (AIDS in multi-ethnic neighborhood) study. *American Journal of Public Health*, 81: 284.

------. 1992b. Prevalence of AIDS-related risk factors on condom use in the United States. *Science*, 258 (13): 1101-6.

Cates, W. 1980. Adolescent abortion in the U.S. *Journal of Adolescent Health Care*, 1 (1): 18-25.

Census of Canada, 1971. *Population and Religious Denominations*. Catalogue No. 92-724, vol. 1, part 3 (Bulletin 1.3.3), September, 1973.

Char, W. & McDermott, J. 1972. Abortion and acute identity crisis in nurses. *American Journal of Psychiatry*, 128 (February): 952-57.

Chilman, C. 1974. Some psychosocial aspects of female sexuality. *The Family Coordinator*, 23 (2): 123-31.

------. 1979. *Adolescent Sexuality in a Changing American Society: Social and Psychological Perspectives*. Washington, DC: U.S. Government Printing Office. Publication No. (MIH) 79-1426.

Chilman, C. 1980. Toward a reconceptualization of adolescent sexuality. In C. Chilman, ed. *Adolescent Pregnancy and Childbearing*. Washington, DC: U.S. Government Printing Office. Publication No. 81-2077: 101-27.

Cho, L., Grabile, W. & Bogue, D. 1970. *Differential Current Fertility in the United States*. Community and Family Study Center, University of Chicago.

Christensen, H. & Meissner, H. 1953. Studies in child spacing: Premarital unwanted pregnancy as a factor in divorce. *American Sociological Review*, 18: 641-44.

Christmon, K. 1988. Perceived role performance and unwed adolescent fathers. Fourth National Symposium on Doctoral Research and Social Work Practice, The Ohio State University: 81-92.

Claman, D., Williams, B. & Wogan, L. 1969. Reaction of unmarried girls to pregnancy. *Canadian Medical Association Journal*, 101 (September): 1-7.

Clark et al. 1968. Sequels of unwanted pregnancy: a follow-up of patients referred for psychiatric opinion. *Lancet*, 2: 501-3.

Clothier, F. 1943. Psychological implications of unmarried parenthood. *American Journal of Orthopsychiatry*, 13: 531-49.

Cobliner, G. 1970. Teen-age out-of-wedlock pregnancy. *Bulletin of the New York Academy of Medicine*, 46 (June): 438-47.

Cobliner, G., Schulman, H. & Romney, S. 1973. The termination of adolescent out-of-wedlock pregnancies and the prospects for their primary prevention. *American Journal of Obstetrics and Gynecology*, 115 (3): 432-44.

Coe, B. & Blum, M. 1972. The out-of-wedlock pregnancy. *Obstetrics and Gynecology*, 40: 807-12.

Cohen, L. & Roth, S. 1984. Coping with abortion. *Journal of Human Stress*, 10 (3): 140-45.

Collins, A. 1985. *The Big Evasion: Abortion, the Issue That Won't Go Away*. Toronto, Ont.: Lester & Orpen Dannys Ltd.

Combs, M. & Welch, S. 1982. Blacks, whites and attitudes toward abortion. *Public Opinion Quarterly*, 46: 510-20.

Committee on Government Operations, House of Representatives. 1989. Medical and psychological impact of abortion, 101st Congress, First Session, March 16, House Report Vol. 135 (33).

Committee on the Operation of the Abortion Law (COAL). 1977. *Report of the Committee*. Catalogue No. J2-30/1977. Ottawa: Supply and Services Canada.

Cook, R. 1989. An anti-abortion ruling would go against the global grain. *The Globe and Mail*, August 8: A7.

Cooksey, E. 1990. Factors in the resolution of adolescent premarital pregnancies. *Demography*, 27: 207-10.

Cormier, C. & Cormier, S. 1985. *Interviewing Strategies for Helpers*. 2d ed. Monterey, CA: Cole Publishing Co.

Crosby, M. & English, A. 1991. Mandatory parental involvement/judicial bypass laws: Do they promote adolescents' health. *Journal of Adolescent Health*, 12 (2): 143-47.

Cutright, P. 1971. Illegitimacy: myth, causes and cures. *Family Planning Perspectives*, 3 (January): 26-48.

Cutright, P. & Smith, H. 1988. Intermediate determinants of racial differences in 1980 U.S. nonmarital fertility rates. *Family Planning Perspectives*, 20 (3): 119-23.

Cvetkovich, G. & Grote, B. 1982. In I. Stuart & C. Wells, eds. *Pregnancy in Adolescence*. New York: Van Nostrand Reinhold Co.

Cvetkovich, G., Grote, B., Bjorseth, A. & Sarkissian, J. 1975. On the psychology of adolescents' use of contraceptives. *Journal of Sex Research*, 11: 256-70.

Dagg, P. 1990. The psychological sequelae of therapeutic abortion - denied and completed. *American Journal of Psychiatry*, 148 (5): 578-85.

Daily, E. & Nicholas, N. 1972. Use of contraception control methods before pregnancies terminating in birth or a requested abortion in New York City municipal hospitals. *American Journal of Public Health*, 62: 1544-45.

Daily, E., Nicholas, F. & Pakter, J. 1973. Repeat abortion in New York City: 1970-72. *Family Planning Perspectives*, 5 (Spring): 83-93.

Danielson, R., Marcy, S., Plunkett, A., Wiest, W. & Greenlick, M. 1990. Reproductive health counseling for young men: What does it do? *Family Planning Perspectives*, 22 (3): 115-21.

Dauber, B., Zalar, M. & Goldstein, p. 1972. Abortion counseling and behavior change. *Family Planning Perspectives*, 4 (2): 23-27.

David, H. 1971. Mental health and family planning. *Family Planning Perspectives*, 3 (April): 20-23.

David, H., Dytrych, Z., Matejcek, Z. & Schuller, V., eds. 1988. *Born Unwanted: Developmental Effects of Denied Abortion.* Prague: Springer Publishing Company.

Davis, J. 1978. *General Social Surveys, 1972-1978: Cumulative Data.* Chicago: National Opinion Research Center.

De Beauvoir, S. 1953. *The Second Sex.* New York: Alfred A. Knopf.

Dehler, D. 1972. On abortion policy. *Journal of the Ontario Association of Children's Aid Societies*, (November): 5-12.

DeLamater, J. & MacCorquodale, P. 1978. Premarital contraceptive use: A test of two models. *Journal of Marriage and the Family*, 40: 235-47.

Delmore, T., Kalagian, W. & Loewen, I. 1991. Follow-up of adolescent oral contraceptive users. *Canadian Journal of Public Health*, 82: 277-278.

Dembo, M. & Lundell, B. 1979. Factors affecting adolescent contraceptive practices: Implications for sex education. *Adolescence*, 15 (56): 657-64.

Deschin, C. 1963. Research interviewing in sensitive subject areas. *Social Work*, April: 3-18.

Deutsch, H. 1945. *The Psychology of Women: A Psychoanalytic Interpretation*, vol. 2. New York: Grune & Stratton Inc., 1945.

Diamond, M., Steinhoff, P., Palmore, J. & Smith, R. 1973. Sexuality, birth control and abortion: a decision-making sequence. *Journal of Biosocial Science*, 5: 374-361.

Dixon, P., Strano, D. & Willingham. 1984. Locus of control and decision to abort. *Psychological Reports*, 54: 547-53.

Dominion Bureau of Statistics News. 1970. Therapeutic abortions in Canada.

Donnai, P., Charles, N. & Harris, R. 1981. Attitudes of patients after "genetic" termination of pregnancy. *British Medical Journal*, 282: 621.

Dryfoos, J. 1988. School-based health clinics: Three years of experience. *Family Planning Perspectives*, 20 (4): 193-200.

Dunbar, F. 1967. Psychosomatic approach to abortion and the abortion habit. In H. Rosen, ed. *Abortion in America*. Boston: Beacon Press.

Dytrych, M., Matejcek, Z. & Schuller, V. 1986. Psychosocak development of children born from unwanted pregnancies. Workshop: Life Styles, Contraception, and Parenthood. Amsterdam.

Ebaugh, F. & Heuser, K. 1947. Psychiatric aspects of therapeutic abortion. *Postgraduate Medicine*, 2: 325-32.

Ebaugh, H. & Haney, A. 1985. Abortion attitudes in the United States: continuities and discontinuities. In P. Sachdev, ed. *Perspectives on Abortion.* Metuchen, NJ: Scarecrow Press, Inc.

Ehrmann, W. 1969. Changing sexual mores. In E. Ginsberg, ed. *Values and Ideas of American Youth.* New York: Free Press, 1969.

Eisen, M. & Zellman, G. 1984. Factors predicting pregnancy resolution decision satisfaction of unmarried adolescents. *Journal of Genetic Psychology*, 145: 223-31.

------. 1987. Changes in the incidence of sexual intercourse of unmarried teenagers following a community-based sex education program. *Journal of Sex Research*, 23: 527-33.

Eisen, M., Zellman, G. & McAllister, A. 1990. Evaluating the impact of a theory-based sexuality and contraceptive education program. *Family Planning Perspectives*, 22 (6): 261-71.

Ekblad, M. 1955. Induced abortion on psychiatric grounds: Follow-up study of 479 women. *Acta Psychiatrica Scandanavia*, Supplement 99, 18: 1-238.

Elkind, D. 1967. Egocentrism in adolescence. *Child Development*, 38: 1025-34.

Ewing, J. & Rouse, B. 1973. Therapeutic abortion and a prior psychiatric history. *American Journal of Psychiatry*, 130 (January): 37-40.

Family Planning Perspectives, 1990. Documents, 22 (4) (July/August): 177-81.

Family Planning Perspectives (Digest). 1990. French Trials of RU 486 find 96 percent abortion rate in pregnancies of less than seven weeks. *Family Planning Perspectives*, 22 (3): 134-35.

Farmer. C. 1973. Decision making in therapeutic abortion. In G. Horbin, ed. *Experience with Abortion.* London: Cambridge University Press.

Figley, C. & Scroggins, L. 1978. Putting the "family" in Family Planning Services. *Advances in Planned Parenthood*, 13 (3): 75-77.

Fine, M. 1988. Sexuality, schooling and adolescent females: The missing discourse of desire. *Harvard Educational Review*, 58: 29-41.

Fischman, S. 1977. Delivery or abortion in inner-city adolescents. *American Journal of Orthopsychiatry*, 47: 127-33.

Fisher, W. 1978. *Affective, Attitudinal and Normative Determinants of Contraceptive Behavior among University Men*. Ph.D. Dissertation, Purdue University.

Fleck, S. 1970. Some psychiatric aspects of abortion. *Journal of Nervous and Mental Diseases*, 151 (July): 42-50.

Fleissig, A. 1991. Unwanted pregnancies and the use of contraception: changes from 1984 to 1989. *British Medical Journal*, 302: 147-52.

Ford, C., Castelnuovo-Tedesco, P. & Long, K. 1971. Abortion: Is it a therapeutic procedure in psychiatry? *Journal of the American Medical Association*, 218 (November): 1173-78.

------. 1972. Women who seek therapeutic abortions: a comparison with women who complete their pregnancies. *American Journal of Psychiatry*, 129 (November): 546-52.

Forrest, J. & Singh, S. 1990. The sexual and reproductive behavior of American women, 1982-1988. *Family Planning Perspectives*, 22 (5): 206-14.

Forssman, H. & Thuwe, I. 1966. One hundred and twenty children born after application for therapeutic abortion refused. *Acta Psychiatrica Scandanavia*, 42: 71-88.

Francke, L. 1978. *The Ambivalence of Abortion*. New York: Random House.

Franz, W. & Reardon, D. 1992. Differential impact of abortion on adolescents and adults. *Adolescence*, 27 (105): 161-72.

Fraser, G. 1991. Supreme Court supports B.C. decision that fetus is a person. *Globe and Mail*, March 22: 1.

Freeman, E., Rickels, K., Huggins, R., et al. 1980a. Emotional distress patterns among women having first or repeat abortions. *Obstetrics and Gynecology*, 55: 630-36.

------. 1980b. Adolescent contraceptive use: Comparison of male and female attitudes and information. *American Journal of Public Health*, 70 (8): 790-97.

------. 1981. Emotional distress patterns among urban black women having first or repeat abortions: a one-year follow up. *Advances in Planned Parenthood*, 16 (3): 91-97.

Freidman, C., Greenspan, R. & Mittleman, F. 1974. The decision-making process and the outcome of therapeutic abortion. *American Journal of Psychiatry*, 131 (12): 1332-37.

Freundt, L. 1973. Investigation of women admitted to hospital with abortion. *Acta Psychiatrica Scandanavia*, supplement 242. Munksgaard, Copenhagen: 1-217.

Freundt, L. 1970. Premarital pregnancy among black teenagers. *Transaction*, (May): 52-55.

Friedlander, M., Kaul, T. & Stimel, C. 1984. Abortion: Predicting the complexity of the decision-making process. *Women and Health*, 9 (1): 43-54.

Furstenberg, F. 1976. *Unplanned Parenthood: The Social Consequences of Teenage Childbearing*. New York: Free Press.

Furstenberg, F., Gordis, L. & Markowitz, M. 1969. Birth control knowledge and attitudes among unmarried pregnant adolescents: a preliminary report. *Journal of Marriage and the Family*, February: 34-42.

Furstenberg, F., Moore, K. & Peterson, J. 1985. Sex education and sexual experience among adolescents. *American Journal of Public Health*, 75 (11): 1331-32.

Furstenberg, F., Morgan, S., Moore, K. & Peterson, J. 1987. Race differences in the timing of first intercourse. *American Sociological Review*, 52: 511-18.

Gabrielson, I., Goldsmith, S., Potts, L., Mathews, V. & Gabrielson, M. 1971. Attitudes towards abortion: effects on contraceptive practice. *American Journal of Public Health*, 61 (April): 730-38.

Galdston, I. 1958. Other aspects of abortion problem: psychiatric aspects. In M. Calderone, ed. *Abortion in the United States*. New York: Hoeber-Harper.

Gallup Poll. 1984. Canadian attitudes toward sexuality. *Tellus, Journal of Planned Parenthood Association of Canada*, 30 September: 27-30.

Gardner, R. 1972. *Abortion: The Personal Dilemma*. Grand Rapids, MI: William B. Eerdmans Publishing Company.

Garner, W. 1970. Cited in J. Nunnally, Jr. *Introduction to Psychological Measurement*. New York: McGraw-Hill Book Company.

Gebhard, P., Pomeroy, W., Martin, C. & Christenson, C. 1958. *Pregnancy, Birth and Abortion.* New York: Harper and Brothers, Publishers.

Gillaspie, M., Ton Vergart, E. & Kingma, J. 1988. Secular trends in abortion attitudes: 1975-1980-1985. *Journal of Psychology,* 122 (4): 323-41.

Ginsburg, H. & Opper, S. 1988. *Piaget's Theory of Intellectual Development.* 3d ed. Englewood Cliffs, NJ: Prentice-Hall.

Glasser, P. & Navarre, E. 1965. Structural problems of the one-parent family. *Journal of Social Issues,* 216: 98-109.

Glenc, F. 1974. Early and late complications after therapeutic abortion. *American Journal of Obstetrics and Gynecology,* 118 (January): 34-35.

Goldsmith, S. 1969. San Francisco's teen clinic: meeting the sex education and birth control needs of the sexually active schoolgirl. *Family Planning Perspectives,* 1 (October): 23-26.

Goldsmith, S., Gabrielson, M., Gabrielson, I., Mathews, V. & Potts, L. 1972. Teenagers, sex and contraception. *Family Planning Perspectives,* 4 (1): 32-38.

Golstein, P. & Stewart, G. 1972. Trends in therapeutic abortion in San Francisco. *American Journal of Public Health,* 62 (May): 695-99.

Gordon, R. 1980. *Interviewing: Strategies, Techniques and Tactics.* 3d ed. Homewood, IL: Dorsey Press.

Gottschalk, L., Tichner, J., Piker, H. & Stewart, S. 1964. Psychosocial factors associated with pregnancy in adolescent girls: a preliminary report. *Journal of Nervous and Mental Diseases,* 138: 524-34.

Gough, H. 1979. Some factors related to men's stated unwillingness to use a male contraceptive pill. *Journal of Sex Research,* 15 (1): 27-37.

Granberg, D. & Granberg, B. 1985. Social bases of support and opposition to legalized abortion. In P. Sachdev, ed. *Perspectives on Abortion.* Metuchen, NJ: Scarecrow Press: 191-204.

Grauer, H. 1972. A study of contraception as related to unwanted pregnancy. *Canadian Medical Association Journal,* 107 (October): 739-41.

Green, J. 1970. *Introduction to Measurement and Evaluation.* New York: Dodd, Mead & Company.

Greenberger, N. & Connor, K. 1991. Parental notice and consent for abortion: Out of step with family law principles and policies, comment. *Family Planning Perspectives*, 23 (1): 246-52.

Greenglass, E. 1976. *After Abortion*. Don Mills, Ont.: Longman Canada Ltd.

------. 1977. Therapeutic abortion, fertility plans, and psychological sequelae. *American Journal of Orthopsychiatry*, 47 (January): 119-26.

Greenglass, E. 1981. A Canadian study of psychological adjustment after abortion. In P. Sachdev, ed. *Abortion: Readings and Research*, Toronto: Butterworths: 76-90.

Greer, G. 1984. *Sex and Destiny: The Politics of Human Fertility*. London: Martin Seeker & Warburg Ltd.

Grotevant, H. & Cooper, C. 1986. Individuation in family relationships. *Human Development*, 56: 415-28.

Group for the Advancement of Psychiatry. 1970. *The Right to Abortion*. New York: Charles Scribner's Sons.

Guilford, J. 1954. *Psychosomatic Methods*. 2d ed. New York: Mcgraw-Hill.

Hall, R. 1971. Induced abortion in New York City. *American Journal of Obstetrics and Gynecology*, 110 (July): 601-11.

Hamilton, J. 1984. Quoted in Rip van Winkle period ends for puerperal psychiatric problems. *Journal of the American Medical Association*, 27 (April): 2061-67.

Hamilton, V. 1966. Cited by N. Simon and A. Senturia. Psychiatric sequelae of abortion: Review of the literature, 1935-1964. *Archives of General Psychiatry*, 15 (October): 378-89.

Handy, J. 1982. Psychological and social aspects of induced abortion. *British Journal of Clinical Psychology*, 21 (1): 29-41.

Hanson, S., Myers, D. & Ginsburg, A. 1987. The role of responsibility and knowledge in reducing teenage out-of-wedlock childbearing. *Journal of Marriage and the Family*, 49: 241-51.

Haring, B. 1970. Cited in D. Callahan. *Abortion: Law, Choice and Morality*. New York: Macmillian Company.

Harrison, D., Bennett, W. & Globett, G. 1969. Attitudes of rural youth toward premarital sexual permissiveness. *Journal of Marriage and the Family*, 31 (November).

Harter, C. & Beasley, J. 1967. A survey concerning induced abortions in New Orleans. *American Journal of Public Health*, 57 (November): 1937-47.

Health Reports. 1989. *Therapeutic Abortions 1989. Ottawa: Statistics Canada*, Supplement no 9, 1991, (1).

Health Reports. 1990. *Therapeutic Abortions 1990*, Supplement no 9, 1991, 3 (4).

Hefferman, R. & Lynch, W. 1953. What is the status of therapeutic abortion in modern obstetrics? *American Journal of Obstetrics and Gynecology*, 66: 335-45.

Heineman, R. 1973. The evolution of an abortion counseling service in an adoption agency. *Child Welfare*, LII (April): 253-60.

Henker, F. 1973. Abortion applicants in Arkansas. *Journal of the Arkansas Medical Society*, 69 (March): 293-95.

Henshaw, S. 1986. Trends in Abortion, 1982-1984. *Family Planning Perspectives*, 18 (1): 34.

------. 1991. The accessibility of abortion services in the United States. *Family Planning Perspectives*, 23 (6): 246-52.

------. 1992. Abortion trends in 1987 and 1988: Age and race. *Family Planning Perspectives*, 24 (2): 85-86.

Henshaw, S. & Kost, K. 1992. Parental involvement in minors' abortion decision. *Family Planning Perspectives*, 24 (5): 196-213.

Henshaw, S. & O'Reilly, K. 1983. Characteristics of abortion patients in the United States, 1979 and 1980. *Family Planning Perspectives*, 15 (1): 5-16.

Henshaw, S. & Silverman, J. 1988. The characteristics and prior contraceptive use of U.S. abortion patients. *Family Planning Perspectives*, 20 (4): 158-168.

Henshaw, S. & Van Vort, J. 1989. Teenage abortion, birth and pregnancy statistics: an update. *Family Planning Perspectives*, 21 (2): 85-88.

------. 1990. Abortion services in the U.S., 1987 and 1988. *Family Planning Perspectives*, 22 (3): 102-108.

------, eds. 1992. *Abortion Factbook, 1992 Edition: Readings, Trends and State and Local Data to 1988*. New York: Alan Guttmacher Institute.

Henshaw, S., Koonin, L. & Smith, J. 1991. Characteristics of U.S. women having abortions, 1987. *Family Planning Perspectives*, 23 (2): 75-81.

Henshaw, S., Binkin, N., Blaine, E. & Smith, J. 1985. A portrait of American women who obtain abortions. *Family Planning Perspectives*, 17 (2): 90-96.

Hentoff, M. 1970. Cited in D. Callahan, *Abortion: Law, Choice and Morality*. New York: Macmillan Company.

Hepworth, D. 1964. The clinical implications of perceptual distortions in forced marriages. *Social Casework*, 45 (December): 579-85.

Hepworth, P. 1975. *Family Planning and Abortion Services and Family Life Education Programs, vol. 5*. Ottawa: Canadian council on Social Development.

Herold, E. 1984. *Sexual behavior of Canadian Young People*. Toronto: Fitzhenry & Whiteside.

Herold, E. & Goodwin, M. 1980. A comparison of younger and older adolescent females attending birth control clinics. *Canadian Family Physician*, 26: 687-94.

Hill, R., Stycos, J. & Back, K. 1959. *The Family Planning and Population Control: A Puerto Rican Experiment in Social Change*. Chapel Hill: University of North Carolina Press.

Hobart, C. 1972. Sexual permissiveness in young English and French Canadians. *Journal of Marriage and the Family*, 34 (May): 292-303.

Hofferth, S., Kahn, J. & Baldwin, W. 1987. Premarital sexual activity among U.S. teenage women over the past three decades. *Family Planning Perspectives*, 19 (2): 46-53.

Hogan, D. & Kitagawa, E. 1985. The impact of social status, family structure and neighborhood on the fertility of black adolescents. *American Journal of Sociology*, 90: 825-55.

Hogue, C. 1986. Impact of abortion on subsequent fecundity. *Clinics of Obstetrics and Gynecology*, 13 (1): 95-103.

Hook, K. 1963. Refused abortions: a follow-up study of 249 women whose applications were refused by the National Board of Health in Sweden. *Acta Psychiatrica Scandanavia*, 39, Supplement 168.

------. 1975. The unwanted child: effects on mothers and children of refused applications for abortion. In *Society, Stress and Disease*. Oxford Medical Publications, vol. 2: 187-92.

Hospital Administration in Canada. 1972. The care and treatment of therapeutic abortion patients in Canadian hospitals, January 1 to September 30, 1971: A nation-wide survey. *Hospital Adminstration in Canada*, 14 (March): 25-31.

Hyde, J. 1990. *Understanding Human Sexuality*. 4th ed. New York: McGraw-Hill Publishing Co.

Illsley, R. & Hall, M. 1976. Psychosocial aspects of abortion: a review of issues and needed research. *Bulletin of World Health Organization*, 53: 83-106.

Inazu, J. & Fox, G. 1980. Maternal influence on the sexual behaviors of teenage daughters. *Journal of Family Issues*, 1: 81-99.

Ingham, C. & Simms, M. 1972. Study of applicants for abortion at the Royal Northern Hospital, London. *Journal of Biosocial Science*, 4 (July): 351-69.

Inghe, G. 1972. Cited in Michael B. Bracken et al. Contraceptive practice among New York abortion patients. *American Journal of Obstetrics and Gynecology*, 114 (December): 968.

Janis, I. & Mann, L. 1968. A conflict-theory approach to attitude change and decision-making. In A.G. Greenwald and T.C. Brock, eds. *Psychological Foundations of Attitudes*. New York: Academic Press: 327-60.

Jansson, B. 1965. Mental disorders after abortion. *Acta Psychiatrica Scandanavia*, 41: 87-110.

Joffee, C. 1979. Abortion work: strains, coping strategies, policy implications. *Social Work*, 24: 485-90.

Jones, E., Forrest, J., Henshaw, S., Silverman, J. & Torres, A. 1988. Unintended pregnancy, contraceptive practice and family planning services in developed countries. *Family Planning Perspectives*, 20 (2): 53-67.

Jones. E. & Forrest, J. 1989. Contraceptive failure in the United States: revised estimates from the 1982 National Survey of Family Growth. *Family Planning Perspectives*, 21 (3): 103-9.

Jones, E. et al. 1986. *Teenage Pregnancy in Industrialized Countries*. New Haven: Yale University Press.

Jones, J. & Philliber, S. 1983. Sexually active but not pregnant: A comparison of teens who risk and teens who plan. *Journal of Youth and Adolescence*, 12 (3): 235-51.

Joseph, C. 1985. Factors related to delay for legal abortions performed at a gestational age of 20 weeks or more. *Journal of Biosocial Sciences*, 17: 327-37.

Kaats, G. & Davis, K. 1970. The dynamics of sexual behavior of college students. *Journal of Marriage and the Family*, August: 390-99.

Kadushin, A. 1969. An experience in tape recording interviews: report of an adoptive follow-up study. *Journal of Jewish Communal Services*, 43: 327-33.

Kadushin, A. 1972. *The Social Work Interview*. New York: Columbia University Press.

------. 1988. *Child Welfare Services*. 5th ed. New York: Macmillan Publishing Company, Inc.

------. 1990. *The Social Work Interview*. 3d ed. New York: Columbia University Press.

Kahn, R. & Cannell, C. 1957. *The Dynamics of Interviewing*. New York: John Wiley & Sons, Inc.

Kalmuss, D. 1986. Contraceptive use: A comparison between ever- and never-pregnant adolescents. *Journal of Adolescent Health Care*, 7: 332-37.

Kaltreider, N. 1973. Emotional patterns related to delay of decision to seek legal abortion. *California Medicine*, 118 (May): 23-27.

Kaminsky, B. & Scheckter, L. 1979. Abortion counseling in a general hospital. *Health and Social Work*, 4 (2): 93-103.

Kane, F., Feldman, M., Jain, S. & Lipton, M. 1973. Emotional reactions in abortion services personnel. *Archives of General Psychiatry*, 28 (March): 409-11.

Kane, F., Lachenbruch, P., Lipton, M. & Baram, D. 1973. Motivational factors in abortion patients. *American Journal of Psychiatry*, 130 (March): 290-93.

Kane, F., Lachenbruch, P., Lokey, L., et al. 1971. Motivational factors in abortion patients. *American Journal of Obstetrics and Gynecology*, 110: 1050-54.

Kantner, J. & Allingham, J. 1968. American attitudes on population policy. *Studies in Family Planning*. The Population Council, No. 30 (May): 1-7.

Kantner, J. & Zelnik, M. 1972. Sexual experience of young, unmarried women in the United States. *Family Planning Perspectives*, 4 (October): 9-18.

------. 1973. Contraception and Pregnancy: experience of young, unmarried women in the United States. *Family Planning Perspectives*, 4 (Winter): 21-35.

Katchadourian, H. 1989. *Fundamentals of Human Sexuality*. Toronto: Holt, Rinehart and Winston, Inc.

Kazanjian, A. 1973. A review of the first two years experience. Association for Contraceptive Counseling and Related Areas. Mimeographed, 23 August.

Keith, J., McCreary, C., Collins, K., Smith, C. & Bernstein, I. 1991. Sexual activity and contraceptive use among low-income urban black adolescent females. *Adolescence*, 26 (104): 769-85.

Kenney, A., Guardado, S. & Brown, L. 1989. Sex education and AIDS education in the schools: What states and large school districts are doing. *Family Planning Perspectives*, 21 (2): 56-64.

Kenyon, F. 1969. Termination of pregnancy on psychiatric grounds: A comparative study of 61 cases. *British Journal of Medical Psychology*, 42: 243-53.

Kerenyi, T., Glascock, E. & Horowitz, M. 1973. Reasons for delayed abortion: Results of four hundred interviews. *American Journal of Obstetrics and Gynecology*, 117 (October): 299-311.

Kiesler, F. 1971. Cited in David K. Michelman. Abortion: a psychological study. Ph.D. dissertation, Michigan State University.

Kimball, C. 1970. Some observations regarding unwanted pregnancies and therapeutic abortions. *Obstetrics and Gynecology*, 35 (February): 293-96.

Kinsey, A. & Gebhard, P. 1953. *Sexual Behavior in the Human Female*. Philadelphia: W.B. Saunders Company: 304-7.

Kinsey, A., Pomeroy, W. & Martin, C. 1953. *Sexual Behavior in the Human Male*. Philadelphia: W.B. Saunders Company.

Kirby, D. 1984. *Sexuality Education: An Evaluation of Programs and their Effect*. Santa Cruz, CA: Network Publications.

Kirby, D., Waszak, C. & Ziegler, J. 1991. Six school-based clinics: Their reproductive health services and impact on sexual behavior. *Family Planning Perspectives*, 23 (1): 6-16.

Kirby, D., Barth, R., Leland, N. & Fetro, J. 1991. Reducing the risk: Impact of a new curriculum on sexual risk-taking. *Family Planning Perspectives*, 23 (6): 253-63.

Kirkpatrick, C., Stryker, S. & Buell, P. 1952. An experimental study of attitudes toward male sex behavior with reference to Kinsey findings. *American Sociological Review*, 17 (October): 580-87.

Kiser, C. & Whelpton, P. 1953. Resume of the Indianapolis study of social and psychological factors affecting fertility. *Population Studies*, 7: 95-110.

Klinger, A. 1966. Abortion programs. In B. Berelson et al., eds. *Family Planning and Population Program.* Chicago: University of Chicago.

Klitsch, M. 1991. Antiprogestins and the abortion controversy: a progress report. *Family Planning Perspectives*, 23 (6): 275-82.

Koenig, M. & Zelnik, M. 1982. The risk of premarital first pregnancy in metropolitan-area teenagers: 1976-1979. *Family Planning Perspectives*, 14 (5): 239-47.

Kolbert, K. 1989. Perspectives on the abortion controversy and the role of the Supreme Court. *American Journal of Law and Medicine*, 15 (2-3): 153-68.

Kolstad, P. 1957. Therapeutic abortion: a clinical study based upon 968 cases from a Norwegian hospital, 1940-53. *American Obstetrics and Gynecology Society*, 36, Supplement 6.

Koop, C. 1988. *AIDS and Teenagers: Emerging Issues.* (Hearing before the Select Committee on Children, Youth and Families: House of Representatives, One Hundredth Congress, First Session). Washington, DC: U.S. Government Printing Office.

Kost, K., Forrest, J. & Harlap, S. 1991. Comparing health risks and benefits of contraceptive choices. *Family Planning Perspectives*, 23 (2): 54-61.

Kretzchmar, R. & Norris, A. 1967. Psychiatric implications of therapeutic abortion. *American Journal of Obstetrics and Gynecology*, 198: 368.

Ku, L., Sonenstein, F. & Pleck, J. 1992a. The association of AIDS education and sex education with sexual behavior and condom use among teenage men. *Family Planning Perspectives*, 24 (3): 100-106.

------. 1992b. Patterns of HIV risk and preventative behaviors among teenage men. *Public Health Reports*, 107: 131.

Kumabe, K. 1972. Abortions among women on public assistance in Hawaii: implications for practice. *American Journal of Public Health*, 62: 1538-43.

Kummer, J. 1963. Post-abortion psychiatric illness--a myth? *American Journal of Psychiatry*, 119 (April): 980-83.

------. 1967. A psychiatrist views our abortion enigma. In A. Guttmacher, ed. *The Case for Legalized Abortion.* Berkeley, CA: Diablo Press.

Laidlaw, R. 1966. Cited in R. White. Induced abortions: a survey of their psychiatric implications, complications and indications. *Texas Report on Biology and Medicine*, 24: 543-44.

Lambert, J. 1971. Survey of 3,000 unwanted pregnancies. *British Medical Journal*, 4: 156-60.

Landsberg, M. 1990. Abortion bill should be withdrawn. *Toronto Star*, September 14.

Lask, B. 1975. Short-term psychiatric sequelae to therapeutic termination of pregnancy. *British Journal of Psychiatry*, 126 (2): 173-77.

Latimer, R., McGuire, K., Startsman, F. & Swisshelm, M. 1965. Unmarried mothers who keep their babies. *Journal of Health Research*, 13: 49-61.: 66.

Law Reform Commission. 1989. Crimes against the foetus. Law Reform Commission of Canada, Working Paper 58: Ottawa: Catalogue No. J32-1/58-1989.

Lazarus, A. 1985. Psychiatric sequelae of legalized elective first trimester abortion. *Journal of Psychosomatic Obstetrics and Gynecology*, 4: 141-50.

Lee, N. 1969. *The Search for an Abortionist*. Chicago: University of Chicago Press.

Lehfeldt, H. 1970. Psychological factors. In M. Calderone, ed. *Manual of Family Planning and Contraceptive Practice*. 2d ed. Baltimore: Williams and Wilkins Company.

Leiter, N. 1972. Elective abortion: women in crisis. *New York State Journal of Medicine*, (December 1): 2908-10.

Lemkau, J. 1988. Emotional sequelae of abortion: implications for clinical practice. *Psychology of Women Quarterly*, 12: 461-72.

------. 1991. Post-abortion adjustment of health care professionals in training. *American Journal of Orthopsychiatry*, 61 (1): 92-102.

Levene, H. & Rigney, F. 1970. Law, preventive psychiatry, and therapeutic abortion. *Journal of Nervous and Mental Diseases*, 151 (July): 51-59.

Ley, D. 1955. A follow-up study of unmarried mothers. *Social Casework*, 31: 27-33.

Lidz, T. 1967. Reflection of a psychiatrist. In H. Rosen, ed. *Abortion in America*. Boston: Beacon Press.

Lindemann, C. 1974. *Birth Control and Unmarried Young Women*. New York: Springer Publishing Co.

Linn, S., Schoenbaum, S., Monson, R., et al. 1983. The relationship between induced abortion and the outcome of subsequent pregnancies. *American Journal of Obstetrics and Gynecology*, 146 (2): 136-40.

Lipovenko, D. 1987. Court ruling to protect fetus opens Pandora's box of issues. *Globe and Mail*, April 4: D3.

Lipper, I., Cvejic, H., Benjamin, P. & Kinch, R. 1973. Abortion and the pregnant teenager. *Canadian Medical Journal*, 109 (3): 852-56.

Llewalyn, S. & Pytches, R. 1988. An investigation of anxiety following termination of pregnancy. *Journal of Advanced Nursing*, 13 (4): 468-71.

Lodl, K., McGettigan, A. & Bucy, J. 1985. Women's responses to abortion: implications for post-abortion support. *Journal of Social Work and Human Sexuality*, 3 (2-3): 119-32.

Loesch, J. & Greenberg, N. 1962. Some specific areas of conflicts observed during pregnancy: a comparative study of married and unmarried pregnant women. *American Journal of Orthopsychiatry*, 32 (July): 624-36.

Loewenstein, G. & Furstenberg, F. 1991. Is teenage sexual behavior rational? *Journal of Applied Social Psychology*, 21 (12): 957-86.

Look Magazine, July 28, 1970.

Luker, K. 1975. *Taking Chances: Abortion and the Decision Not to Contracept*. Berkeley: University of California Press.

------. 1984. *Abortion and the Politics of Motherhood*. Berkeley: University of California Press.

Lundberg, S. & Plotnick, R. 1990. Effects of state welfare, abortion and family planning policies on premarital childbearing among white adolescents. *Family Planning Perspectives*, 22 (6): 246-51.

Lyons, J., Larson, D., Huckeba, W., Rogers, J. & Mueller, C. 1988. Research on the psychosocial impact of abortion: A systematic review of the literature 1966 to 1985. In P. Uhlenberg et al., eds. *Values and Public Policy*. Washington, DC: Family Research Council of America.

MacDonald, N., et al. 1990. High-risk STD/HIV behavior among college students. *Journal of the American Medical Association*, 263: 3155-60.

Mace, D. 1972. *Abortion: The Agonizing Decision*. New York: Abingdon Press.

MacIntyre, F. 1970. Cited in D. Callahan. *Abortion: Law, Choice and Morality*. New York: Macmillan Company.

MacIntyre, S. 1977. *Single and Pregnant*. New York: Prodist.

Mahoney, E.R. 1983. *Human Sexuality*. New York: McGraw-Hill.

Major, B. & Cozzarelli, C. 1992. Psychosocial predictors of adjustment to abortion. *Journal of Social Issues*, 48 (3): 121-42.

Major, B., Mueller, P. & Hildebrandt, K. 1985. Attributions, expectations and coping with abortion. *Journal of Personality and Social Psychology*, 48: 585-99.

Major, B., Cozzarelli, C., Sciacchitano, A., Cooper, M., Testa, M. & Mueller, P. 1990. Perceived social support, self efficacy and adjustment to abortion. *Journal of Personality and Social Psychology*, 59: 452-63.

Mackie, R. 1990. Commons restrict abortions, *Globe and Mail*, May 30.

Mallory, G., Rubenstein, L., Drosness, D., Kleiner, G. & Sidel, V. 1972. Factors responsible for delay in obtaining interruption of pregnancy. *Obstetrics and Gynecology*, 40 (October): 556-62.

Malloy, T. 1981. The relationship between therapist-client interpersonal compatibility, sex of therapist and therapeutic outcome. *Journal of Clinical Psychology*, 37 (2): 316-22.

Malmfors, K. 1966. Cited in N. Simon & A. Senturia. Psychiatric sequelae of abortion: Review of the literature, 1935-64. *Archives of General Psychiatry*, (October): 384.

Mandelson, M., Maden, C. & Daling, J. 1992. Low birth weight in relation to multiple induced abortions. *American Journal of Public Health*, 82: 391.

Marder, L. 1970. Psychiatric experience with a liberalized therapeutic abortion law. *American Journal of Psychiatry*, 126 (9): 1230-37.

Martin, C. 1972. Psychological problems of abortion for the unwed teenage girl. Ph.D. dissertation, United States International University.

Masters, W. & Johnson, V. 1970. *Human Sexual Inadequacy*. Boston: Little, Brown and Company.

Masters, W., Johnson, V. & Kolodny, R. 1992. *Human Sexuality*. 4th ed. New York: Harper Collins Publishers.

Mastroianni, L., Donaldson, P., Kane, T. eds. (1990). *Developing New Contraceptives: Obstacles and Opportunities*. Washington, D.C.: National Academy Press.

Matejcek, Z., Dytrych, Z. & Schuller, V. 1980. Follow-up study of children born from unwanted pregnancies. *International Journal of Behavioral Development*, 3: 243-51.

Matejcek, Z., Dytrych, Z. & Schuller, V. 1985. Follow-up study of children born to women denied abortion. In R. Porter and M. O'Connor, eds. *Abortion: Medical Progress and Social Implications*. (CIBA Foundation Symposium 115.) London, Pitman: 136-49.

Mattson, A. 1970. The male therapist and the female adolescent patient. *Journal of the American Academy of Child Psychiatry*, 9: 707-21.

Maxwell, J. 1970. College students' attitudes toward abortion. *The Family Coordinator*, 19 (July): 247-52.

McCance, C., Olley, P. & Edward, V. 1973. Long-term psychiatric follow-up. In G. Horobin, ed. *Experience with Abortion*. London: Cambridge University Press: 245-300.

McCoy, D. 1968. The emotional reaction of women to therapeutic abortion and sterilization. *Journal of Obstetrics and Gynecology*, 75 (October): 1054-57.

McLaren, C. 1990. MDs and the new abortion law. *Globe and Mail*, June 16: D2.

Meikle, S., Peitchinis, J. & Pearce, K. 1985. *Teenage Sexuality*. San Diego, CA: College-Hill Press.

Melamed, L. 1975. Therapeutic abortion in midwestern city. *Psychological Reports*, 37: 1144-49.

Meyerowitz, S., Satloff, A. & Romano, J. 1971. Induced abortion for psychiatric indication. *American Journal of Psychiatry*, 127: 1153-60.

Michelman, D. 1971. Abortion: a psychological study. Ph.D. dissertation, Michigan State University.

Miller, B. & Moore, K. 1990. Adolescent sexual behavior, pregnancy and parenting: research through the 1980's. *Journal of Marriage and the Family*, 52 (November): 1025-44.

Miller, B., McCoy, J., Olson, T. & Wallace, C. 1986. Parental discipline and control attempts in relation to adolescent sexual attitudes and behavior. *Journal of Marriage and the Family*, 48: 503-12.

Miller, C. 1970. Cited in D. Callahan. *Abortion: Law, Choice and Morality*. New York: Macmillan Company.

Miller, J. 1973. Medical abortion in south Australia: a critical assessment of early complications. *Medical Journal of Australia*, 394 (April): 825-30.

Miller, J. 1979. Hospital response to the legalization of abortion in New York state: an analysis of program innovation. *Journal of Health and Social Behavior*, 20: 363-75.

Miller, W. 1976. Sexual and contraceptive behavior in young unmarried women. *Health Care for Women*, 3: 427-53.

Miller, W. 1992. An empirical study of psychosocial antecedents and consequences of induced abortion. *Journal of Social Issues*, 48 (3): 67-93.

Milling, E. 1973. World's largest abortion clinic. *Pageant*, July: 2-7.

Monsour, K. & Stewart, B. 1973. Abortion and sexual behavior in college women. *American Journal of Orthopsychiatry*, 43 (5): 804-14.

Moore, E. 1974. *International Inventory of Information on Induced Abortion*. New York: International Institute for the Study of Human Reproduction, Columbia University.

Moore, K. 1988. *Facts at a Glance*. Washington, DC: Child Trends, Inc.

Moore, K. & Peterson, J. 1989. *The Consequences of Teenage Pregnancy: Final Report*. Washington, DC: Child Trends, Inc.

Moore, K. & Stief, T. 1991. Changes in marriage and fertility behavior: Behaviour vs attitudes of young adults. *Youth and Society*, 22 (3): 362-86.

Moore, K., Simms, M. & Belsey, C. 1986. *Choice and Circumstances*. New Brunswick, NJ: Transaction Books.

Moore, W. 1963. *Social Change*. Englewood Cliffs, NJ: Prentice Hall, Inc.

Morbidity and Mortality Weekly Report. 1992. Sexual Behavior among high school students - Untied States, 1990. 40: 885.

Morrison, D. 1989. Predicting contraceptive efficacy: A discriminant analysis of three groups of adolescent women. *Journal of Applied Social Psychology*, 19 (17): 1431-52.

Moseley, D., Follingstad, D., Harley, H. & Heckel, R. 1981. Psychological factors that predict reaction to abortion. *Journal of Clinical Psychology*, 37: 276-79.

Mosher, W. 1979. Sex guilt and sex myths. *Journal of Sex Research*, 15: 224-34.

------. 1990. Contraceptive practice in the United States, 1982-1988. *Family Planning Perspectives*, 22 (5): 198-205.

Mosher, W. & Horn, M. 1989. First family planning visits by young women. *Family Planning Perspectives*, 21 (1): 33-40.

Mosher, W. & Pratt, W. 1990. Contraceptive use in the United States, 1973-1988. Advanced Data for Vital and Health Statistics, No. 182.

Mueller, P. & Major, B. 1989. Self-blame, self-efficacy and adjustment to abortion. *Journal of Personality and Social Psychology*, 57: 1059-68.

Murphy, J., Symington, B. & Jacobson, S. 1983. Pregnancy-resolution decisions: What if abortions were banned? *The Journal of Reproductive Medicine*, 28 (11): 789-97.

Nadelson, C., Malkah, I., Notman, T. & Gillon, J. 1980. Sexual knowledge and attitudes of adolescents: Relationship to contraceptive use. *Obstetrics and Gynecology*, 55: 340-45.

Nathanson, C. 1985. Physicians, hospitals, and abortion: the influence of attitudes on medical practice. In P. Sachdev, ed. *Perspectives on Abortion*. Metuchen, NJ: Scarecrow Press: 205-20.

Nathanson, C. & Becker, M. 1980. Obstetricians' attitudes and hospital abortion services. *Family Planning Perspectives*, 12: 26-32.

National Center for Health Statistics. 1989. Advance report of final natality statistics, 1987. Monthly Vital Statistics Report, U.S. Department of Health and Human Services.

Newton, J., Brotman, M., McEwan, J. & Owens, C. 1973. Hospital family planning: termination of pregnancy and contraceptive use. *British Medical Journal*, November 3: 280-84.

Niemela, P., Lehtinen, P., Rauramo, L., Hermansson, R., Karjalainen, R., Maki, H. & Stora, C. 1981. The first abortion--and the last? A study of the personality factors underlying repeated failure of contraception. *International Journal of Gynecology and Obstetrics*, 19: 193-200.

Niswander, K. & Patterson, R. 1967. Psychologic reaction to therapeutic abortion: Subjective patient responses. *Obstetrics and Gynecology*, 29 (May): 702-6.

Niswander, K., Singer, J. & Singer, M. 1972. Psychological reaction to therapeutic abortion II: Objective response. *American Journal of Obstetrics and Gynecology*, 114 (September): 29-33.

Noble, D. 1968. Abortion and sterilization: psychiatric problems in therapeutic abortion. In R. Allen, E. Ferster & J. Rubin, eds. *Readings in Law and Psychiatry*. Baltimore: Johns Hopkins Press.

Notman, M. 1975. Teenage pregnancy: The non-use of contraception. *Psychiatric Opinion*, 12: 23-27.

Nunnally, J. 1970. *Introduction to Psychological Measurement*. New York: McGraw-Hill Book Company.

Olsen, J., Weed, S., Nielsen, A. & Jensen, L. 1992. Student evaluation of sex education programs advocating abstinence. *Adolescence*, 27 (106): 369-80.

Olson, L. 1980. Social and psychological correlates of pregnancy resolution among adolescent women: a review. *American Journal of Orthopsychiatry*, 50 (3): 432-45.

Oppenheim, A. 1966. *Questionnaire Design and Attitude Measurement*. New York: Basic Books, Inc., Publishers.

Orentlicher, D. 1989. Webster and the fundamental right to make medical decisions. *American Journal of Law and Medicine*, 15 (2-3): 184-88.

Orr, D., Langefeld, C., Katz, B., Caine, V., Dias, P., Blythe, M. & Jones, R. 1992. Factors associated with condom use among sexually active female adolescents. *Journal of Pediatrics*, 120 (2, pt. 1): 311-17.

Osofsky, J. & Osofsky, H. 1972. The psychological reaction of patients to legalized abortion. *American Journal of Orthopsychiatry*, 42 (January): 48-60.

Palko, M., Lennox, R. & McQuarrie, C. 1971. Current status of family planning in Canada. *Canadian Journal of Public Health*, 62: 509-19.

Pannor, R. 1971. *The Unwed Father - New Approach to Helping Unmarried Young Parents*. New York: Springer Publishing Company, Inc.

Pantelakies, S., et al. 1973. Influence of induced and spontaneous abortions on the outcome of subsequent pregnancies. *American Journal of Obstetrics and Gynecology*, 116 (July): 801-5.

Pare, C. & Raven, H. 1970. Follow-up of patients referred for termination of pregnancy. *Lancet*, 1 (March 28): 635-38.

Patt, S., Rappaport, R. & Barglow, P. 1969. Follow-up of therapeutic abortion. *Archives of General Psychiatry*, 20: 408-14.

Payne, E., Kravitz, A., Malkah, T., Notman, M., Jane, V. & Anderson, M. 1976. Outcome following therapeutic abortion. *Archives of General Psychiatry*, 33 (June): 725-33.

Peck, A. 1968. Therapeutic abortion: Patients, doctors and society. *American Journal of Psychiatry*, 125 (December): 109-16.

Peck, A. & Marcus, H. 1966. Psychiatric sequelae of therapeutic interruption of pregnancy. *Journal of Nervous and Mental Diseases*, 143 (5): 417-25.

Perez-Reyes, M. & Falk, R. 1973. Follow-up after theraputic abortion in early adolescence. *Archives of General Psychiatry*, 28 (January): 120-26.

Perline, E. 1971. *Abortion in Canada*. New Women Series: I. Toronto: New Press.

Peterson, G., Rollins, B. & Thomas, D. 1985. Parent and adolescent conformity: compliance and internalization. *Youth and Society*, 16: 397-420.

Peyton, F., Starry, A. & Leidy, T. 1969. Women's attitudes concerning abortion. *Obstetrics and Gynecology*, 34 (August): 182-88.

Pfeiffer, E. 1970. Psychiatric indications or psychiatric justification of therapeutic abortion. *Archives of General Psychiatry*, 23 (November): 402-7.

Pick de, W. 1980. Toward a predictive model of family planning. *Revista Latinoamericana de Psicologia*, 12: 119-25.

Pierce, R. 1970. *Single and Pregnant*. Boston: Beacon Press.

Pleck, J., Sonenstein, F. & Ku, L. 1990. Contraceptive attitudes and intentions to use condoms in sexually experienced and inexperienced adolescent males. *Journal of Family Issues*, 11 (3): 294-312.

Pliner, A. & Yates, S. 1992. Psychological and legal issues in minors' rights to abortion. *Journal of Social Issues*, 48 (3): 203-16.

Pohlman, E. & Pohlman, J. 1969. *The Psychology of Birth Planning*. Cambridge, MA: Schenkman Publishing Company, Inc.

Pope, B. & Scott, W. 1967. *Psychological Diagnosis in Clinical Practice*. New York: Oxford University Press.

Pope, H. 1969. Negro-white differences in decisions regarding illegitimate children. *Journal of Marriage and the Family*, 31 (November): 756-64.

Potts, M. 1988. Birth control methods in the United States. *Family Planning Perspectives*, 20 (6): 288-97.

Prager, K. 1985. Induced termination of pregnancy: reporting states, 1981. Monthly Vital Statistics Report, 34 (4), Supplement 2. Department of Health and Human Services Publication No. 85-1120. Washington, DC: U.S. Government Printing Office.

Pratt, W. & Hendershot, G. 1984. The use of family planning services by sexually active teenage women. Paper presented at the annual meeting of the Population Association of America, Minneapolis, May 3-5.

Pratt, W. & Horn, M. 1985. Wanted and unwanted childbearing, United States, 1973-1982. *Advanced Data from Vital and Health Statistics*, No. 108. Department of Health and Human Services Publication No. 85-1250. Washington, DC: U.S. Government Printing Office.

Pratt, W., Mosher, W., Bachrach, C. & Horn, M. 1984. Understanding U.S. fertility. *Population Bulletin*, 39 (5): 3-42.

Priegert, P. 1991. Federal abortion bill threatens Ontario plans for full access for women. *Evening Telegram*, January 16: 7.

Rader, G., Bekker, D., Brown, L. & Richardt, C. 1978. Psychological correlates of unwanted pregnancy. *Journal of Abnormal Psychology*, 87: 373-76.

Rains, P. 1971. *Becoming an Unwed Mother*. Chicago: Aldine, Atherton, Inc.

Rainwater, L. 1960. *And the Poor Get Children*. Chicago: Quadrangle Paperbacks.

Redmond, M. 1985. Attitudes of adolescent males toward adolescent pregnancy and fatherhood. *Family Relations*, 34: 337-42.

Reinisch, J., Sanders, S., Hill, C. & Ziemba-Davis, M. 1992. High-risk sexual behavior among heterosexual undergraduates at a midwestern university. *Family Planning Perspectives*, 24 (3): 116-21.

Reis, J. & Herz, E. 1989. An examination of young adolescents' knowledge of and attitude toward sexuality according to perceived contraceptive responsibility. *Journal of Applied Social Psychology*, 19 (3): 231-50.

Reiss, I. 1966. The sexual renaissance: a summary and analysis. *Journal of Social Issues*, 22 (April): 123-37.

------. 1967. *The Social Context of Premarital Sexual Permissiveness*. New York: Holt, Rinehart & Winston.

------. 1968. How and why America's sex standards are changing. *Transaction*, March: 26-32.

Reiss, I., Banwart, A. & Foreman, H. 1975. Premarital contraceptive usage: A study and some theorectical explorations. *Journal of Marriage and the Family*, (August): 619-30.

Reschovsky, J. & Gerner, J. 1991. Contraceptive choice among teenagers: a multivariate analysis. *Lifestyles*, 12 (2): 171-94.

Rheingold, J. 1964. *The Fear of Being Woman*. New York: Grune & Stratton.

Rheingold, J. 1966. *The Mother, Anxiety, and Death*. Boston: Little, Brown & Company.

Richardson, S., Dohrenwend, B. & Klein, D. 1965. *Interviewing*. New York: Basic Books.

Right to be pregnant stresses. *Chicago Tribune*, April 5, 1973.

Richardson, S. & Guttmacher, A., eds. 1967. *Childbearing and Its Social and Psychological Aspects*. Williams & Wilkins Company.

Rindfuss, R., Swicegood, G. & Bumpass, L. 1989. Contraceptive choice in the United States: process, determinants, and change. In R. Bulatao, J. Palamore & S. Ward, eds. *Choosing a Contraceptive: Method Choice in Asia and the United States*. San Francisco: Westview Press.

Robbins, J. 1979. Objective vs subjective responses to abortion. *Journal of Consulting and Clinical Psychology*, 16: 995.

Robbins, J. & DeLamater, J. 1985. Support from significant others and loneliness following induced abortion. *Social Psychiatry*, 20 (2): 92-99.

Robinson, B. 1988a. Teenage pregnancy from the father's perspective. *American Journal of Orthopsychiatry*, 58: 46-51.

Robinson, B. 1988b. *Teenage Fathers*. Lexington, MA: Lexington Books.

Robinson, E. 1991. Twenty years of the sexual revolution, 1965-1985: an update. *Journal of Marriage and the Family*, 53 (1): 216-20.

Robinson, I., King, K. & Balswick, J. 1973. The premarital sexual revolution among college females. *The Family Coordinator*, April: 189-201.

Rogel, M. & Zuehlke, M. 1982. Adolescent contraceptive behavior: influences and implications. In I. Stuart & C. Wells, eds. *Pregnancy in Adolescence*. New York: Van Nostrand Reinhold.

Rogers, J., Boruch, R., Stoms, G. & DeMoya, D. 1991. Impact of Minnesota Parental Notification Law on abortion and birth. *American Journal of Public Health*, 81 (3): 294-98.

Romans-Clarkson, S. 1989. Psychological sequelae of induced abortion. *Australian and New Zealand Journal of Psychiatry*, 23: 555-65.

Romm, M. 1967. Psychoanalytic considerations. In H. Rosen, ed. *Abortion in America*. Boston: Beacon Press.

Rosen, A. & Van Knorring, K. 1989. Attitudes toward abortion methods and participation effects. *Social Behavior*, 4 (2): 71-82.

Rosen, R. 1990. Adolescent pregnancy decision making: Are parents important? *Adolescence*, 15: 43.

Rosenblatt, R. 1991. *Life Itself: Abortion in the American Mind*. New York: Random House.

Rosoff, J. 1989. Sex education in the schools: policies and practices. *Family Planning Perspectives*, 21 (2): 52.

Rossi, A. 1966. Abortion laws and their victims. *Transaction*, September-October: 7-12.

------. Public views on abortion. 1967. In A. Guttmacher, ed. *The Case for Legalized Abortion Now*. Berkeley: Diablo Press.

Rotter, K. 1980. Men and the abortion experience. Ph.D. dissertation, Southern Illinois University, Carbondale, Ill.

Rovinsky, J. & Gusbert, S. 1967. Current trends in therapeutic termination of pregnancy. *American Journal of Obstetrics and Gynecology*, 98: 11-17.

Ryan, I. & Dunn, P. 1988. Association of race, sex, religion, family size and desired number of children on college students' preferred methods of dealing with unplanned pregnancy. *Family Practice Research Journal*, 7 (3): 153-61.

Ryder, N. & Westoff, C. 1971. *Reproduction in the United States, 1965*. Princeton: Princeton University Press.

Sachdev, P., ed. 1981. *Abortion: Readings and Research*. Toronto: Butterworth & Co.

------, ed. 1985. *Perspectives on Abortion*. Metuchen, NJ: Scarecrow Press.

------, ed. 1988. *International Handbook on Abortion*. Westport, CT: Greenwood Press.

------. 1989. *Unlocking the Adoption Files*. Lexington, MA: Lexington Books.

Sachdev, P. 1991a. Birth mothers and their reunion experience with adoptees. Paper presented at the American Adoption Congress, Anaheim, CA, April 9-14.

------. 1991b. Birth Fathers: a neglected element in the adoption equation. *Families in Society*, 72 (3): 131-39.

St. John, C. & Grasmick, H. 1985. Decomposing the Black/White fertility differential. *Social Science Quarterly*, 66: 132-46.

Saltman, J. & Zimmering, S. 1973. *Abortion Today*. Springfield: Charles C. Thomas, Publisher.

Sandberg, E. & Jacobs, R. 1971. Psychology of the misuse and rejection of contraception. In F. Haselkorn, ed. *Family Planning Readings and Case Materials*. New York: Council of Social Work Education.

Sanders, G. & Mullis, R. 1988. Family Influences on sexual attitudes and knowledge as reported by college students. *Adolescence*, 23 (92): 837-45.

Sarrel, P., Holley, M. & Anderson, G. 1968. The young unwed mother. *Journal of the American College of Obstetricians and Gynecologists*, 32 (December): 741-47.

Sauber, M. & Rubenstein, E. 1965. *Experiences of the Unwed Mother as a Parent*. Research Department, The Community Council of Greater New York, Inc.

Schofield, M. 1965. *The Sexual Behavior of Young People*. London: Longmans Green.

Schoneberg, C. 1970. Abortion and adoption. *Child Welfare*, 49 (December): 544.

Schur, E. 1965. *Crimes without Victims: Deviant Behavior and Public Policy*. Englewood Cliffs, NJ: Prentice-Hall, Inc.

Schwartz, R. 1968. Psychiatry and the abortion laws: an overview. *Comprehensive Psychiatry*, 9: 99-117.

Selltiz, C., Wrightsman, L. & Cook, S. 1976. *Research Methods in Social Relations*. 3d ed. New York: Holt, Rinehart & Winston.

Senay, E. 1970. Therapeutic abortion. *Archives of General Psychiatry*, 23 (November): 408-15.

Shah, F. & Zelnik, M. 1981. Parent and peer influences on sexual behavior, contraceptive use and pregnancy experience of young women. *Journal of Marriage and the Family*, 43: 339-48.

Shainess, N. 1970. Abortion is no man's business. *Psychology Today*, 3 (May): 18-22.

Shanmugan, N. & Wood, C. 1970. Unwed mothers: a study of 100 girls in Melbourne, Victoria. *The Australia and New Zealand Journal of Sociology*, 6 (April): 51-55.

Shepler, L. 1991. Values, gender and the abortion question: A feminist perspective. In Nada L. Stotland, ed. *Psychiatric Aspects of Abortion*. Washington, DC: American Psychiatric Press, Inc.

Shostak, A. & McLouth, G. 1984. *Men and Abortion*. New York: Praeger Publishers.

Shulman, L. 1989. *The Skills of Helping*. 3d ed. Itasca, ILL: F.E. Peacock Publishers.

Shusterman, L. 1976. The psychosocial factors of the abortion experience: a critical review. *Psychology of Women Quarterly*, 1 (1): 79-106.

------. 1979. Predicting the psychological consequences of abortion. *Social Science and Medicine*, 13A: 683-89.

Silverman, J., Torres, A. & Forrest, J. 1987. Barriers to contraceptive services. *Family Planning Perspectives*, 19: 94.

Simms, M. & Smith, C. 1986. The teenage mothers and their partners. London: Department of Health and Social Security, Research Report No. 15, Her Majesty's Stationary Office.

Simon, N. & Senturia, A. 1966. Psychiatric sequelae of abortion: review of the literature, 1935-64. *Archives of General Psychiatry*, 15 (October): 378-89.

Simon, N., Senturia, A. & Rothman, D. 1967. Psychiatric illness following therapeutic abortion. *American Journal of Psychiatry*, 124 (July): 59-65.

Singh, B. & Williams, J. 1983. Attitudes and behavioral intentions about abortion. *Population and Environment*, 6 (2): 89-95.

Skerry, P. 1978. The class conflict over abortion. *Public Interest*, 52: 69-84.

Sloane, R. 1969. The unwanted pregnancy. *New England Journal of Medicine*, 28 (May): 1206-13.

Slonim-Nevo, V. 1988. Abortion among Israeli women after interruption in contraceptive use. *Health and Social Social Work*, 13 (2): 137-44.

Smigel, E. & Seiden, R. 1969. The decline and fall of the double standards. In J. Hadden & M. Borgatta, eds. *Marriage and the Family: A Comprehensive Reader*. Peacock Publishers, Inc.

Smith, E. 1972. Counseling for women who seek abortion. *Social Work*, March: 62-68.

------. 1973. A follow-up study of women who request abortion. *American Journal of Orthopsychiatry*, 43 (July): 574-85.

Smith, M. 1979. How men who accompany women to abortion service perceive the impact of abortion upon the relationship and themselves. Ph.D. dissertation, University of Iowa, Iowa City, IA.

Smith, T. 1991. Adult sexual behavior in 1989: number of partners, frequency of intercourse and risk of AIDS. *Family Planning Perspectives*, 23 (3): 102-7.

Sonenstein, F., Pleck, J. & Ku, L. 1989. Sexual activity, condom use and AIDS awareness among adolescent males. *Family Planning Perspectives*, 21(4): 153-58.

------. 1991. Levels of sexual activity among adolescent males in the United States. *Family Planning Perspectives*, 23 (4): 162-67.

Sorenson, R. 1973. *Adolescent Sexuality in Contemporary America*. New York: World Publishing.

Spanier, G. 1977. Sources of sex information and premarital sexual behavior. *Journal of Sex Research*, 13: 73-88.

Spees, E. 1987. College students' sexual attitudes and behaviors, 1974-1985: A review of the literature. *Journal of College Student Personnel*, 28 (2): 135-40.

Sprey, J. 1969. On the institutionalization of sexuality. *Journal of Marriage and the Family*, August: 43.

Statistics Canada. 1974. *1971 Census of Canada*. Ottawa: Publication Sales Division. Catalogue No. 94-791 (AE-7), April.

------. 1972. *Therapeutic Abortion in Canada, 1971*. Ottawa: Health and Welfare Division. May 3.

------. 1973. *Therapeutic Abortion in Canada, 1972*. Catalogue No. 82-211 Annual.

------. 1989. *The Family in Canada*. Ottatwa: Publication Sales, Catalogue #89-509.

Steele, B. & Pollock, C. 1968. A psychiatric study of parents who abuse infants and small children. In R. Helfer and H. Kempe, eds. *The Battered Child*. Chicago: University of Chicago Press: 103-47.

Steinhoff, P., Smith, R., Palmore, J., et al. 1979. Women who obtain repeat abortions: a study based on record linkage. *Family Planning Perspectives*, 11: 30-38.

Stewart, G. & Goldstein, P. 1972. Medical and surgical complications of therapeutic abortion. *Obstetrics and Gynecology*, 40: 539-50.

Strassberg, D. & Moore, M. 1985. Effects of film model on the psychological and physical stress of abortion. *Journal of Sex Education and Therapy*, 11 (2): 46-50.

Stroup, H. 1969. Philosophy predicts and projects. *The Future of the Family*. New York: Family Service Association of America.

Struder, M. & Thornton, A. 1989. The multifaceted impact of religiosity on adolescent sexual experience and contraceptive usage: A reply to Shornack and Ahmed. *Journal of Marriage and the Family*, 51: 1085-88.

Sullivan, G. & Watt, S. n.d. Legalized abortion: myths and misconceptions. Mimeographed. Toronto General Hospital, Toronto, Ontario.

Swenson, I., Erickson, D., Ehlinger, E., Carlson, G. & Swany, S. 1989. Fertility, menstrual characteristics and contraceptive practices among white, black, and Southeast Asian refugee adolescents. *Adolescence*, 24: 647-54.

Szafran, R. & Clagett, A. 1988. Variable predictors of attitudes toward the legalization of abortion. *Social Indicators Research*, 20 (3): 271-90.

Talan, K. & Kimball, C. 1972. Characteristics of 100 women psychiatrically evaluated for therapeutic abortion. *Archives of General Psychiatry*, 26 (June): 571-77.

Tanfer, K. 1987. Patterns of premarital cohabitation among never-married women in the United States. *Journal of Marriage and the Family*, 49: 483.

Tanfer, K., Cubbins, L. & Brewster, K. 1992. Determinants of contraceptive choice among single women in the United States. *Family Planning Perspectives*, 24 (4): 155-61.

Taussig, F. 1936. *Abortion, Spontaneous and Induced*. St. Louis, Missouri: C.V. Mosby Company.

Thompson, L. 1978. Influence of parents, peers, and partners on the contraceptive use of college men and women. *Journal of Marriage and the Family*, (August): 481-92.

Thorton, A. & Camburn, D. 1987. The influence of the family on premarital sexual attitudes and behavior. *Demography*, 24 (3): 323-40.

Thurstone, P. 1969. Therapeutic abortion. *Journal of the American Medical Association*, 209 (July): 229-31.

Tietze, C. 1979. *Induced Abortion: 1979.* New York: The Population Council.

Tietze, C., Forrest, J. & Henshaw, S. 1988. United States of America. In P. Sachdev, ed. *International Handbook on Abortion.* Westport, CT: Greenwood Press.

Tietze, C., Pakter, J. & Berger, G. 1973. Mortality with legal abortion in New York City, 1970-72. A preliminary report. *Journal of the American Medical Association,* 225 (July 30): 507-9.

Tillack, W., Tyler, C., Pacquette, R. & Jones, P. 1972. A study of premarital pregnancy. *American Journal of Public Health,* 62 (May): 676-79.

Todd, N. 1972. Follow-up of patients recommended for therapeutic abortion. *British Journal of Psychiatry,* 120: 645-46.

Torres, A. & Forrest, J. 1988. Why do women have abortions? *Family Planning Perspectives,* 20 (4): 169-76.

Tredgold, R. 1964. Psychiatric indications for termination of pregnancy. *Lancet,* 2: 1251-54.

Trent, K. & Griner, E. 1991. Differences in race, marital status and education among women obtaining abortions. *Social Forces,* 69 (4): 1121-41.

Trippett, F. 1969. The unending quest for fun. *Reader's Digest,* December: 2.

Truax, C. & Carkhuff, R. 1967. *Toward Effective Counseling and Psychotherapy: Training and Practice.* Chicago: Aldine Press.

Truax, C. & Mitchell, K. 1971. Research on certain therapist interpersonal skills in relation to process and outcome. In A. Bergin and S. Garfield, eds. *Handbook of Psychotherapy and Behavior Change,* 2d ed. New York: John Wiley & Sons.

Trussell, J. & Kost, K. (1987). Contraceptive failure in the United States: A critical review of the literature. *Studies in Family Planning,* 18 (5): 237-283.

Trussell, J. & Westoff, D. 1980. Contraceptive practice and trends in coital frequency. *Family Planning Perspectives,* 12 (5): 246-49.

Tuttle, E. 1962. Serving the unmarried mother who keeps her child. *Social Casework,* 43 (October): 415-27.

Tyler, C., Tillack, W., Smith, J. & Hatcher, R. 1970. Assessment of a family planning program: contraceptive services and fertility in Atlanta, Georgia. *Family Planning Perspectives,* 2 (March): 25-29.

U.S. Centers for Disease Control, National Center for HEALTH Statistics, 1990. Quoted in *Public Health Policy Implications of Abortion*. Washington, DC: The American College of Obstetricians and Gynecologists.

Ullman, A. 1972. Social work service to abortion patients. *Social Casework*, October: 481-89.

Urquhart, D. & Templeton, A. 1991. Psychiatric morbidity and acceptability following medical and surgical methods of induced abortion. *British Journal of Obstetrics and Gynecology*, 98: 396.

Valk, A. 1974. *Morality and Law in Canadian Politics: The Abortion Controversy*. Dorval: Palm Publishers.

Vincent, C. 1961. *Unmarried Mothers*. New York: Free Press.

Vital Statistics (Canada), vol. 1. *Births 1971*. Catalogue No. 84-204 Annual.

Volkhart, E., ed. 1951. *Social Behavior and Personality: Contributions of W.I. Thomas to Theory and Social Research*. New York: Social Science Research Council.

Wallerstein, J., Kurtz, P. & Bar-Din, M. 1972. Psychological sequelae of therapeutic abortion in young, umarried women. *Archives of General Psychiatry*, 27 (December): 828-32.

Wallston, K., Maides, S. & Wallston, P. 1976. Health-related information seeking as a function of health-related locus of control and health values. *Journal of Research in Personalities*, 10: 215-22.

Walter, G. 1970. Psychological and emotional consequences of elective abortion. *Obstetrics and Gynecology*, 36 (September): 482-91.

Walters, J. 1969. Pregnancy in young adolescents. *Southern Medical Journal*, 62 (June): 655-58.

Watters, W. 1980. Mental health consequences of abortion and refused abortion. *Canadian Journal of Psychiatry*, 25 (1): 68-73.

Werman, D. & Raft, D. 1973. Some psychiatric problems related to therapeutic abortion. *North Carolina Medical Journal*, 34 (4): 274-75.

Westfall, J., Kallail, K. & Walling, A. 1991. Abortion attitudes and practices of family and general practice physicians. *Journal of Family Practice*, 33 (1): 47-51.

Westoff, C. 1988. Contraceptive paths towards reduction of unintended pregnancy and abortion. *Family Planning Perspectives*, 20 (1): 4-12.

Westoff, C., Moore, E. & Ryder, N. 1969. The structure of attitudes toward abortion. *Millbank Memorial Fund Quarterly*, 47, Part 1 (January): 11-37.

Weston, F. 1973. Psychiatric sequelae to legal abortion in South Australia. *Medical Journal of Australia*, 1 (February 17): 350-54.

Whelpton, P., Campbell, A. & Patterson, J. 1966. *Fertility and Family Planning in the United States*. Princeton, NJ: Princeton University Press.

Whelpton, P., Feedman, R. & Campbell, A. 1959. *Family Planning, Sterility and Population Growth*. New York: McGraw-Hill Book Company.

Whelpton, P., & Kiser, C. 1966. Cited in P. Whelpton, A. Campbell & J. Patterson. *Fertility and Family Planning in the United States*. Princeton, NJ: Princeton University Press.

White, L. 1990. Determinants of divorce: A review of research in the eighties. *Journal of Marriage and the Family*, 52 (November): 904-912.

White, R. 1966. Induced abortions: a survey of their psychiatric implications, complications and indications. *Texas Report on Biology and Medicine*, 24: 531-38.

Whittaker, J. & Garbarino, J. 1983. *Social Support Networks: Informal Helping in the Human Services*. New York: Aldine Publishing Co.

Whittington, H. 1960. Evaluation of therapeutic abortion as an element of preventative psychiatry. *American Journal of Psychiatry*, 126 (March): 1224-29.

Williams, L. & Prat, W. 1990. Wanted and Unwanted Childbearing in the United States: 1973-88. *Advance Data for Vital and Health Statistics*, No. 189.

Wilmoth, G. 1988. Depression and abortion: a brief review. *Population and Environmental Psychology News*, 14 (1): 9-12.

Wilmoth, G., Alteriis, M. & Bussell, D. 1992. Prevalence of psychological risks following legal abortions. *Journal of Social Issues*, 48 (3): 37-66.

Wilson, D. 1952. Psychiatric implications in abortion. *Virginia Medical Monthly*, 79 (August): 448-51.

Winter, L. 1988. The role of sexual self-concept in the use of contraceptives. *Family Planning Perspectives*, 20 (3): 123-27.

Wolfish, M. 1973. Adolescent sexuality. *Practitioner*, 210 (February): 226-31.

Worthington, E., Larson, D., Lyons, J. & Brubaker, M. 1991. Mandatory parental involvement prior to adolescent abortion. *Journal of Adolescent Health*, 12 (2): 138-42.

Wright, H. 1965. *Eighty Unmarried Mothers Who Kept Their Babies*. Department of Social Welfare, State of California, May.

Yarber, W. & Greer, J. 1986. The relationship between sexual attitudes of parents and their college daughters and sons sexual attitudes on sexual behavior. *Journal of School Health*, 56 (2): 68-72.

Young, A., Berkman, B. & Rehr, H. 1973. Women who seek abortion: a study. *Social Work*, May: 60-65.

Young, L. 1954. *Out-of-Wedlock*. New York: McGraw-Hill Company, Inc.

Yurdin, M. 1970. Recent trends in illegitimacy--implications for practice. *Child Welfare*, 49 (July): 373-75.

Zabin, L., Hirsch, M., Smith, E., Streett, R. & Hardy, J. 1986. Evaluation of a pregnancy prevention program for urban teenagers. *Family Planning Perspectives*, 18 (3): 119-26.

Zabin, L., Kantner, J. & Zelnik, M. 1979. The risk of adolescent pregnancy in the first months of intercourse. *Family Planning Perspectives*, 11: 215.

Zelnik, M. & Kantner, J. 1974. The resolution of teenage first pregnancies. *Family Planning Perspectives*, 6 (Spring): 74-80.

------. 1980. Sexual activity, contraceptive use and pregnancy among metropolitan area teenagers: 1971-1979. *Family Planning Perspectives*, 12 (5): 230-37.

Zelnik, M. & Kim, Y. 1982. Sex education and its association with teenage sexual activity, pregnancy and contraceptive use. *Family Planning Perspectives*, 14 (3): 117-26.

Zilbergeld, B. 1983. *The Shrinking of America*. New York: Little & Brown.

Zimmerman, M. 1977. *Passage through Abortion*. New York: Praeger Publishers.

Zozaya, F., Fernandez, O. & Ayala, L. 1972. Cited in M. Bracken et al. Contraceptive practice among New York abortion patients. *American Journal of Obstetrics and Gynecology*, 114 (December): 968.

Index

About the Author

PAUL SACHDEV, Ph.D., is Professor in the School of Social Work at Memorial University of Newfoundland. An authority on reproductive health care, and on family and child welfare, he has edited four books: *International Handbook on Abortion* (Greenwood, 1988), *Perspectives on Abortion* (1985), *Adoption: Current Issues and Trends* (1984), *Abortion: Readings and Research* (1981), and is the author of *Unlocking the Adoption Files* (1989). Paul Sachdev is the recipient of several national and international research and travel awards. He received Memorial University President's Award for Outstanding Research. He is also an international editor of the journal *Medicine and Law*.